THIS BOOK IS DEDICATED TO:
Judge J. Randall Wyatt Jr.
Division II, Criminal Court
Nashville, Tennessee

Chief of Police Steve Anderson
Nashville Police Department
Nashville, Tennessee

Chief of Police Deborah Y. Faulkner
Franklin Police Department
Franklin, Tennessee

Retired Chief of Police Joe D. Casey
Metropolitan Police Department
Nashville, Tennessee

Retired Lieutenant Tim Durham
Metropolitan Police Department
Nashville, Tennessee

Retired Captain Ken Pence

Angel On My Shoulder

Vanderbilt Professor, PhD
Metropolitan Police Department
Nashville, Tennessee

Bill Hamblin Retired Captain
Metropolitan Police Department
Nashville, Tennessee

My sincere appreciation to my wife, Patsy for her endless dedication and hard work in helping me with the Novel.

This book would not have been possible without her long hours in organizing this amazing Journey of My Life and my granddaughter Olivia Taylor McEwen who was very instrumental in organizing and completing this novel. For which I am very grateful.

Angel On My Shoulder

PREFACE

This book is about my life, from childhood, being a caddy for my father, going to school and playing golf, going into the Navy and boy was that a trip being seasick all the time, workingat A&P in Louisville, Ky. I had a wife and three kids that depended on me; my job with A&P was going nowhere. I was really worried about what to do, until I talked with my sister in Nashville, Tn.

After giving it a lot of thought, my family and I packed up and left Louisville, Kentucky to relocate in Nashville, Tennessee. I began the process of becoming a Police Officer. I never thought, beyond my wildest dreams that just over a year later, while working in my Squad Car that someone, not even 20 years old would shoot me 5 times with a 32 Cal. Pistol intending to kill me. A couple of years later I confronted a suspect that had just robbed a Furniture Store. I had spotted the subject who was walking at a fast pace as he rounded the corner of 3rd Avenue North and Church Street. He saw me in my Patrol Car and started running. He entered Central Parking Garage and was running up a ramp. He grabbed a man by his coat and pointed the gun barrel at the man's head threatening to kill him.

So relive my life's true story, from childhood to a Retired Lieutenant with the Police Department. My life may have not been the best in the world, but I survived. I learned a lot of things which you shouldn't do and a lot of hard knocks makes one want to have more in life.

Angel On My Shoulder

Ride with me as my Career unfolds with the Nashville Police Department, starting in the Prisoner Processing Section, Recruit School, West Station, South Station, Police Training Academy as an Instructor, SWAT Team calls, CID ~ Auto Theft and finally 5 years in the Vice Section.

Police work is not easy, Rules are changing all the time regarding Police Procedure's. Experience the Car Chases, Shootings, Burglaries, Domestic Disturbance, Face to Face confutations and Life and Death incidents. These calls are relived every time a Police Officer puts on the Uniform and puts the key into the Patrol Car and begins their tour of duty.

It's all in this book, Life and Death as it unfolds both on and off duty. This is unlike any Police Book that has ever printed. So turn the page and begin a Journey that you will never forget. You will probably read this Book more than once.

Enjoy this ride that I had while working in the Police Department, both good and bad. Oh, well life goes on but somehow you remember things every now and then and it doesn't seem like it was that far back. Pictures are good because they seem to freeze time, but the memories are even better, they will forever linger on. Some are good, some are bad, some you can laugh about and others just make you cry.

Angel On My Shoulder

PREFACE

This book is about my life, from childhood, being a caddy for my father, going to school and playing golf, going into the Navy and boy was that a trip being seasick all the time, working at A&P in Louisville, Ky. I had a wife and three kids that depended on me; my job with A&P was going nowhere. I was really worried about what to do, until I talked with my sister in Nashville, Tn.

After giving it a lot of thought, my family and I packed up and left Louisville, Kentucky to relocate in Nashville, Tennessee. I began the process of becoming a Police Officer. I never thought, beyond my wildest dreams that just over a year later, while working in my Squad Car that someone, not even 20 years old would shoot me 5 times with a 32 Cal. Pistol intending to kill me.

A couple of years later I confronted a suspect that had just robbed a Furniture Store. I had spotted the subject who was walking at a fast pace as he rounded the corner of 3rd Avenue North and Church Street. He saw me in my Patrol Car and started running. He entered Central Parking Garage and was going up a ramp. He grabbed a man by his coat and pointed the gun barrel at the man's head threatening to kill him.

So relive my life's true story, from childhood, playing golf and then joining the Navy. My life may have not been the best in the world, but I survived. I learned a lot of things which you shouldn't do and a lot of hard knocks makes you want to have more in life.

Ride with me as my Career unfolds with the Nashville Police Department, starting in the Prisoner Processing Section, Recruit School, West Station, South Station, Police Training Academy as an Instructor, SWAT Team calls, CID ~ Auto Theft and finally 5 years in the Vice Section.

Angel On My Shoulder

Police work is not easy, Rules are changing all the time regarding Police Procedure's. Experience the Car Chases, Shootings, Burglaries, Domestic Disturbance, Face to Face confutations and Life and Death incidents. These calls are relived every time a Police Officer puts on the Uniform and puts the key into the Patrol Car and starts their tour of duty.

It's all in this book, Life and Death as it unfolds both on and off duty. This is unlike any Police Book that has ever printed.

So turn the page and begin a Journey that you will never forget. You will probably read this Book more than once.

Enjoy this ride that I had while working in the Police Department, both good and bad.

Oh, well life goes on but somehow you remember things every now and then and it doesn't seem like it was that far back. Pictures are good because they seem to freeze time, but the memories are even better. Some are good, some are bad, some you can laugh about and thers just make you cry.

Yet the memories will forever linger on and on.

Angel On My Shoulder

A NEW BEGINNING

There were no Police Officer Trainee classes due to start for several months so I took a position in the Prisoner Processing Section as a Service Technician. I was making a whopping $400.00 gross a month. This was in January 1969. However with myself and
my wife and three kids, there wasn't much money left over for any extra activities. Times were hard, but at least we had food on the table and not on food stamps. I have never received any type of Government assistance in my life for anything.

My first job with the Police Department entailed working in the Prisoner Processing Section which is commonly known as the Booking Room. This is the Prisoner's second part of the Booking process after going before the committing Magistrate, so that a Warrant can be obtained.

I learned a lot in the Booking Room, which I took with me to the streets later on. I learned very quickly how a person can be real calm one minute and a crazed maniac real fast. Sometimes it would take four or five Police Officers to contain the outraged subject. I worked the 11 PM to 7 AM shift, which was difficult to become acclimated too. But, I finally had a job that I really enjoyed going to work.

On one such night a large black female was brought into the Processing Section, I began to type her information onto the Arrest slip. I was separated from the Prisoner's only by a thick mesh wire for obvious reasons. This was so that they could not harm the person on the other side of the screen in anyway. They could spit on you and they did quite often, I always tried to keep back a little way. You never know who has what kind of a disease.

Angel On My Shoulder

The large female seemed very polite, but the Arresting Officer was trying to give her a hard time. I told the Officer to step back, so that I could get her information. She looked at me and winked and said, "Thank you." I told her no problem. I began to ask her name, nickname, address, date of birth, social security number and phone number. I could tell that she was a rather very large woman, but I tried not to provoke her. She had been charged with Disorderly Conduct, which was a Simple Misdemeanor. She seemed personable enough if not disrespected. I was very polite to her with very little effort to try and avoid a screaming match. I asked her if she had a nickname and she replied, "Big Tussie." When I asked for her weight, she stated, 400 pound sweetie." I looked at her and said, "you certainly don't look like you weigh that much." She replied, "Yeah baby and I've got forty pounds of tits, she then placed her hands under each breast and bounced then up and down." She was wearing a sack dress with no belt, her shoes were flip flops. Her hair was short and somewhat matted. This was one huge strong woman.

Later on I was told by several Officers that she loved to fight and she always won. One Officer said one night she took on four Officers at the same time and if she didn't want to be put in a Patrol Car, then there was no way they could force her to get in. It took the Paddy Wagon to Transport her because of the large door opening in the rear of the vehicle.

I had heard stories of her holding two Police Officers off the ground while each one was holding onto to her arms, trying to bend them to get the handcuffs on her. This did not faze her at all. If the Officers could not calm her down they would call a Supervisor or Superior Officer that she knew and when they arrived on the scene they would talk her into cooperating by voluntarily getting into the transport wagon. His is the only way to control her and it always took three pairs of handcuffs linked together to subdue her.

This night must have been a good one, because I had no problem talking to her and she seemed to have a good sense of humor, you know everybody likes to be treated with a little respect sometimes.

I learned a lot in the Booking Room, you can't treat people like dogs during an arrest, after all they are still a person with feelings. Well, that is to a point, sometimes you can't help but use force. This is the only job in which I have really enjoyed going to work. But, what I really want is to be a Police Officer. I believe that I have what it takes to perform the duties of an Officer. It's just my wife has told me many times that this was a stupid mistake I was making. Maybe so, but I know that I wanted a career change and a job that was exciting. I feel like with this job, I can provide for my family.

I knew the training that I received here in the Prisoner Processing would be of help to me after I became a Police Officer, I could hardly wait until I went to the Academy. After watching the Police Officer's come into the Booking Room and to see them in their uniform, I thought this would be a privilege to wear the uniform. I am going to set my goals to become a Police Officer.

After submitting my application and passing the written and physical agility testing, I began my training in the basement of the Old Ben West Building. I started Police Officer Training School in July 1969.

The training wasn't bad. I had learned a lot while I was in the Navy about discipline, following orders, etc. I felt that this is what I was meant to do with my life. The physical agility was somewhat strenuous but challenging. There was no running at all. As far as the tests that we had to take, if you listened while the Instructors were talking and think about only what you hear, then the rest is not so bad.

Angel On My Shoulder

I was a marksman in the Navy and I had the privilege of qualifying with a 45 cal. automatic pistol, so the Firearms part of the Training was interesting and fun. I was fortunate enough to have the best pistol score in our class and I won a box of 38 cal. cartridges as a reward.

There were a lot of Rules and Regulations to remember, but I knew that if I went by these Rules and Regulations that I could make it through my Probationary period after Graduation. Most of all you have to believe in yourself and really want something bad enough to fight for it. I knew it would be a challenge, but I thought just bring it on.

After Graduating from the Police Academy, I was assigned at the West Sector as a Rookie. Police life came at me hard and fast. I soon learned that Rules were not to go by, but to get fired by. It took me a while to understand this, but the old timers had some good advice and some not so good advice. You more or less just have to go by your gut instinct. These older Police Officers would not trust a new Rookie unless they took a drink of Alcohol while on duty. I took a sip and it tasted awful, I did this just so I would not be treated like an outcast. I would have preferred a sip of beer instead. I found out very quickly that this was going to be rough until I had some time on the Police Department.

One night my partner and I had a slow night and he asked me if I wanted to go shoot some rats? He added we can drive down to the Feed Store with the lights off and speed around back, turn the headlights on and start shooting. The rats were gorging themselves on the piles of corn which was spilled from the boxcars while off-loading the feed.

We sped around back hanging half way out the window and starting shooting. There must have been two hundred rats that were scurrying everywhere while we were firing our pistols. We each fired 6 rounds and only killing about 7 rats! They were huge.

Angel On My Shoulder

We backed the Patrol Car back to the front of the Feed Store and re-loaded our guns. My partner said that this kind of keeps the rats in check.

About thirty minutes later our Supervisor called on the radio for us to meet him several blocks away from the Feed Store. We told him that we only fired a total of 12 rounds. He said that he didn't care how many rounds that we fired, but to stop this horseplay, at least for tonight. He closed by adding the caller of the Restaurant which was just 2 blocks away said that it sounded like a War Zone. He also said that the patrons of the Restaurant were really scared because they did not know what was going on. We told the Sergeant that we would not be shooting rats anymore, at least for tonight anyway.

Police at this time were not paid for Court Time and this was a sore spot for me. On my previous job in Louisville, Kentucky, I had joined the Union and I knew the meaning of Contract Negotiations, every three years between the Union and the Management. After all, time is our most precious commodity.

My wife was right about one thing, The females are everywhere; I came in contact with them only as a Police Officer. Their conduct and their language had certainly changed over the years. The profanity that they used was as blunt as a person could get. The revolution of the female was very prevalent at this day in time. I learned that Police Officers have a very high divorce rate, very high as a matter of fact.

The last part of the year seemed to fly by, because everything was new and exciting. Most of the time I had a different partner and when the Shift Lieutenant put me on his Detail, I
was on the day shift and I rode solo. The shifts rotated from days to nights and then to mornings. It was hard to get adjusted to a proper sleeping habit, because just when you became accustomed to one shift, it was time to change again.

Angel On My Shoulder

Also working extra jobs disrupted my sleep pattern and it made living at home very hectic, especially with children running around all the time. In and out of the house slamming doors all the time, but they are just kids. It seemed like the only time my wife wanted to vacuum the floors is when I had just laid down for a nap or just to try and get a little rest. Oh well, it is what it is.

I also enrolled in Aquinas Junior College to start on my journey to get a Criminal Justice Diploma. I capitalized on the GI Bill which was a great help in paying an extra $260.00 a month. Also the Police Department paid all of the Tuition fees. This was offered to any Police Officer who wanted to better their Education. With a 2 year Degree you would get a 3% raise and with a 4 year or Bachelor Degree you would get a 6% raise. This was a very good incentive for the Police Officers. J. Randall Wyatt Jr. was a teacher at Aquinas Junior College, this was the first time that I had seen him since his near fatal wreck. His class was on Evidence and he made it very interesting. After his Tour of Duty in the Marines, he joined the Police Department in Nashville, went to College, Law School and he became a Prosecuting Attorney and a few years later he became a Judge in Criminal Court, Div. II. His classes he taught at Aquinas were at night.

My partner and I would arrest a drunk on occasion. If it was close to shift change and the suspect fell asleep in the rear seat of our Patrol Car, then we would drive to the Police Station and park next to another Patrol Car and then we would place the drunk suspect in the rear of the unattended squad car, making sure that no one saw us. This could be done only on the night shift, because you had the darkness to our advantage.

We then casually drove to the area where the Patrol Cars were parked when not in use at the side of the building and then we walked to where our personal cars were parked. My partner having 15+ years of Service told me

Angel On My Shoulder

as we neared our vehicles to drive safely home and then he would say, "just remember Rookie I'll teach you how to get even with someone you don't like and you'll never break a sweat." This will become a Supervisor's problem, not ours he added.

"Get some rest Joe and I'll see you tomorrow night and we will see what we can get into."

Later on, I had heard stories of how drunks were put into Telephone Booths near the shift change so that he becomes the next shift's problem. Oh so Sad, but oh so true!

On several occasions I would see Big Tussie on the streets, but I never had any problems with her because I treated her with respect and I never talked down to her. I knew that there was no way that I could handle her by myself, I always called for backup. There are some things that just can't be done by yourself. So you then go to Plan B.

Most of the time when I came into contact with her she would say, "I remember you from the Booking Room, you were always nice to me and you always treated me with respect and never once did you make fun of my weight like most of the other personnel in the Prisoner Processing Section. They always said well, look Miss Fat Ass is back. You know Joe, I respect you."

Every now and then when we met I would give her a hug. I didn't try to reach around her
 because I knew that my arms weren't long enough. After the hug she would step back, smile and
wink at me. Several years later she just disappeared, no one knew what happened to her. She told me on one occasion that she had a heart problem, so I guess her heart just gave out.

After being on the streets for less than 6 months, I made a huge mistake one night that almost cost me my life. I was not prepared for what was about to happen to my life. I disregarded safety and did what is known as Tomb Stone Courage, by going into a dangerous situation alone. This should not be handled by just one Officer. I was almost murdered and left to die beside my Patrol Car by two thugs from out of town. These two thugs had been robbing elderly people of their Social Security money after returning home from the grocery store.

The near death experience is closing in on me fast.

Angel On My Shoulder

ANGEL ON MY SHOULDER ~ PART 1

A POLICE OFFICER'S TRUE STORY

Would this day be any different than any other day in the lives for the Men and Women in Blue? Police Officer's daily encounters of domestic problems, issuing traffic tickets, wrecks, fatalities, shootings, assaults, robberies, thefts and burglaries.   If you could name it, they worked and investigated it. With some encounters the adrenaline would flow faster through their system, increasing plaque buildup in their arteries, assuring hypertension and heart disease later on in life. The training they received as a Police Trainee would help, but as each shift was worked, more wisdom was gained I had been out of the Academy only six months and was a Rookie at the West Station along with the other members of his graduating class. However being a Veteran, with 4 years spent in the U. S. Navy gained me a lot of experience that a non-Veteran Police Officer did not possess.

Being the oldest member of the Recruit Class made me wonder if quitting my job in Louisville, Kentucky to become a Police Officer was the right choice. The pay for a Police Officer was a lot less than what I had been making as a forklift operator at the
A & P Warehouse, plus being a member of the Teamsters Union had its advantages, a guaranteed pay raise every three years, job security and a Teamsters Pension at the age of 65. However I was unhappy in my work and wanted more from life. I worked the late shift and it was always cold in the freezer where I spent most of my time. When I was tired and wanted to sleep on the job I'd find some pallets of food that were stacked up and then I would get in the middle of them and slept for 15 to 30 minutes which was just enough to get through the end of the shift. My home life wasn't

must better either. Having 3 small children and a wife that did work but she managed to take care of the three children. They loved their mother very much and she adored them. The house could have shown a little more work, dishes were stacked high on the sink. When I came home all that I wanted was piece and a little quite time. No such thing for me, peace and quiet was far from what

I had. It was always something going on. When I bought a motorcycle and went for a ride, this is where I would let off steam. Sometimes I would ride for an hour or more and not realizing the time. This was so soothing to my hectic life style. I talked with the other guys at work and they said that's the way it is with them too. This made me feel a little better. All I wanted was to have a happy home life and have a job that I enjoyed. This haunted me, because I didn't know what to do about it. There weren't that many jobs in Louisville which would fit into what I wanted to do. I seemed to be torn between a rock and a hard place about what to do with the rest of my life. I was a good provider for my family, but still I wanted more from life than this job had to offer. The thought of working

at A&P for another 35 years was appalling. Knowing that I would have to sell the house before a move of any kind could be made. I got a part – time job at a Service Station making a whopping 85 cents an hour.

Remembering what I had read in a magazine at the doctor's office, that great strides would be made in Law Enforcement in the coming decades, regarding pay increases, promotions, career opportunities and pension benefits. Not many people would attempt to make this drastic change in mid-life. Having a family in Nashville, was also a deciding factor in my career change.

Only time would tell if I made the right choice, from a forklift operator in Louisville, Ky. to a Police Officer in Nashville, TN.

I was 32 when I made this mid-life career change. My thoughts were how to better provide for my three children and a stay at home wife, this was a major career change and a very

Angel On My Shoulder

scary to attempt. All in all I did love being a Police Officer and I knew that moving back to Nashville was the right move.

No one really knew what would take place in his next 8 hour shift as a Police-man. No one can prepare for the unknown, but a Policeman needs to be alert and aware of his or her surroundings at all times and become an expert on reading the body language of the people they came in contact with. This was easier said than done, because no two people are alike in their actions. They just have to go with their gut instincts and pray that it works out because their life could depend upon it. When you are actually involved in an incident, things seem to take on a different outlook.

It was March 6th, 1970 and roll call at 1700 hours at the West Police Station had begun. As I stood at attention with the other Officer's, patiently waiting for our assignments, when the Sergeant barked out McEwen….Here Sir…Car 21 because Pique called in sick. McKinley….Here Sir…Car 22, in a deep voice replied the heavy set Officer, a retired Army Sergeant who had been known to write more tickets than anyone in the Department. Durham….Here Sir…Car 23. Durham graduated from the Academy with me. Johnson….Here Sir…Car 24. Johnson, Durham and McEwen were close friends and they were a tight knit group, always backing each other up during their 8 hour shifts while patrolling the streets. Officers rode solo because of the shortage of

manpower, Sergeant Harold continued to give out the remaining assignments of cars to the rest of the Officers. Harold was a 15 year Veteran who stood 6 foot 1 and weighed 200 lbs. His appearance was rugged and when he stared at you he meant business. He was a good Sergeant to work for and tough as nails. Listen up he always said. "Stay in your sector; do not wander too far out of your zone and whatever you do, do not wreck any more cars or you will be doubling up with someone else. Okay men get your subpoenas from Sgt. Dunbar, be safe. You're Dismissed!!!"

The 16 Officer's walked outside to the waiting Squad Cars, motors still running. The seats were still warm from the day shifts

Angel On My Shoulder

smell. It was customary to leave the cars running due to the high mileage as many of the vehicles would not restart, if turned off.

There were only 16 Officers for the entire West Nashville Sector, a very large area with far too few Officers. However there were Traffic Officers along with Specialized Squads working and plain clothes. The West Patrol Officers knew the Traffic Officers and the Specialized Squads would help out if a Zone Car happened to need backup or be in a sticky situation. They seemed to be one big family. Well, that is sometimes.

      I opened the car door scanning my home for the next 8 hours, what a piece of shit this car is, I thought, as I listened to the sputtering motor. Candy wrappers on the floor, ashtray full of cigarette butts and a moldy musty smell permeated from inside the patrol car. I tossed my briefcase onto the passenger's seat, got in and shut the door. I glanced at the Motorola Radio with 2 channels, West frequency and County Wide. The radio was outdated but it was all the department had to offer, this was my only
lifeline to headquarters and to the rest of the Police Cars in the West Sector. There were no Walkie-Talkies back then. I backed up, put the vehicle in drive, headed to the gas pumps which was located right at the West Sector, this was a good thing for the Officers, at least they didn't have to drive all the way back to town just to get gas. This just to get gas. This saved them a lot of valuable time. I waited for the attendant to fill my gas tank and check the oil, 15 minutes later I headed towards my zone. The only thing that bothered me was that the old veterans were leery of new the Rookies, they were wondering if the New Officers would keep their mouths shut or be a snitch.

      A lot of rules to follow and easy to sway from rules and regulations. I thought this is the only job that you get in trouble by working extra hard. It's too late now, but I was wondering, did I make a mistake by leaving Louisville.

      Unbeknown to me that the die was cast on this chilly night for events to unfold involving 2 Lewisburg, Tn. teens. This night

Angel On My Shoulder

was to be a night I would never forget as I would dance with the angel of death before my shift was over and DANCE I did!!

Meanwhile in Lewisburg a 19 year old, named Roy Allen pulled his white 4 door Olds into the driveway of a friend and partner in crime William McClain. Roy honked the horn and William bounced off the porch and trotted to the car. Opened the door
and got in. Wuz up Roy, you're running late, we have to hurry if we plan on making any money before those old mother fuckers get back home before dark. I need at least $400.00 to pay my bills and my monthly payment is due at the Barber College, Roy said. I paid mine last week replied William. Roy drove back to town and turned onto the entrance of I-65 and headed towards Nashville, driving in the right lane, doing the speed limit. "Roy, we ain't gonna get there if you don't speed up," said William. I isn't drawing no attention to us. We'll get there just shut up William and sit back and relax, I
knows what I doing, how many times have we done this? "Not enough," replied William.

William hollered "watch out Roy that car almost hit us!" I see him, that's why I slowed down. No calls for me on the Police radio as I drove several miles in the country to my home. I pulled into my driveway and drove to the back of the house where my 3 children were playing. Lisa 8, Joe 6 and Eric 5. They ran to the Police car shoving and trying to push each other out of the way, to see who would get the closest to the driver's door first. "Are we going to the park tomorrow?? Are we, are we daddy? They yelled in unison!"

"You betcha we are, about 9 AM, I replied!" Their faces lit up and all three hollered at the same time, Oh Boy! So mind your mother and be good, BE GOOD, knowing these three kids they were always getting into something, what one didn't think of the other two would. I just thought I'd come home to confirm that we were going to the Park tomorrow.

Angel On My Shoulder

"I forgot my flashlight." "I know where it is daddy," Eric yelled, "I'll get it for you." He took off at breakneck speed and was back in a few seconds. How did you know where it was?

UUH...UUH, "I was playing with it earlier," Eric said sheepishly. He handed the flashlight to his daddy who tossed it into the passenger's seat, tell your mother I will be home around 2 AM. Daddy....Daddy....Turn the blue lights on, come on daddy let me do it, no I want to do it first, no I'm gonna do it first. "I'm the oldest," Lisa replied, "but I'm the youngest" replied Eric and then Joe Joe spoke up and said, "but I am the tallest." "But I found daddy's flashlight," replied Eric. Each child was trying their best to get in the open window to be the first to turn the lights on. OK, OK, just a minute kids, I'll let each of you do it, but one at a time. Then daddy has to get back to work. I let each one turn on the switch that activated the overhead blue lights, each time one threw the switch they would all step back and their eyes showed great delight as they watched the spinning blue lights. I leaned my head out of the window and kissed the children on their cold and dirty cheeks and began to ease the Patrol Car into gear and out the gravel driveway onto the blacktop road. All three children ran as fast as they could to the end of the driveway to watch my car
disappear over the hill. Little did they know, no park tomorrow, plus they would not see their daddy for three weeks. As I was leaving I wondered why my wife didn't come out to see me? I know she is not cleaning up the house or washing dishes because they are probably stacked high enough now. I wonder if she will ever take as much time on the house as she does her hair and her make-up. Oh well, I've got to get back in my zone and see what's happening. I hope this will be a slow night; I could stand an easy one for a change. I bet if I flipped a coin and called heads it would be tails. My luck has got to change.

It would be dark in another hour I thought as I headed back into civilization, out of the rural scenery and back into the busy streets of Nashville.

Angel On My Shoulder

Meanwhile, Roy and William had reached Nashville and they pulling into the Kroger parking area. "This is going to be a good night," said Roy. William added, "how do you know?" "Do you think you are a mind reader or one of them kind of people that can tell the future!" Roy said, "OK William I'm pulling over to the rear of the parking lot where we can watch these old people coming out the grocery store. You drive, I'll be the hit man." Roy stopped the Olds, put it into park and they swapped seats. We have to watch ourselves, we're the only black men among these whities!!   Roy watched the customers leaving the Kroger Store and go to their cars.

"There's the two we want!!" Roy said in a startled voice! They watched as the elderly couple pushed the shopping cart to the rear of a 4 door Buick. The old man opened the trunk and began to place the bags of groceries into the trunk of the car which was parked in the Kroger's parking lot with plenty of light. They thought they were safe here because there was always a lot of people coming and going and usually a hired Security Guard was there around the first
week of the month to give a safe feeling for the elderly. The elderly man and wife were wearing glasses. Roy said "this will be like shooting fish in a barrel. Get right behind them, they will never notice us, they are old and slow. This hit will be good for at least $200.00
bucks." The hunters had spotted their prey and were slowly closing in.

Roy and William had developed a plan to rob old people during their tenure at the Barber College in Nashville. William would drive the car and follow the couple home and when they would start getting the groceries out of their car, Roy would walk up to the
man slapping him in the face with his open hand knocking his glasses off. This would make a positive I.D. almost impossible. A simple, foolproof and profitable operation that had been repeated many times over and over with great success. The two thugs had successfully robbed elderly people over 30 different times in the past 3 months.

Angel On My Shoulder

Just a week earlier I had taken a report from an elderly woman who was a victim of a purse snatching and she would not release her pocket book until she had been dragged half way across the asphalt on the street where she lived. She paid the price though, her right leg was skinned up pretty bad and her ankle was sprained. She could not give a good detailed description of the suspects, except that he was male black. She said that when he knocked her glasses off her vision was blurred. She stated that they
were in a white car, but she could not tell what kind it was.

I figured that these are the same two black males that we are looking for tonight. Finding them would be rather difficult, however I still need to give it my best shot, they have got to be stopped.
    I thought if everyone would give 100% while they were working, more arrest's would be made. However a lot the Police Officer's just lay back and wait for their shift to end. Most of all they don't engage in aggressive Patrol Tactics like they should.
On this night after locating their next prey, Roy and William followed them home to the back of an apartment complex where they lived. Roy pulled his car in about 15 feet behind the elderly couple and they did not notice the stranger approaching. Roy walked up to the man from behind slapping him on the right side of his face knocking his glasses to the ground. Roy then ripped the old man's rear pocket taking his billfold and in one sweeping motion slapped the old woman in the face knocking her down, putting a gash in her left leg and knocking her glasses off and grabbing her purse. This took only a few
seconds for this crime to happen. Roy then ran back to the waiting parked Olds and the two thugs sped away and flow into disappeared over the hill heading towards Hillsboro Road. Roy would go through the billfold taking only bills and then tossing the wallet out of the window. He would keep anything else of value before throwing the purse away. Getting rid of any incriminating evidence was the Rule and it seemed to be working.
    I had just finished writing a moving traffic violation at 31st and Poston Ave., when a robbery was broadcast over the radio.

Angel On My Shoulder

The incident had taken place behind the apartment complex parking lot, located at Murphy Road and West End. I put my Patrol car in drive and headed towards West End, making a quick turn at the traffic was light as I sped to the Crime Scene. I'm only a few blocks away thought. I can be there in a matter of seconds. Maybe I might be able to get a lead on these thugs. These two have plagued this area for the past 3 months, robbing numerous elderly people. They
were victims of brutal assaults, bruised elbows and knees where they had been knocked down. Older people cut more easily because their skin is fragile just like they are.

William and Roy drove around Love Circle with Roy tossing credit cards, empty billfold, papers and etc. out the window of the white Olds. The street they were on was narrow and winding with cars parked on the side of the road leaving barely enough room for a car to pass. The cars were parked on the side of the road because the houses were built on a slope and had no garages or driveways. There was not much room between the houses, probably 10 to 15 feet at the most. Love Circle used to be a hangout for kids to park with their dates. This was on a hill overlooking Nashville and it had a beautiful view of downtown.

Roy kept hollering at William to slow down, slow down, we don't want to get stopped for speeding. They crossed Natchez Trace and drove onto Belcourt to 25th Avenue turning left and stopping at the corner, stop this damn car now.
Stop, damn it William stop this damn car. We've been here before, don't you remember anything. Stop!!! Stop!!! What is wrong with you? William stopped the car and Roy opened the passenger's door, jumped out leaving the door agape, with the interior light on and as he hurriedly walked towards the shotgun house at the corner of 25th and Blakemore,

Roy stepped onto the porch, opened the screen door and went inside without knocking.
Meanwhile I drove behind the Apartment Complex onto the parking area where I saw Detective Roberts filling out a report.

Angel On My Shoulder

This was a nice section of town and mostly older and business people lived. The Apartment house was on a hill with parking under

the covered carports. This was surrounded by hedges and greenery. When I stopped my Patrol Car near Detective Roberts and said "what do you have?" Mac, all we have is 2 black males driving a white Olds. One with an afro and he's wearing a blue jacket,

they left headed towards the Village on Love Circle. "How long ago" I asked? About 4 or 5 minutes ago. The couple had just cashed their Social Security checks. "Be careful Mac, these fuckers are very dangerous" the Detective said. I grinned at the Detective and said, "So am I." I then drove left onto Love Circle headed towards Hillsboro Village, planning to do a grid search from Natchez Trace to Hillsboro Road. It's like looking for a needle in a haystack I thought, hell they could be anywhere now…white car, 2 male blacks…white car, 2 male blacks. I just kept saying over and over. I was about 6 miles out of my regular zone now because not much was going on out towards the county line.

Across Natchez Trace I looked right and left at every intersection. This was an older well-established part of town. Searching for the white Olds. My heart was pounding hard as I drove past 28th Avenue South. They're close I thought, I can feel it. The time was 9:05 P.M. March 6, 1970, just 2 days after my 34th birthday. My steely blue eyes searched every car as he drove past 27th Ave. South, I could feel my heart pounding harder and harder. My arm pits were getting sweaty. On past 26th Ave. South, that

ended into Blakemore. I looked to the right and said, "God Damn" there's the white Olds with a black male behind the wheel. The passenger door was open and the dome light was on. Son of a Bitch this could be the car. I eased my Patrol car past the Olds and pulled into 24th Ave. South slowly so not to arouse suspicion to the person behind the wheel of the Olds. Backing out, I headed towards to the parked Olds a block away.

Angel On My Shoulder

I reached for the mike to radio that I had found the car, but the air was jumping with Police calls about this robbery. I then flipped to County Wide, same problem. Damn I thought we need more channels because we can't get air time in an emergency and this is certainly an emergency, no one knows that I have found the white Olds. Damn, I need back up, but there's no time. I felt like the suspects would be leaving any second now. The old clunker that I was driving would do 75 MPH tops. If they tried to get away I would not be able to keep up with them. Fuck it I thought, I can take these pricks.

Little did I know that the decision I was about to make would probably change my life forever. After being on the streets for 6 months, I made a huge mistake that almost cost me my life. Disregarding safety and full of tombstone courage, I continued alone. This type of decision is known in Officer Training as the John Wayne Syndrome, (Tombstone Courage). Many young Officers has made this mistake, which often has fatal outcomes. I walked into a dangerous situation alone. I knew better, I knew that I should of waited for backup, but I didn't.

As I headed my Patrol car towards the white Olds, I noticed the License Plate number on the Olds was RA0572. I then turned onto 25th Avenue and pulled a few feet past the Olds facing in the opposite direction and stopping my Police Car. Still I had not
been able to get air time, I can do this, I kept thinking over and over to myself. Just remember what was taught in class about safety. Hell, here I am without back-up and no one knows where I am or that I have found the car that was used in the robbery.

Damn, what was I thinking. I guess I'm going to do this without backup. I can do this. Just take time to and breathe. I approached the white Olds after getting out of my Patrol Car.

A black male was sitting in the driver's seat, illuminated by the overhead dome light. The time was 9:13 P.M., my heart was pounding harder than before. This was the first time that these two thugs had ever actually been seen after committing a crime and visibly seen by a Police Officer. I knew that I had to stop

Angel On My Shoulder

them. I stood a shade over 6 foot 1 inch with my Police boots on, weighing 212 lbs., this gave me a false sense of security.

I started to thinking back at a time when I was in the Navy and stationed in Orange, Texas where I was participating in a boxing match. I was hit with a left hook and was knocked unconscious. My heart was beating faster and faster by the minute now, damn, take it

easy I thought, just breathe in deeply and let it out, stay calm don't rush anything. What the Hell am I doing here without back up. I can do this, I can do this, I kept thinking just remember your training, just improvise and get it done. Keep your cool and focus, don't

let this get out of hand, just focus.

"Roy, Roy get out of here, there's a Police car out here." The excited home owner yelled, "Quick!! Quick!! Go out the back way Roy," yelled the man cause he won't see you going out the back way into the alley.

"Now, Roy damn it Roy, he's coming closer. Go! Go! Roy get the hell out of here, you gotta go, now." Roy ran through the kitchen and out the rear door to the rear alley behind the house, crossed 25th Ave. South and made his way towards Blakemore under the cover of darkness by utilizing a vacant lot beside the Police Cruiser. Roy pulled a 32 Caliber pistol from his waist band as he approached the Police Car. Roy thought I'm getting close now, I've really got to be quiet. Roy approached McEwen from the rear, getting within eight feet of him, Roy stopped, took aim and started to squeeze the trigger.

Damn he's a big mother fucker. Silently, Roy said to himself, "You ain't taking me down, I'm gonna put you down you fucking Cop."

Across the street Mrs. Beasley was looking out her front living room window, when she saw what was about to happen to this Police Officer and he was by himself. Quick Honey, she called to her husband, a Police Car is stopped in front of the house across

Angel On My Shoulder

the street and there is someone sneaking up on the Cop. Quick!....Quick!.... Honey, call 911, hurry up I just feel like something bad is about to happen. She was transfixed on the Officer as the events were unfolding. Hurry, Honey this Officer needs some help

there's 2 of them. Call 911, now.

As I approached the driver I tapped on the car door and asked, "What are you doing here boy? With my flashlight in my left hand and my right hand on my pistol, I tried to get a good firm hold on the oversized grips, unsnapping the Pistol strap with my thumb, I could feel the sweat trickling down my back. This is an eerie feeling I thought, I feel like something is about to happen. Maybe I should have waited for air time. Again, I asked the male what he was doing, "Uh, Uh, waiting on Roy, was his reply."

Where is he?" I asked as I shined my flashlight on the suspect. He's uh, he's uh, speak up boy, Uh, he's where? He's inside that house uh, uh, over there Sir, pointing over his right shoulder. Roy was barely 8 feet away from the Police Officer who was beside the Olds, talking to William when Roy pointed the revolver at the back of McEwen's body and began squeezing the trigger. The hammer started to move back on the gun. Roy's hand was trembling as he aimed point blank at the Police Officer.

"Give me some I.D. asshole and keep your hands where I can see them," barked McEwen. I began pulling my pistol from it's leather holster. This is not good, I thought, something is wrong. I looked over the top of the olds to the shotgun house for any sign of movement. Not noticing anything my eyes focused back on the driver of the Olds.

I looked at the suspect whose eyes were focused ahead looking over the top of the steering wheel. I did not know it at the time, but the driver had spotted Roy just a few feet from the Officer, Roy was pointing his gun right at the Cop. I slowly cleared my

pistol from the Holster. Roy squeezed the trigger on his revolver and the hammer fell…firing the gun, BANG…BANG…BANG…BANG, four terrifying shots rang out hitting me in the left elbow, my left side and bouncing off a rib and

Angel On My Shoulder

stopping near my spine. Number 3 & 4 did the most damage. The 3rd bullet went through my liver and lung and pushed a rib out two inches on his right side. Number 4 went into my liver exploding the main artery in the liver and stopping in my right lung. Blood began pouring from the severed artery and gushed into my right chest cavity. The time was 9:45 P.M., March 6, 1970.

Little did I know that I had four bullet holes in my liver. There were 2 entrance and 2 exit wounds to my liver which is always considered to be fatal.

My legs buckled as I fell to the ground. The flashlight dropped from my left hand as I grabbed the chrome door handle on the Olds, trying to pull myself back up, then drawing my weapon and firing into the vehicle, shooting the suspect in the arm and the

stomach. You Son of a Bitch, I snarled , then pointing my revolver up to the suspects head and began squeezing the trigger when two more shots rang out from Roy's gun.

The fifth bullet whizzed past my head and the sixth bullet hit me in the back of my neck. It was a through and through wound. This knocked me back down again, my hand reached for the chrome door handle again to pull myself back up.

Meanwhile Mrs. Beasley was still watching from her window the horrifying events, that was taking place. She began screaming, "Oh my God the Policeman has been shot. Where are the other Police cars, they should be here by now. Honey, Call the police again! Oh my God! Oh my God!"

A few seconds earlier Roy watched in horror as I got up after being shot 5 times from a distance of eight feet. Roy then raised his pistol and aimed for my head. I'll put this fucker down for good on this volley, Roy thought. Roy had not realized at this point that he had fired all six rounds, he clicked the trigger 2 more times, but nothing happened.

Six shots and his gun was empty. Then I returned and fired once at Roy barely grazing his head and traveling through the window of a house across the street, lodging in the living room wall just barely missing a woman who was watching as this tragic event unfolded.

Angel On My Shoulder

When I was shot I knew I was a dead man, the pain was horrible. It felt like someone had hit me with a hard fist and put a hot poker in my body. The burning sensation was intense with excruciating pain. My body felt paralyzed. I knew that I didn't have long to live. It was impossible to breathe in, the pain was unbearable with every breath I tried to take. I could feel my shirt becoming soaked with blood and I knew that I was bleeding badly. It was hard for me to move but I knew that I had to try and fight this pain. It became more painful and harder to move, harder to think, grunting with each breath from the bullet holes in his body. I knew that I had to fight back. I was trying to keep a count on the number of shots. I had fired three times and knew I only had three rounds left in my revolver. Each breath was labored as each one made it harder to breath than the previous one. My face was sweaty and my vision was getting blurred. Thinking that I had only seconds before I would pass out, I knew that I had to do something and fast.

Roy turned and ran to the vacant lot on the west side of 25th Ave. South. I aimed my gun back towards the driver as he was trying to exit out the opened right door of the parked vehicle before I could shoot him again. All that was visible of the suspect was the

soles of his shoes as he dove out of the passengers door and disappeared into the darkness of the night.

I then took two steps to the left fender of my Patrol Car and using my left arm to help support my buckling legs, I fired the remaining three rounds from my 38. Revolver at the shooter but Roy kept on running.

I then swung around my opened car door and half fell and half sat in the driver's seat, tossing my empty revolver on the passenger's seat. I planned on ramming the suspects automobile with my patrol car if I was still conscious if they came back to get

their car and drive away. I knew that if I kept the car here, they would be caught. I had to stay awake. I kept fighting to stay awake. Think about my kids, think about my kids, I kept saying it

Angel On My Shoulder

over and over. Who would teach them the things that I can about life and the pitfalls in it. I was sweating more now and getting dizzier by the minute. Not knowing how much longer I could keep from passing out. Breathing was labored and coming in gasps.

I knew that if I passed out they would come back and kill me. I thought about why in the hell did I leave Louisville, I had a good job, my kids had a big

swimming pool that I built and had everything for a blue collar worker could want. I guess I was running on pure adrenaline. However unlike the stories I have heard about a person's life flashing before their eyes, this didn't happen to me. NOT SO. I was super pissed because I didn't kill that prick that was in the car and didn't hit the other suspect in the head as he was running away. Things were happening to fast and I knew I had to keep my wits about me. Surely someone will be here soon to back me up. However I looked ahead of my unit dash board and saw the other suspect running, illuminated by the squad cars headlights, he was bent over holding his stomach and looking back in my direction as he headed towards the alley. I shot that prick twice, point blank, hitting him in the stomach, I thought they'll catch him, because he'll have to seek medical

attention for those gunshot wounds. Maybe he'll bleed out and then he can't hurt any other elderly person. I'll run this prick down if he shows up again, I thought. My legs would not move to the brake petal or the accelerator. Damn, Damn, I need some help badly, no one knows what has happened to me or my location. I'm in deep shit this time, I thought as I reached for the microphone, the radio was silent at this time as I yelled for help. Taking my left arm I lifted my leg and placed it on the brake petal so I could put the car in reverse and retreat from the kill zone. I turned the emergency lights and

began to idle my Patrol car backwards onto Blakemore. I looked at the street sign and because of darkness and my vision being blurred I thought the street sign read Belcourt.

However I was really on Blakemore. With the emergency lights on I knew that they would be able to spot my unit from 21st Ave. South and also Natchez Trace. I then turned the spotlight

Angel On My Shoulder

towards the alley and put the headlights on bright which illuminated the Olds.

If they come back I'll ram their fucking car. If I can keep the car here they'll be caught, I said silently to myself. God Damn I'm hurt bad, it was hard to reach for the mike, but I knew that help had to get here fast because I thought that the window of

opportunity was closing fast. I began calling Headquarters for help but my speech was getting slurred from the lack of not being able to breath. I was hurting really bad now.   I could feel my life coming to a horrible ending and I knew that I would die in the street.

BELOW IS THE ACTUAL TRANSMISSION OF MARCH 6, 1970 OF THE ROBBERY
        BY TWO THUGS FROM LEWISBURG
MARCH 6, 1970   CONTINENTAL APARTMENTS ON WEST END, LAST SEEN RUNNING NORTH, CORRECTION, LAST SEEN RUNNING SOUTH IN THE REAR PARKING LOT, CONTINENTAL APTS,
        AUTHORITY CAR 22 AND CAR 12.
DISPATCHER 10-4
TIME   21:43   SIGNAL 12
DISPATCHER 40
DISPATCHER   ATTENTION ALL CARS, WANTED FOR CONNECTION FROM
    10-53 FROM A PURSE SNATCHING BY CAR 22 AND CAR 12,
                    MALE COLORED, 5'7" TO 5'10" TALL, APPROXIMATELY
    NINETEEN YEARS OLD AND WEARING A BROWN CAP,
    BROWN SWEATER OR BROWN COAT, DARK PANTS. LAST
 RUNNING SOUTH IN REAR OF THE CONTINENTAL APARTMENTS ON WEST END, 3300 BLOCK. KIA234
                9:44
25   15 TO 10

Angel On My Shoulder

20   10-4

25   SIGNAL 12 SERGEANT 10-4

DISPATCHER   24-23739

24   10-4

45   PUT US OUT AT 16TH AND JO JOHNSON FOR A FEW

DISPATCHER WAS THAT 45 AT 16TH AND JO JOHNSON

45 10-4

TIME   21:45

45 PUT US 10-8

DISPATCHER 106   21 TO 22 SIGNAL 12 MAC

22   10-4   SIGNAL 12

DISPATCHER   40

TIME   21:46

CAR 25 TO HEADQUARTERS

DISPATCHER 25

CAR 25 PUT US 10-7 AT BOOK   BELOW IS WHERE
OFFICER McEWEN CALLED FOR HELP   AFTER BEING
SHOT

McEWEN 10-55 10-55 I'VE BEEN HIT, 26TH AND BELCOURT.
10-55

DISPATCHER ATTENTION ALL CARS. ALL CARS 10-55, 26TH
AVE. SO. AND BELCOURT.

McEWEN GET AN AMBULANCE BABY, I'VE BEEN HIT ABOUT 5
TIMES.

        GET'EM BABY I'M HURTING BAD

DISPATCHER   10-4

McEWEN   26TH AVE. SOUTH AND BELCOURT LICENSE
NUMBER RA-0572.

        ALL GOD A MIGHTY I'M FAINTING FAST. GET ME AN
                AMBULANCE BABY.

DISPATCHER REPEAT WHAT INFORMATION YOU HAVE ON
        HIM.

McEWEN MALE COLORED, BLUE, BLUE, GOD DAMN I HAVE
BEEN HIT. I

Angel On My Shoulder

THINK I HIT ONE OF THEM. HE ROLLED OUT OF THE CAR.

DISPATCHER   GIVE ME THE LICENSE NUMBER AGAIN.

McEWEN   THE CAR IS IN FRONT OF ME, A WHITE OLDSMOBILE RA-0572.
HE'S RUNNING TOWARDS, OH GOD.HE'S RUNNING TOWARDS.
I'M FAINTING FAST. HE HAS ON A BLUE SWEATER AND ABOUT 20 YEARS OLD. A GUY MUST OF COME IN BEHIND ME.
I'M HIT IN THE NECK AND EVERY WHERE ELSE. BABY I'M FAINTING FAST, GET ME AN AMBULANCE OUT HERE.
GET ME AN AMBULANCE OUT HERE.
DISPATCHER   GET HIM ON THE WAY
CAR 102   WHAT'S GOING ON.
DISPATCHER 10-55 WE BELIEVE SOMEONE HAS BEEN SHOT AT 26TH AND BELCOURT
CAR 102   10-4
CAR 30   CLEAR THE AIR

CAR 106   HAVE YOU A 10-47 ON THE WAY?   10-47   SIGNAL 10
DISPATCHER   10-4

CAR 342   YOU GOT ONE IN ROUTE?

DISPATCHER   10-4
CAR 24   GIVE US THAT LICENSE NUMBER

DISPATCHER THE CAR IS RIGHT THERE RA-0572 OLDSMOBILE
CAR 24   10-4

UNKNOWN   SUBJECT IN BLUE SWEATER LEFT THERE RUNNING,

Angel On My Shoulder

DIDN'T GET THE DIRECTION OF IT.

CAR 343   HE RAN DOWN TOWARDS 21ST.

DISPATCHER   ATTENTION ALL CARS SUBJECT RAN
TOWARDS 21ST,
     TOWARD 21st   CLEAR THE AIR….. CLEAR THE AIR…..
                    CLEAR THE AIR…..
CAR 22   10-55   10-55 GET ME AN AMBULANCE AT 26TH AND
                    BELCOURT OFFICER BEEN HURT.

DISPATCHER   10-4 GO AHEAD 22
CAR 22   10-47 26TH AND BLAKEMORE 26TH AND
BLAKEMORE
DISPATCHER 10-4
CAR 10   IS THAT BLAKEMORE OR BELCOURT?   .
DISPATCHER WE'VE GOT 26TH AND BELCOURT AND 26TH
AND BLAKEMORE
        BOTH MAC SAID BLAKEMORE.
UNKNOWN   DISPATCHER IT IS BLAKEMORE

DISPATCHER 106 SIGNAL 12
DISPATCHER HEADQUARTERS ANY SERGEANTS ON THE
SCENE 26TH AND BELCOURT

CAR 10 I AM AT NATCHEZ TRACE, I'LL BE THERE IN JUST A
MINUTE
DISPATCHER 10-4
DISPATCHER 102
CAR 30 TO HEADQUARTERS
DISPATCHER 30

CAR 30   CALL THE HOSPITAL TELL THEM TO BE
WAITING FOR HIM HE

Angel On My Shoulder

IS HURTING BAD.

DISPATCHER GOING TO VANDERBILT
CAR 30   10-4
CAR 30   TO HEADQUARTERS
DISPATCHER 30
CAR 30   CALL EMERGENCY ROOM VANDERBILT TELL
THEM WE ARE
     ON THE WAY. IT'S A GUN SHOT WOUND AND HE IS
HURTING BAD.

DISPATCHER 10-4 30, WE HAVE CALLED VANDERBILT AND
TOLD THEM TO BE READY FOR HIM.

In the background I heard several sirens and I knew that the
cavalry was on the way. But, in the alley Roy and William met,
Roy said we have to get the car or we're fucked. They headed
back towards the parked Olds.

     I tried to breathe, but I fell from the Patrol Car onto the
asphalt. I was on my back with my right arm under the Patrol Car,
I have to get up, I cannot breathe. I was grabbing for anything to
get leverage, unknowing that I had touched the hot exhaust pipe
burning all the skin from my right thumb. I then scooted a little left
to clear my arm from underneath the Patrol Car when I heard a
voice. I'm here to help you Officer, I live across the street and I
saw the whole thing. I've got a rifle so they can't take their car. Be
careful I gasped trying to tell the man, the incoming Police might
think you're the one who shot me and shoot your ass. I called the
Police Station and told them what had happened. They should
have been here before now.
     The next person on the scene was Officer McKinley from
an adjoining zone who knelt beside the critically wounded Officer.
Get me an ambulance Mac, I'm dying as I gasped. As my head
fell back onto the cold asphalt, my eyes were halfway closed.

Angel On My Shoulder

I could hear the bagpipes softly playing Amazing Grace and thinking, my God what will my children do if I die, thinking to myself I should have stayed in Louisville at A & P, driving a forklift, no danger of getting my ass shot up and the money I gave up to become
a Policeman.

While McKinley went to his car to radio for help, the two suspects appeared on 25th Ave. South at the alley intersection. Mr. Beasley pointed the rifle at the pair and they both fled down the alley towards Hillsboro Road.

Sgt. Joe Harold arrived on the scene and told Mr. Beasley to get back on his porch for his own safety. He unzipped McEwen's blue field jacket and yanked his tie off. "God dam it," Harold said, "where is the fucking bone box?" which was a ambulance from a local Funeral Home because they were equipped with an oxygen mask. He unbuttoned the downed Officer's shirt which was dripping wet with sweat and blood.

I was gasping to breathe, I need air I can't breathe, where are they? They are on the way, Mac, just take it easy. Man I'm dying. The right side of his chest was oozing blood. He could feel blood oozing from the right side of his neck wound from the exit hole of the bullet. I was worried about being paralyzed from the neck shot and become a talking head unable to even kill yourself if you wanted too.

The sirens were growing closer as Roy and William ran down the alley towards Hillsboro Road. William was holding his stomach with both arms crossed and partially bent over. We have to split up Roy said to William. I'm going to my sister's house on 13th Ave. South, near Hawkins. That Mother fucking Cop shot me in the stomach, yelled William. What did you expect him to do kiss you? Fuck you Roy, I'm burning in my gut real bad. I don't know why the Cop didn't drop, I shot the fucker six times in the chest.

Hell I think I shot him in the head also and the fucker was still standing before I started running. They passed 22nd heading south and Roy told William "I'll see you back home.

Angel On My Shoulder

"Roy ran between two houses and vanished."

Back at the scene an ambulance from Pettis Owen and Woods Funeral Home managed to get through the maze of Police Cars coming from all over Nashville to join in the search for the two suspects.

The ambulance attendant, Rickey McWright jumped from the ambulance, opened the rear door, pulled the gurney from the rear of the vehicle and rolled the gurney towards the fallen Policeman. Several Police Officers ran to his side and together they picked up the wounded Officer and placed him onto the gurney. The Police Officers continued to arrive at the scene. Everyone thought that there was no way the Joe could survive this brutal gun attack. He was wheeled quickly into the rear of the ambulance and pushed inside and immediately the ambulance took off. Rickey was reaching for the oxygen mask, "I can breathe out, but I can't breathe in," I told Rickey. The oxygen mask was placed over my face and Rickey asked, is that any better? "Hell no, that didn't help a bit." Unbeknown to McEwen, the reason he could not inhale was because blood was pouring into his chest cavity and not allowing his right lung to properly expand while inhaling and thus causing tremendous pain.

"Hey Sarge," the driver yelled, "General Hospital, hell no replied Sgt. Dorman, take Joe to Vanderbilt. You're a lot closer to Vanderbilt than General." The ambulance driver placed the vehicle in drive and sped from the crime scene with the siren and ambulance
lights on and dodging all the Police Cars that were still pouring into the crime scene.

Within two minutes the ambulance was backing into the Emergency entrance where a hoard of Doctors and Nurses were waiting at the door. Wheeling McEwen into the hallway and into the Emergency Room, a Nurse began cutting McEwen's blue jacket from his left arm and across his chest. Another assistant did the same procedure on his right arm. The jacket was removed in seconds. They quickly began cutting his bloody shirt off.

Angel On My Shoulder

One Doctor began barking orders…give me a cut down…start an IV…Blood type….call the Blood Bank and tell them we are going to need a lot of blood…What type someone yelled? "A Negative" replied McEwen…"10 per cent rare"…We will still have to type you, to be sure Officer. The Doctor barked not the left arm, my God is this your first time to do a cut down, the cut down is on the right arm. "The fucker shot me in the neck, am I going to be paralyzed" asked McEwen? Can you wiggle your toes?....Can you wiggle your feet?....McEwen had no trouble wiggling his toes or feet.

"You're OK Joe on that part," replied the Doctor. I can't inhale McEwen told the Doctor. Someone began checking his right chest area with a stethoscope, listening for any abnormal lung sounds. The Doctor stated he's definitely down on his right side.

"What's your name," the Doctor asked? Joe…OK, Joe we are going to put a chest tube in your right side. I believe it will help you breathe a little better.

"Please…Please…Please knock me out"… I begged. Can't just yet Joe, we need X- Rays first. A female Nurse was holding McEwen's head steady. Her hands felt cool and smooth to his face. Hang in there Joe, replied the Nurse. He glanced up at her and said, thank you. Will you be with me when I go to X-Ray? I can if you want me too. Little did he know, but weeks later this same Nurse would come to his room and check up on his progress. About the time that they were going to take me to X-Ray Detective Nichols came into the Emergency Room and said, I have to talk to Joe, just for a second Doc. Make it brief. There were so many Doctors, Nurses and other assistants, trying to save him. Blood was all over the gurney. His Police jacket, shirt, pants were on the floor, soaked with blood.

"We need these clothes for evidence," Det. Nichols said. "OK, but right now we have to get this Officer to X-Ray. Someone will put all his belongings in a plastic sack and hold it for you."

Nichols leaned over right next to Joe's face and said "Gimmie something just anything."

Hurry up this man has to go to X-Ray STAT.

Angel On My Shoulder

Joe said to the Detective, there were two black males, one inside the house and the other one was in the white Olds, in the driver's seat. One sneaked up behind me and shot the shit out of me. I shot the driver twice point blank and maybe the shooter, as he ran away….the Olds belongs to the robbers. The Detective leaned towards McEwen and said, "Joe we are going to catch these Mother Fuckers, one way or another." He put his mouth up to McEwen's left ear and whispered, if we don't blow them away first. "They're in for one hell of an ass beating, so help me God!!" Nichols added, son we are here for you and we know you are strong and God is with you.

OHHHHH Fuck what the hell was that!! The Doctor had shoved a chest tube between McEwen's 3rd and 4th ribs on his right side. The large tube was the size of a little finger. Blood squirted from the end of the tube splattering the Dr's white coat. I can breathe a little better now Doc, but I'm really hurting bad. Damn I'm hurting, Doc, 'gimmie' something. Not yet Joe, we might have to tube you again, they can't do it in X-Ray, we have to do it here after the Tech's get through.

The Dr. placed the end of the chest tube into a clear jug, which began to fill up rapidly. One of the Dr's said, "we'll have to do exploratory surgery." An Assistant asked where are the bullet holes, I don't see any entrance wounds? I replied, "I was shot in my side, back and neck. God Dam it, the Mother Fucker sneaked up behind me." Little did I know that this exploratory surgery would leave a 22" scar across my chest and 4" past his belly button.

Take him to X-Ray STAT, two Assistants and the nurse that was holding his head began to push the gurney down the long hall to X-Ray, while another held the jug for the chest tube. A spare jug was placed on the gurney to use if the first one filled up, which it
was already half full with the blood from McEwen's chest.

Det. Nichols was walking along with Joe, assuring him that everything was going to be OK. He turned and started back towards the ER entrance, thinking that there is no way in hell that

Angel On My Shoulder

he could survive this ordeal. There were Officers all around the ER, both
inside and outside of the building, waiting to hear any news of Joe.

When a fellow Officer is in trouble, they all come together, and this is their Brotherhood. They all consider themselves as one big family.

 "You three start scrubbing up, we'll take him to the Operating Room as soon as they get through with X-Ray. The Chief Surgeon should arrive soon, from where ever in the hell he is," one of the Doctors stated as he left the ER.

Meanwhile at 9:25 P.M. on White Bridge Road, Officer McEwen's sister and her boyfriend were headed home, they were listening to the music on the Radio, when suddenly the music stopped and an announcement was given. We interrupt this program
to bring you breaking News! A Metro Police Officer has been shot several times at 25th and Blakemore and has been taken to Vanderbilt ER. As this story unfolds, listen tothe Ten O'clock news. Joan screamed, "That's my brother that was shot!" How do you
know, asked Mark? There are more than 800 Cops in Nashville. I just know it's him, turn around and get me to Vanderbilt now. Mark slowly pulled into a parking lot adjoining White Bridge Road.

"Don't fuck around Mark, she demanded, get going or I'll drive."

Six minutes later Joan opened the car door and ran past two Policeman at the Emergency entrance. Just as McEwen was being wheeled back from X-Ray, she cried, "Oh Brother!" Tears began to stream down her cheeks streaking her eye liner. I heard my sister's voice and he said, take care of my kids, Sis. They are going to need a lot of help. He disappeared down the hall towards X-Ray. Joan stood frozen in fear in the hall-way when she overheard two Interns talking. Not knowing she was McEwen's sister.

One said nobody makes it on a liver wound, let alone it being he was hit twice. No tell what the other bullets did to his body. Joan

Angel On My Shoulder

collapsed where she stood. Several Police Officers picked her up and placed her in a waiting room chair.

At 25th and Blakemore a Police Captain arrived the same time Major Joe Casey drove up. Major, I just saw Joe in Emergency, he's turned ashen gray. There's no way in hell he can come out of this. I want every fucking male black moving stopped and checked out. Fuck probable cause, we're not stopping until we find those bastards.
Nobody goes home until these pricks are caught!

Dr. John Foster, the Chief Surgeon at Vanderbilt just finished his Gin Spritzer at the Country Club when a waiter came up to him and said, "Dr. Foster you have an important, emergency phone call at the Waiter's station."
Dr. Foster excused himself from his party and walked hurriedly behind the waiter to the phone. "Hello," he said.

Dr. Foster, this is Juanita at the Emergency Room. Dr. Killebrew told me to call, he needs you to come to the E.R. ASAP....We have a Metro Police Officer that has been shot all to hell. He's in X-Ray now. Dr. Killebrew said he is bleeding profusely and needs to be opened up. Exploratory surgery is what he recommended but we need your help badly.
Dr. Foster said, I'll be there in five minutes. He hung up the phone and left by the side door without telling anyone what was happening. Four and a half minutes later he pulled into the E.R. parking lot, to his marked space. He unbuttoned his black tuxedo coat and removed his bow tie as he half walked, half ran through the
E.R. doors to the Nurses' Station. He told Juanita, "I'm going to scrub up, tell Dr. Killebrew where I am."

Dr. Foster thought there aren't any Police Officers on the streets because they're all here. He asked one of the Officers, "who's minding the streets, in a joking manner."

Angel On My Shoulder

The Officer's reply was, who gives a damn, one of our brothers is down. There's enough left to hunt the suspects down, all we ask is that you take care of Joe.

An Assistant Chief arrived on the scene and his first order of business was to impound the Olds and have it towed to the Police Garage for processing. "They won't go towards West End," he said it's 100% white…They'll head towards Edgehill or Granny White Pike. He told the Sarge to get the 10 and 30 series cars to Granny White Pike and work back, check every Beer Joint, dumpster and Alley in that area. Check every swinging Dick walking or riding. Anything on wheels, time is vital. If anyone becomes irate, tell them to call the Chief tomorrow. We don't have any time to explain. Get 20 and 40 series to start this sector and work east. Major Casey will head up the TACT Squad and Traffic Cars. We are going to blanket this area all the way to the Interstate.

Has anybody bothered to get a listing on this Olds? I did replied a Patrolman, it's registered to a Roy Allen in Lewisburg, Tn. The Chief said, somebody call the Dispatcher and tell the T.H.P. to cover the exit ramp in Lewisburg. One of the Patrolman mumbled, as he walked to his car, " too many Chiefs and not enough Indians" This is what happens when Police Officers work alone and they are aggressive Cops and not some laid back Chicken Shit just waiting to write tickets and answer calls and doing nothing else. McEwen was the type that got into situations all the time, always ending up
where the action was. The older Cops call this running hot or hot dogging.

Angel On My Shoulder

"Officer," the technician said, "Joe please try to be still so we can get X-rays that are not blurred." I replied, "I can't breathe and I can't be still because of the pain." The nurse then said, "One more Officer and we'll be through."

The Nurse that held my head steady with me in X-ray said, "Joe I'll give you something for pain just as soon as they take one more picture."

"Let's do it, OK!!" I blinked my eyes. "Okay we're through; take him to the OR STAT." the nurse shouted. "Okay Joe," the Nurse said "here is something for pain." She injected the clear
fluid into my IV and the relief was almost instant. The technicians began rolling the gurney down the long corridor to the awaiting elevator.

I stated, "that's much better now" and then
raised my head up looking down and over my feet and the hall was dark." I worriedly questioned, "Who's that? Who's that coming our way? Is he coming after me?" To me the hall seemed dark, but I could see an image of a person. I blinked my eyes and said, "He's wearing a cape and a scythe is across his shoulder." He wasn't walking he was just gliding down the hall. "Holy Shit," I cried, "It's...It's the Reaper!"

"Hold on Joe," the nurse said, "you're just hallucinating from the morphine I gave you, it has opium in it.

"He's waiving for me to come to him fuck him, get him away from me," I screamed, get him away!!! The nurse gave me a little more morphine and my head fell back onto the pillow. my mouth was half open and my eyes rolled back showing only the white.

"We might have to tube him, How's he breathing?"
one of the technician's said.

"He's breathing okay, but he looks bad, his color is gone! He's ashen, and that doesn't look good, I hope the OR is waiting on him."

The other nurse replied, "They might not have much time, he seems to be going downhill fast." I could hear them talking but I couldn't speak. The elevator door closed and it went upward to the OR floor.

I felt someone place their hand under the back of my neck, making an arch so I could be tubed prior to surgery.

" Restrain his arms and legs," someone said. I could feel the straps being tightened around my wrists and ankles. "Keep him light and I mean light," a Doctor told the Anesthesiologist. I was terrified. They are going to do exploratory surgery on me and not put me completely asleep. I felt the scalpel going across my chest, they seemed to cut and pull in a rough manner. I felt my toes curl upwards as the cutting continued. I wished they would put me to sleep; having my arms and legs strapped down was unbearable. I saw orange and heard the sound of the balloons being rubbed together and that was the last thing I remembered   until four days later I woke up.

BELOW IS THE EXACT SUMMARY OF THE OPERATION IN WHICH   24 UNITS OF BLOOD WAS GIVEN TO McEWEN DURING HIS 4 HOUR .   OPERATION.
PREOPERATIVE DIAGONSIS: GUNSHOT WOUND OF THE CHEST AND ABDOMEN.

POSTOPERATIVE CLINICAL DIAGNOSIS: SAME, WITH EXPLOSION   LESION OF THE RIGHT LOBE OF THE LIVER, PENETRATION OF THE   DIAPHRAGM AND RIGHT LOWER LOBE.
OPERATION: EXPLORATION BY THORACO-ABDOMINAL INCISION

WITH THE RIGHT HEPATIC LOBECTOMY AND INSERTION OF T-   TUBE INTO THE COMMON DUCT.

SURGEONS: DR. JOHN FOSTER AND DR. JAMES THRELKEL

THIS IS A 34 YEAR OLD MALE, POLICE OFFICER WHO WAS   ALLEGEDLY SHOT AT LEAST FIVE TIMES. THE PATIENT WAS SEEN   IN THE EMERGENCY ROOM OF THIS HOSPITAL

Angel On My Shoulder

WITHIN SEVERAL MINUTES OF THE TIME OF THE WOUNDS…HE   HAS BEEN HYPOTENSIVE, BUT HE REMAINED ALERT   THROUGHOUT. THE PATIENT HAS A THROUGH-AND-THROUGH

WOUND OF THE POSTERIOR ASPECT OF THE NECK. HE HAS A   THROUGH-AND-THROUGH WOUND OF THE LEFT UPPER ARM. HE   HAS A WOUND OF ENTRANCE ON THE LEFT MID-AXILLARY LINE AT THE LEVEL OF THE 10TH RIB. HE HAS TWO WOUNDS OF ENTRANCE   ON THE RIGHT MID-SCAPULAR LINE ABOUT THE 6TH RIB LEVEL.

CHEST TUBE WAS INSERTED AND SEVERAL HUNDRED CC. OF   BLOOD WAS REMOVED FROM THE RIGHT CHEST AREA.

THE ABDOMEN WAS QUITE DISTENDED AND TENDER. THE   PATIENT WAS TAKEN TO THE OPERATING ROOM WITH THE   SUSPECTED DIAGNOSIS OF GUNSHOT WOUNDS TO THE

ABDOMEN AND RUPTERED SPLEEN. THE PATIENT WAS PUT ON THE OPERATING TABLE IN THE SUPINE POSITION AND SATISFACTORY ENDOTRACHEAL ANESTHESIA WAS INDUCED. THE BLOOD WAS RUNNING BY MULTIPLE CUTDOWS. AFTER THE ABDOMEN AND CHEST WERE PREPPED AND DRAPED

IN THE USUAL FASHION, A MIDLINE ABDOMINAL INCISION WAS   MADE AND DEEPENED TO THE PERITONEAL CAVITY. ON ENTERING THE PERITONEAL CAVITY, SEVERAL LITERS OF

BRIGHT RED BLOOD WERE ENCOUNTERED. EXPLORATION WAS   FIRST IN THE LEFT UPPER QUADRANT WHERE THE SPLEEN WAS FOUND TO BE INTACT AND NOT BLEEDING. THERE WAS SOME RETROPERITONEAL   HEMATOMA IN THE AREA OF THE KIDNEY. HOWEVER,

HIS PREOPERATIVE URINE HAD SHOWN NO RED CELLS AND   THE KIDNEY WAS UNREMARKABLE TO PALPATION. THERE WAS NO BLOOD WELLING FROM THE

Angel On My Shoulder

UPPER LEFT QUADRANTAFTER   THIS HAD BEEN REMOVED BY SUCTION.

ATTENTION WAS THEN TURNED TO THE RIGHT UPER QUADRANT WHERE TWO LARGE STELLATE EXPLOSION TYPE   LACERATIONS OF THE RIGHT LOBE OF THE LIVER

WERE SEEN. FROM THESE WAS WELLING LARGE AMOUNTS OF   RED BLOOD. THE FREE BLOOD IN THE PERITONEAL CAVITY WAS ASPIRATED WHILE PRESSURE WAS HELD ON THE LIVER AND   BLOOD WAS PUMPED INTO THE PATIENT. WITH THE INDUCTION   OF ANESTHESIA HIS PRESSURE HAD DROPPED AND HE WAS

HYPOTENSIVE FOR A SIGNIFICANT PORTION OF THE   PROCEDURE. MASSIVE AMOUNTS OF BLOOD WERE

PUMPED DURING THE PROCEDURE. AFTER THE PATIENT'S   CONDITION WAS STABILIZED, LARGE CHROMIC LIVER SUTURES   WERE PLACED IN THE FIGURE-OF-EIGHT FASHION

THROUGH THE WOUND AND THE BLEEDING APPEARED TO BE   CONTROLLED.

ATTENTION WAS THEN TURNED TO THE EXPLORATION OF   THE REMAINDER OF THE ABDOMEN. TWO WOUNDS IN THE   DIAPHRAGM WERE SEEN WITH SOME BLOOD

COMING OUT OF THE CHEST. THE STOMACH WAS UNREMARKABLE. THERE WAS SOME BLOOD IN THE RETROPERITONEAL SPACE ABOVE THE PANCREAS. THE LESSER SAC WAS OPENED AND THIS WAS EXAMINED. THERE WERE NO WOUNDS OF THE PANCREAS SEEN.

THE ENTIRE BOWEL WAS RUN AND THERE WERE NO WOUNDS   IDENTIFIED. THE COLON WAS WITHOUT INJURY. FOLLOWING   THIS EXPLORATION, ATTENTION WAS AGAIN TURNED TO THE   LIVER AND IT WAS FOUND TO BE BLEEDING PROFUSELY.

AGAIN ATTEMPTS WERE MADE TO OVERSEW THE WOUND USING LARGE CHROMIC LIVER SUTURES. ONCE MORE THIS PROVED UNSUCCESSFUL AND THE PATIENT BLED TO

Angel On My Shoulder

THE POINT OF BEING UNABLE TO GET A BLOOD PRESSURE.
AGAIN PRESSURE WAS APPLIED AND THE BLOOD PUMPED
INTO THE PATIENT. THE INCISION WAS EXTENDED INTO
THE

RIGHT CHEST ALONG THE EIGHTH INTERCOSTAL
SPACE AND THE   DIAPHRAGM WAS DIVIDED DOWN
TOWARD THE VENA CAVA.   SEVERAL LITERS OF
BLOOD WERE REMOVED FROM THE CHEST.   THE CHEST
CAVITY WAS EXAMINED AND FOUND TO BE FREE OF

BLEEDING SITES. IT WAS FELT THAT THE BLOOD
ENTERED THE   CHEST THROUGH HOLES IN THE
DIAPHRAGM. HOLES IN THE   DIAPHRAGM WERE
THEREFORE OVERSEWN. THE CHEST WAS   AGAIN
EXAMINED AND FOUND TO BE FREE OF BLEEDING SITES. A

SLUG WAS FOUND SITTING UNDER A CRUSHED
LATERAL RIB.   THIS WAS REMOVED WITHOUT
DIFFUCILITY AND MARKED. THERE   WAS ANOTHER
SLUG IDENTIFIED IN THE LATERAL EDGE OF THE   RIGHT
LOWER LOBE LUNG. THERE WAS AN AREA OF

HEMORRHAGE AND CONTUSION. IT WAS ELECTED
TO LEAVE THIS   SLUG IN PLACE RATHER THAN VIOLATE
THE LUNG AND CAUSE   FURTHER PULMONARY
DISTRUCTION. ON ONE OCCASION IT

BECAME NECESSARY TO REMOVE AND TO APPLY
MASSAGE TO   THE HEART THROUGH THE
PERICARDIUM FROM THE RIGHT SIDE. THE PATIENT
PROMPTLY HAD REINSTITUTION OF CARDIC   ACTIVITY
AND HAD RETURN OF BLOOD PRESSURE, AFTER SOME

MORE BLOOD WAS GIVEN. LARGE HEMATOMA
DEVELOPED SUBCAPSULARLY IN THE LIVER AND IT
BECAME APPARENT THAT THERE WAS AN IMPOSSIBILITY
TO CONTROL THE BLEEDING

WITH SUTURE. THEREFORE, HEPATIC LOBECTOMY
WAS CARRIED   OUT REMOVING THE MAJOR PORTION
OF THE RIGHT LOBE. LINE   OF DISSECTION WAS
CHOSEN JUST TO THE

Angel On My Shoulder

RIGHT OF THE LINE DRAWN BETWEEN THE NECK OF THE   GALLBLADDER AND THE VENA CAVA. IT WAS NECESSARY TO   REMOVE THIS MUCH LIVER SO TO REMOVE ALL THE
DAMAGED TISSUE.

SHARP INCISION WAS MADE THROUGH THE CAPSULE OF THE LIVER AND THEN USING THE HANDLE OF THE   KNIFE AND BLUNT DISSECTION THE LIVER WAS
DIVIDED. REMOVAL OF THE LIVER WEIGHING 850 GRAMS AND MEASURING 20.0 X 18.0 X 12.0. ALL POINTS OF RESISTANCE   BEING VESSELS AND BILE DUCTS WERE DOUBLY
CLAMPED AND DIVIDED BETWEEN CLAMPS. THE RIGHT LOBE OF   THE LIVER WAS ACHIEVED BY TYING ALL POINTS WITH 3-0 PLAIN   GUT. COMPLETE HEMOSTASIS WAS ACHIEVED AND THERE WAS   NO FURTHER SIGNIFICANT BLEEDING. THIS AREA WAS
COPIOUSLY IRRIGATED AND PACKED. THE COMMON DUCT WAS   THEN EXPOSED AND USUING TWO FINE SILK ARTERIAL SUTURES   AS GUIDE STITCHES, INCISION WAS MADE
IN THE COMMON DUCT AND #12 RUBBER T-TUBE WAS INSERTED.   T-TUBE WAS BROUGHT OUT VIA STAB WOUND LOW ON THE   RIGHT FLANK. THE COMMON DUCT WAS CLOSED
USING INTERRUPTED SERIES OF 4-0 CHROMIC SUTURES. THE   RIGHT UPPER QUADRAN WAS AGAIN REEXPLORED AND FOUND   TO BE FREE OF BLEEDING SITES AND THERE WAS
NO SIGNIFICANT LEAKAGE OR DRAINAGE FROM THE LIVER. AGAIN   THE AREA WAS COPIOUSLY IRRIGATED. A LARGE CLEAR   SILASTIC CHEST TUBE WAS THEN INSERTED
LOW IN THE MID-AXILLARY LINE AND BROUGHT UP THE   POSTERIOR GUTTER ALONG THE DOME OF THE

Angel On My Shoulder

DIAPHRAGM. THE DIAPHRAGMATIC WOUND WAS THEN CLOSED USING A #5 TEVDEK SUTURE. A HOLE IN THE DIAPHRAGM HAS PREVIOUSLY CLOSED. THROUGH-AND-THROUGH LARGE PENROSE DRAINS WERE THEN PLACED FROM STAB WOUNDS IN THE ASPECT OF THE RIGHT FLANK TO THE ANTERIOR ABDOMINAL WALL. THESE DRAINS WERE LEAD ALONG THE BROAD LIVER BED AND THE OMENTUM WAS LAID TO COVER THE DRAINS AND THE LIVER BED. A LARGE SARATOGA SUMP WAS THEN LAID INTO THE RIGHT UPPER QUADRANT JUST OUTSIDE THE OMENTRUM AND EXITED VIA STAB WOUND IN THE RIGHT FLANK.

THE PENROSE DRAIN WAS PLACED DOWN TO THE COMMON DUCT WHERE THE T-TUBE HAD BEEN PLACED AND ALSO EXITED BY STAB WOUND IN THE RIGHT UPPER QUADRANT. THREE PENROSE DRAINS WERE THEN EXITED FROM THE UPPER QUADRANT STAB WOUND. THESE DRAINED THE LEFT GUTTER AT THE AREA OF THE SPLENIC FLEXUREM WHERE THE HEMATOMA HAD BEEN EXPLORED IN THAT AREA. FOLLOWING THIS, THE WOUNDS WERE CLOSED IN LAYERS. THE FASCIA WAS CLOSED WITH O-POLYDEK SUTURES. THE INTERCOASTAL INCISION WAS CLOSED IN TWO LAYERS, WITH INTERRUPTED SYNTHETIC MATERIAL. SUBCUTANEOUS TISSUE WAS COPIOUSLY IRRIGATED AND CLOSED WITH INTERRUPTED 3-0 PLAIN. THE SKIN WAS CLOSED WITH INTERRUPTED 4-0 POLYDEK STITCHES IN A LOOSE FASHION. THE PATIENT TOLERATED THE PROCEDURE IN A PRECARIOUS FASHION. HE WAS GIVEN THE TOTAL OF 24 UNITS OF BLOOD DURING THE PROCEDURE. THE PATIENT REQUIRED ADDITIONAL CUTDOWN

Angel On My Shoulder

DURING THE PROCEDURE. HE WAS GIVEN BICARB AND CALCIUM AND ANTIBOTICS AND IV FLUIDS. THERE WAS NO SIGNIFICANT BLEEDING AT THE TERMINATION OF THE PROCEDURE. THE PATIENT'S BLOOD PRESSURE WAS STABLE AT 140 SYSTOLIC AND THE PULSE WAS AROUND 100. DRY, STERILE DRESSINGS WERE APPLIED AND ALL THE DRAINS WERE COVERED AND THE PATIENT WAS TAKEN TO THE INTENSIVE CARE UNIT IN CRITICAL CONDITION. THE PATIENT AWAKENED PROMPTLY ON CESSATION OF ANESTHESIA AND ISALERT AND COHERENT. HE IS MAKING URINE.

I was in ICU and seemed to be doing as well as expected, but there were thirteen tubes still in my chest and elsewhere.

Things seemed to be making progress back at the scene of the shooting.

"MAJOR! I have a call from dispatch about a subject with blood on his shirt and he is at an address near Hawkins. They wouldn't let him in!" Sgt. Roberts said excitedly. "This could be our shooter!" the Major said. "Send one car to the address and 5 more units to to the area. He's on foot near Hawkins."

Meanwhile the driver of the Olds managed to get to his friend's house. "William," his friend said as he pulled the bandages tight, "you have to get a doctor to look at this tomorrow. It's pretty bad. You can tell the doc you were playing with your gun, and it went off." Then he helped William to his feet, got him in the car and drove him back to Lewisburg.

William replied, "how is Roy going to explain about his Olds in Nashville?" James said "he'll have to file a stolen car report or something, man I don't know. I do know, this is bad, really fucking bad, and I'm taking a hell of a risk by transporting you home." James continued, "You owe me big time. Man you know when a Cop gets shot those Police go crazy and never let up, it really becomes personal for them. They will go to any means and leave no stone unturned until the suspects are caught. Do you know if the Cop that got shot can or can't I.D. you? Can

Angel On My Shoulder

you? Man oh man you're in deep shit. I might add…that an ass whipping is in store for somebody. Man I'd hate to be in your shoes. You've got to be careful and keep your mouth shut. Don't forget to make a report on the Olds being stolen."

William replied, "OK! OK! Man what in the hell have I done, I really messed up this time."

James scoffed, "Was it worth the amount that you got from those old people?" "Hell no, it wasn't worth the mess I'm in now." "What am I going to do?" William worriedly asked.
"Don't ask me, I'm glad that it's you and not me. God help you, man." James concluded.

The Lieutenant at the crime scene said "Get this car towed to the garage for processing ASAP, out of this damp air. I mean nobody is to touch this car or anything inside without using gloves. We got to catch these guys fast. Keep these civilians back. Who the hell was supposed to tape this area off. This isn't a practice, it's for real. McEwen's life is at stake, we've got to find
something. There's too many milling around, rubber necking." He then added, "Sarge, get all the cars back in service except the first one on the scene. We can't catch these thugs with 8 or 10 Officers just standing around with their hands in their pockets scratching their nuts!!! Move!! Move!! now!! Son of a bitch, what a night." replied the Lieutenant.

This was hard to take, one of their own had been taken down and they were going to do everything they could to try and find these shooters.

"Stop!! Stop the car Tim!" Sam stated, in an excited tone. "Turn off the motor its making too much noise."
the ignition off and they sat silently in their Patrol listening for any
sound that could lead them to the shooter. All at once they heard dogs barking in the area, "Ease down the street real slow Tim. I have a good hunch that those two are close around here.

Angel On My Shoulder

There's a lot of hedges in front of these old houses. It's a good place to hide because they are so close to each other and there are lot of bushes they could hide under. They could be behind them. Go slow Tim, we just might get lucky."

The Patrol car crept down 14th Avenue South for another two blocks and Officer Durham said softly, "stop, I think I saw something across the street behind the hedge, someone just ducked down." Sam jumped from the car and crossed the street in   a dead run and turned his flashlight on just as he jumped the two   foot hedge. Lying just to the left of his feet was a male/black   huddled next to the base of the hedge. "Tim, over here," Sam   yelled. "Don't you move you mother fucker or you're a dead man.   Hands behind your back…do it now!" Tim was   beside Sam in an instant and together they handcuffed the suspect. "Where's the gun?" Sam asked.

"I don't, remember," was the suspects reply.

"How about this for remembering," as Sam hit the male black in his right rib cage with a closed fist. "You want some more, or are you going to start remembering now you mother fucker? What's your name?"

"Roy," "Roy what," again Sam punched him, this time in the stomach. Roy bent over in agony…

"Well," said Sam.

"I asked you Roy what? Ok you want some more"

"No sir, UH, UH sir, Allen is my last name. Roy replied.

Sam then asked again, "The gun, where is the gun?"

"I uh, well uh uh I threw it in the hedge, over there Officer." Roy shakily stated.

Sam shined his flashlight and he then spotted a blue steel revolver in the hedge. He retrieved the gun by the butt to keep from
smudging any of the fingerprints.

"You shouldn't have hit me Officer," Roy squeaked.

"Really," Sam said, "how about this." as he began slapping Roy's face back and forth several times.

Angel On My Shoulder

"HELP… HELP…HELP…somebody help me, I ain't did nothing," Roy screamed as Sam shut him up with another punch to the stomach.

Together the two Officers half ran and half dragged the reeling suspect to the Patrol Car. Once back inside the car, Sam picked up the mike and called dispatch to let them know that they had found one of the suspects and they believed it was the shooter and to notify CID that they were on their way to headquarters. All the while Roy was yelling," I ain't did nothing…call me a lawyer."

"Ok" said Sam, "you're a lawyer mother fucker."

"I mean call me a real lawyer."

Once more, Sam replied "OK you're a real lawyer asshole."

"This ain't right, I knows I have my rights."

"Yeah you have rights just like the Police Officer fighting for his life right now." Tim leaned over the front seat and bitch slapped Roy across the mouth with a loud popping noise.

Tim turned toward Sam and said, "I wonder who's going to notify Joe's dad, You know Red's real tight with the Mayor, I'd hate for him to find out over the TV News, or in the newspaper tomorrow. Joe's kids are going to be devastated, they worshiped their dad. We ought to go by and tell them after we drop this turd off at headquarters."

I awoke one morning and I was in Intensive Care and Judge J.Randall Wyatt Jr. and his wife, Kay, was standing beside my   bed. What a Great Day this was, our paths crossed again. Randall   is one of my closest friends. Over 6 decades, I've known this man. I felt I was on the right track to getting well now. This was a great surprise to wake up and see him standing by my bedside.

On the fifth day the Dr. came in and removed a feeding tube from my nose and told me that he was going to remove the chest tube in my right side. He took a 4 X 4 gauze and put something on it.

He said, "Joe in order to remove the chest tube you will have to take a deep breath and hold it. This is very important,

Angel On My Shoulder

because if you let the air out of your lungs they will collapse so this why you have to keep them fully inflated. This is going to hurt pretty bad, but you will feel much better after this is done. Are you ready? I'll count to three and then take a deep breath and hold it until I tell you it is OK to let it out."

I nodded and held my breath. he pulled out the chest tube and quickly placed the 4 X 4 gauze over the hole, while someone else taped over it.

"Can you tell any difference now, Joe." The Doctor asked?

"Not now, but it hurt like hell when you took it out. It felt like you pulled a rasp out of my lungs." I stated. "Now when you eat something, it won't have such a bad taste." The doctor added.

"I know, the food has tasted awful." Each morning very early the Doc came by to change the fluid soaked dressing that covered the hole where the tube was. I had what is known as a parachute covering that was laced back and forth across my chest, when they took the dressing from my chest there was six pen rose drains coming from my chest area. They looked like they were rubber or a large noodle. Each one had a safety pen stuck to it, to keep it from
retracting back into my chest. The Dr. would take and hold the drain tube, remove the safety pin and advance the pen rose tube approximately an inch and a half. As he was advancing
these drains a large amount of fluid seeped from the hole that he was working on. This fluid was soaked up with numerous gauze patches. He would then put the safety pin in a new hole and cut off the part that he had pulled out. The fluid had an orange color to it. He stated that this fluid was loaded with bacteria. It had a funny smell to it. He did this to all 6 holes that was on my chest and then put clean dressing back on. He then covered my entire chest with one big piece of gauze and replaced the parachute covering back up. This was quite an ordeal, but I got a pain shot every time they did this which wasn't so bad. This went on for about a week until all the pen rose drains were pulled out of my chest cavities.

Several days after I had been shot the Doctor came into my room and he said that he was amazed at how much of my liver had grown back in such a short time. Even though it had

Angel On My Shoulder

grown back, but there was no filtering tissue to it. One of the Interns said that if he not seen the X-Ray, he would not of believed it.

On March 27th, 1970 my previous partner David L. Cook came to me in the Hospital and asked me if I would be his best man at his wedding. I told him that I would, but I might be a little shaky because I had lost almost 34 lbs. since the shooting and my legs were kind of weak. We went through the Police Recruit Academy at the same time and on occasion we worked together in the same Patrol Car. The wedding took place in the Vanderbilt Hospital Chapel with the Rev. Harold Sorrell, Pastor of the Lockland Baptist Church who read the marriage Vows to David and Helen. Also present was Mrs. McEwen.

The very next day I was discharged from the Hospital to finish my recovery at home. I was always upbeat and full of pep and energy, but now I feel totally drained.

ANGEL ON MY SHOULDER - PART 3
SECOND SURGERY March 20, 1970

I was in a private room at Vanderbilt watching TV on this chilly day, and I was wearing pajama bottoms with no top and the sheet draped across my waist. I was thinking about the surgery in two days, only this time it would be a cakewalk compared to the night I was shot.

Dr. Foster would remove a bullet beneath the right side of my chest that had slowly moved from the lower part of his chest cavity to just beneath the skin. There would be a ½" incision and pop the bullet out, and put 2 stitches in. This would take about 10 minutes tops. Then back to my private room, more tests, blood workup and on and on.

My interest in the TV stopped when I heard the door open and in walked the Nurse that first saw me in the ER the night I was shot. "You don't remember me, do you Mac," she said. I shook my head from side to side. "I'm Patsy, the one that was holding your head steady when you came into emergency room. You had tubes going in and out of you. After the X-Rays we were headed to the elevator to go up to the OR when
I gave you a shot of morphine after that you got pretty mixed up. You thought you had seen the Grim Reaper, you put your right hand on mine and looked at me with those blue eyes and winked and said, "Come to see me as soon as possible." Then your eyes closed and I left the gurney at the Operating Room. I tried numerous times to see you but there was
always a crowd, either the TV News Media, the Mayor, Chief of Police, numerous Police Officers and the Newspaper reporters. So here I am with no one else around."

While she was talking all I could think about was 5' 8, about 25 years old, 160 lbs., brown hair, nice lips, a small waist and a nice ass and large breasts. Wow is she Sexy looking. Damn, I must be dreaming, I thought.

I was looking into her brown Jane Russell eyes that no man would forget, among all her other features. "You know, Patsyif I were standing up right now, I would be weak in the knees."

Patsy smiled and said, "You are kidding me aren't you, Joe?"

I said," No, I promise you I'm not kidding, I really mean it."

"I just got back in town from a monthly seminar and you were the main topic of the surgeons. Everyone was astounded on how you survived 2 wounds to the liver. How about a total of 4 holes, 2 entrance and 2 exit wounds. You are the first in fourteen before you who never made it off the operating table. So you see, someone was watching over you that night. I know a lot of people that were keeping you in their prayers. Did you know that the liver is the only organ that replaces itself if the remaining part is healthy?"

"No," I replied, "but I do now."

Patsy said, "Dr. Foster mentioned by you not being a smoker it kept your lungs from collapsing. You bled out 2 times on the operating table and you had no pulse. I'm going to call you Mighty Mouse."

"That sounds good to me," I replied.

Patsy stated, "March 6th was and I had 14 days off and tonight I start the grave-yard shift. I haven't been here but I've been keeping up with your progress from Beverly and the newspapers. You have lost some weight." she quipped, "how much?"

I said, "I came in weighing 212 lbs. and as of today I tipped the scales at 178 lbs."

Patsy shook her head in disbelief. "Wow, 34 lbs. in 14 days must be some kind of a record." She stood beside my bed and looked at my 22 inch scar across my chest which extended belomy

Angel On My Shoulder

belly button. She said, "so that's what an exploratory surgery scar looks like. It is the first one I've ever seen. Dr. Foster opened you up like a cheap suit. He came in the emergency room in a tuxedo. He must have been to some gathering of the minds," she added.

Patsy looked at my baby blue eyes and wondered where this was going to lead, probably nowhere but maybe, just maybe. "Oh! by the way I brought you some Vitamin E to rub on your scar, this will help keep the keloids down some." She turned sideways by my bed and pulled her uniform up just above her knees and sat on the bed putting her right leg atop of the bed sheet and her left leg was on the floor. A lot of leg exposed, I was thinking as he looked in her direction.

My vision was focused on her thigh all the way to her crotch. Beautiful legs I thought as he enjoyed the view, smooth as silk and very warm to touch. Patsy looked at me and raising her left eyebrow, smiled approvingly.

She took the small jar from her uniform pocket, unscrewing the lid and then sticking her index finger in the jar, withdrawing a glob of Vitamin E and she began rubbing it gently on my scar. "Is that tender," she asked.
"No not a bit," I replied. She continued to rub the salve slowly down to his belly button and below. She pushed the sheet down past the ending of the scar. Her elbow brushed against my penis, which began filling with blood almost immediately. She looked at me and said, " I think someone wants out from under the sheet." Her hand remained on his abdomen with her fingers spread apart, moving ever so slightly up and down.

I placed his right hand on her knee which was exposed and felt very smooth. She looked at me in the eyes and using her left hand pushing his hand further up her uniform to a creamy white thigh. Son of a bitch Iwas thinking, I must be dreaming.

Angel On My Shoulder

She looked at the scar and said, "I'll be back at work tonight at 1:00 AM, would you like me to check on you and see if you are feeling all right?" "Please do." I said in an excited reply! "Don't stand me up," he quipped. " Don't take your sleeping pill tonight, I want you 100% awake. " my hand touched her crotch and said, "I know I shouldn't wish my time away, but I wish it was 1 AM right now."

"Don't worry, just relax, I'll be back and don't forget I have 7 days left on this shift. Do you feel up to this," she asked. "Look at the sheet," I whispered, "and tell me what you think."

Patsy said, " OOH yeah!!! See ya tonight Officer, we'll do some undercover work." Patsy started walking towards the door and Joe was looking at her nice round ass as she went out the door and turned right into the hallway. He took a deep breath and thought I'm in no hurry to be discharged… SOMETIMES LIFE IS SO GOOD!!!

As Joe lay in bed watching the clock, 1 AM came and went. He kept watching TV which he had on mute, all he could think about was when she would be walking through the door. 1:15 AM came and went. More TV with no sound, just silence and shadows bouncing off the wall. It seemed as though time had stood still. 1:30 AM when the door opened. My heart starting beating so fast it scared me, but there she was Long Tall Sally.

Patsy closed the door and slid a large chair in front of the door. She turned and looked at me. I had a big smile on my face. I was so glad to see her. "Just being extra careful," she said. "I was late because of an emergency. What!! Did you think I would stand you up? I have been waiting for this moment, just as much as you have, I hope."

I replied, "I didn't know but I sure hoped you would come. "I've been counting the hours and minutes since you left my room earlier today. I am a nervous wreck, I've got a lump in my throat," I said.

Angel On My Shoulder

"Just nerves," she replied. "I can take care of that, no problem. Just lay there and let the Nurse take care of you. I promise I'll take it easy." She was beside the bed now and she leaned over and gave me an electrifying KISS. Her lips felt hot and moist on my lips and my eyes rolled back in my head. I groaned long and low until she pulled back the sheet and said, "How was that Mighty Mouse?"

I replied, "absolutely out of this world!!!"

Patsy pulled the sheet down further and saw that I was buck naked, however I was ready for battle. My Soldier was ready to do battle and it was at attention.

"I'm not wearing any underpants," she pulled her uniform up past her waist and placed her left knee beside my hip and then swung her right leg over my body straddling him. She raised her body up some and using her left hand guiding my soldier into the honey hole. "Would you like a repeat performance in a couple of hours?" she quipped.

"Absolutely, positively, and most assuredly," I replied.

"This is going to be a good week," she said, "I've 6 more nights after tonight before I'm scheduled for 2 weeks off." She got down from my bed and pulled her uniform down, slipped into her shoes and moved towards the door, sliding the chair back to its original place. She turned towards me and said, "get some sleep you're going to need it. I'll wake you up in a little while and we can play hide the weenie again." "2nd time is always better and it usually last longer." She opened the door and walked out looking back to see a big grin on my face.

I thought, I'm sure glad I didn't get shot in the dick!! What a bummer that would have been. I thought this is a good dose of Poor Man's morphine as I drifted off to sleep with a big smile on my face. my regular nurse came in to check on me and couldn't help but notice that I had a smile upon my face. I didn't even wake up when she was taking my blood pressure, she turned out the light and shut the door thinking I did not seem to be in any pain,

Angel On My Shoulder

because I was sleeping soundly. She thought I must be feeling better.

Several days had passed and Nurse Patsy had not been back to his room. I was thinking I knew it was too good to be true. As i laid in bed trying to watch TV, his mind kept wandering back to Patsy. Thinking what did I do wrong or what didn't I do, I'll guess it will always be a mystery. About that time the door was pushed open and just a little single rose was all I could see, when from behind the door she appeared, "I guess you were wondering what happened to me? I got real sick and was out for a while. I'm feeling better now that I know that you are still here, don't get me wrong but I couldn't wait to get back to work. Have you missed me Joe,"

i replied "Hell Yes, I was thinking that I must have done something to make you mad at me." "No way," she replied.

"Joe, I have never thrown myself at any man until I met you. I've had only two men In my life. The first was at the Senior Prom, it was a one night thing with no meaning at all, the second was my husband who died three years ago from a brain tumor. Three years, no one has ever kissed me, let alone touched me, I don't know what it is about you, but that night while you were on you way to the OR and you winked at me, I felt electrified!! I haven't stopped thinking about you since." She added, "I would come to the Intensive Care and just stare at you while you were in an inert state. Here I stand like a school girl captivated with a man who's married with three children. I have about as much of a chance as a snowball in hell to be with you, but you know I don't know what I will feel in ten minutes from now or tomorrow, but I do know that things change and what seems to be impossible now could be very doable next week, next month or next year. I want you Mighty Mouse, you're all I think about. I wake up thinking about you and you're the last thing I think about at night. I want to cool this fire within me, or make it like a volcano. I'm willing to try but don't lead me on, after a short while let me know if it's a go or just a wash. I'm a very patient person and usually get what I want,

Angel On My Shoulder

usually but not always. I live one mile from here making it very convenient for

you to come by on your way home when you start your trial about the two that almost killed you."

I replied, "you're right I am married with three children that I love dearly, as for my wife, she is, well, she's a person that I tolerate because of my children. The house is always dirty, I mean dirty dishes and dirty clothes all over the house. I never get a kind word from her. It is always about her and her needs. Don't get me wrong she is a great Mother, but as far as a wife. She is lacking in what it takes to make a man happy. As for you, you are a breath of fresh air, that seems to make me want to get out of this bed and start living again."

"With that being said, I understand where you are coming from and I respect your feelings. I only hope I can make you happy, even if it is just for a little while." "I brought you something." She gleamed.

"What?" I replied. "I brought you a box of Trojans." "We don't need them," I said.

"Look there is no room in my life for a child."

"Don't worry" I said, "six years ago Eric was born I knew I had to do something, I figured one more kid and I would fuck myself away from the table and have to start eating off of a TV tray. So I went to New Albany, Indiana to see a Dr. Richardson, who gave me a vasectomy for $125.00 cash. So you see I now shoot blanks."

Patsy replied, "Well it just keeps getting better and better. I've met the Tennessee

Angel On My Shoulder

Stud, AKA: Mighty Mouse. You can just sit or lay back and enjoy the ride. One more thing I bought a new open front bra. I have just one small problem."

"What's that" I asked.

"I'll show you." Patsy opened her Nurse's uniform and let it fall to the floor, exposing her two large breasts that were bulging out of her new bra. She added, when I bend over, like when I want to fluff your pillow, like this. She put both arms on each side of my pillow to fluff it up and both breasts fell out and landed in my face.

I immediately put my hands around the right breast and kissed the erect nipple. Her areola was at least three inches in diameter. Real sexy, I thought as I moved his face side to side. "What size are these melons," I asked.

"Well I wear a 42 Double D and they are real."

"Honey," I stated "You don't have to convince me that they are real. A man can tell if they are real or not. Believe me these babies are not only big they are spectacular. I could play with these for hours and hours", I added.

Well Patsy replied "We don't have hours; we only have a few minutes." She went towards the door and placed the chair in front of it again. "This will give us a little alone time. Ok!" She raised up and swung her right leg over me and straddled my body like she had done before. In a few minutes the hospital bed began shaking and rocking. I felt Patsy's side and she began to get sweaty and sticky.

"Damn" Patsy said, "I wish we were at my house so I could scream! Might Mouse you're going where no man has ever gone. You are in virgin territory. How does it feel" she asked.

"Tight good and tight," Joe replied. "I can't last much longer," I said it's been a while.

Just as Patsy was getting off the bed, her leg hit the Nurse's button, "Joe are you all right, do you need anything?"

I replied, "I'm sorry, I hit it by mistake."

Angel On My Shoulder

"Are you sure you are alright?"

"Yes. I was just trying to turn off the TV and I hit the wrong button."

"OK then Joe, I'll check on you In a little bit, it's almost time for your vitals to be taken."

They both giggled, "Boy that was a close call, we'll have to put that out of our way the next time. I can come back around 3 AM, if you want me too."

"Absolutely" I said, "I'll promise to do better then."

"You did just fine Mighty Mouse, you rang my chimes just right," she quipped.

Off the bed she slid and while she was putting her uniform back on I was spellbound with her beauty. She bent over and kissed me with a long wet kiss that made it hard for me to focus, because my eyes were watery with awe.

She pulled away. "That was really good, as good as it gets."

He was thinking again "Sometimes Life Is Good."

She pulled the sheet up to my chest and giving me one more kiss she said, "see you later Mighty Mouse."

At 3:15 AM she came back to my room and the Nurse at the desk, said "he's sleeping soundly, I took his vitals and he never opened his eyes or moved."

"Oh, that's OK, I was just going to see how he was doing."

The floor Nurse said, "he seems to be improving very well. Shall I tell him you came by?"

Patsy replied, "just tell him that the Nurse that took care of him in the ER was here asking about him."

The floor nurse asked, "Your name is?" "I'm sorry my name

Angel On My Shoulder

is Patsy. I work in the ER."

The floor nurse casually said, "I guess you see a lot down there."

Patsy continued, "Oh yeah. Well I have to get back down there my break is about over."

I did not see Patsy for quite some time. Well, I guess it was too good to be true. Anyway, she sure made me a happy one for a while. All I could do was to think about the time we had spent together in my private room and on my bed. I started thinking about the kids. I knew that they were in school and it would be impossible for them to come see me. i also knew that my wife had no one to keep the kids while she came to see me. Their house was a far distance from the hospital, it was almost out in the county in Kingston Springs. My mom came to see me once, she drove up from Naples Florida with her husband a very wealthy man. They brought me a five lb. bag of naval oranges from Florida and a back scratcher. I didn't expect much from my mom because she left me to live with my dad when I was just 15 years old. She moved back to Kentucky and played the piano and sang in my aunt's restaurant, the Indiana Café.

Over a week had passed and she was not around. No phone call, nothing. Oh well,I was thinking it was great while it lasted. Someone was knocking on the door, "come on in,"

I shouted. "Damn, where have you been? I have been worried about you." I said to the nurse. "I had to go to St. Thomas to help out in their ER. I have been calling the Nurses' to see how you were doing." Patsy continued, "I think they started wondering why I was calling so much. I understand you have been giving them a hard time."
"Well it is hard just lying here in this bed alone." I added. "I'm sorry, I should have tried to come see you. The work at St.

Angel On My Shoulder

Thomas is a lot harder than it is here. The staff there is nice and friendly. Enough about that, Damn you look good Joe. I sure have missed you. I understand that you might be leaving pretty soon. Please don't forget me, you have my address and my phone number, call me when you can. I would love to hear from you. If,
you know what I mean." Patsy swooned. "Come here, I will show you how much I missed you."

I said, "You know Mighty Mouse's Soldier has missed you too!!" Patsy said, "I'll see what I can do about that around 4 AM. That is, if it is OK with you big boy."
"Ok, so now I am a big boy?" I said in a flirty manor. "You know what I mean. I have missed you a lot.

I still think about when you arrived in the ER and I was cutting your jacket, shirt and t-shirt off. I had to steady your head while they Dr's examined you trying to figure out what to do. I told one new doctor how about X-Rays to see what damage had been done. I think this was his first time to ever see anyone shot up like you were. He was in awe of what to do."

"You know Joe, I've seen your sister, Joan is that her name?"
"Yeah, that's her name."

"She's not too friendly is she?"
"You can say that. But you know, I don't think I ever saw your wife."
I replied, "She doesn't come too much, her excuse was she has to take care of the kids."

She added, "That's not a very good excuse for someone who was shot up like you were. It looks like she could have gotten someone to watch the kids. Oh well, at least I had you and that is saying something. I have really missed you,"
I told her, "Patsy you have been a breath of fresh

Angel On My Shoulder

air. Please don't go away that long again."

"Do you know when they are going to let you go home?"

"No I don't. But I am not looking forward to going home at all. Do you have a spare bedroom," I asked.

"NO she replied, but I do have a king size bed."

"Damn that sounds good." I said to her. "What's that noise?"

"That's my beeper, there's another emergency coming in. I've got to go but first here is a good luck kiss. Just one more kiss, OK. Joe I have to go, but I'll be back. See ya, Mighty Mouse."

She started toward the door and turned real quick and came back to give me another big wet kiss.

My eyes went back in my head again. I had forgotten what your kiss was like. "Give me just another peck." I can do better than that and she planted another one on my lips.

"That's all for now Joe, I have to go." She said to me.

I pleaded, "I'll write you an excuse for being late!"

"I don't think it would work. I'll see you later gator. I love you Mighty Mouse." she said as she went out the door.

Damn did I hear her right, when she said I love you Mighty Mouse. Damn sweet dreams tonight.

Angel On My Shoulder

ANGEL ON MY SHOULDER – PART 4 THIRD OPERATION

Approximately 3 months after leaving Vanderbilt Hospital, I began having back muscle spasms, every couple of days. I made an appointment to see the Dr. at Vanderbilt. After a series of tests he advised me, the bullet that entered my left side and ended up close to my spine, was irritating some back nerves and the bullet needs to come out. He told me this would not be a bad operation, but at the same time it would not be a cake walk because of the nerves that were close to where the bullet had stopped.

I checked into the Hospital a week later and was placed in a private room a day before surgery. Memories of the day I was shot came to mind, I lived the incident over and over in my mind. I have to stop this; I have got to put that incident in the past and prepare myself for this this operation ahead of me. I started thinking about the trial and how long it would be, hell that's too far off to think about it anymore. I've just got to get my mind set on this surgery. But, how do I put this out of my mind. Hell, I almost died
that night, but I guess the old Man upstairs had more for me to do, what it is I don't know but I guess I'll find out. I began to realize what posttraumatic stress disorder, PTSD, means and
how it affects the mind.

The nurse gave me a super strong laxative that really cleaned me out. After surgery the Dr. came to see me and asked how I was doing. I was a little sore but other than that everything seemed alright. He told me they had trouble finding the bullet even though the X-Ray that was hanging on the wall before me. The Dr. stated; although you can see it on the X-Ray, when we cut into your abdomen there are intestines, that sometimes causes problems.

However we did remove the bullet and a Detective from the Police Department came by and picked it up."

The Dr. said, "I see no reason for you not to go home tomorrow, just take it easy and I'll see you in 6 weeks." He added, "by the way I left you with another scar that is 10" long, but at least we didn't have to make another 22" scar like the first surgery on your chest and abdomen."

"But, Doc when can I go back to work?" I asked him.

"Joe are you serious, this was not major surgery but it was extensive, an invasion of your body again. So, I say at least at 6 months. We will talk about this again after you come back in 6 weeks for a checkup so I can look at my handy work. We'll talk more about this subject then."

"Ok, Doc you're the boss."

"Oh, by the way somebody told me to tell Mighty Mouse hello. Joe, would you happen to know who that is?"

"Yeah, I sure do." I chuckled.

"Have a good night's sleep and I'll see you in the morning to sign you out of here."

The Dr. added, "take care of yourself Joe and you will have a long and healthy life. Limit the amount of alcohol you drink and of course no cigarettes or cigars. Abuse yourself and your life will be cut short, real short. You can count on that and just remember that you were saved for a reason Joe, so take advantage of this miracle. You must have had a Guardian Angel watching over you the night you were shot. The best of luck to you and your family."

"Hey Doc," I said, "I just want to thank you and all the others that had a hand in saving my life. I know that words can't really say what I feel, but I really do mean it. Thanks again Doc, you know every time I look at this scar, I'll think of you."

"OK, Joe that's a first for me. See you Joe in about 6 weeks for a check-up."

"OK, I'll be there."

Angel On My Shoulder

The next morning the Doc came by to check me out. "OK, Joe just remember what I told you, take care of yourself, no heavy lifting, stooping or bending for a while. The organs in your body still have to adjust to what has happened to them. You know you were traumatized pretty good."

I responded, "I understand Doc, I know I'm going to be down for a while. I promise to follow orders; I don't want to go through this again. Thanks again Doc for all your patience and understanding."

"Gotta go Joe, I've got another couple of patients to see." He said to me before leaving the hospital room.

After I went home I just laid around watching TV and trying not to remember what all had transpired on that night I was injured. Sometimes I would walk out back and sit in a swing which I had under a big tree on my back lot. This was quite peaceful being in the country with all the surroundings and solitude. It was not unusual to see a deer run across the back of the yards in this section where we lived. We were far enough off the highway that you couldn't hear the noise of passing cars.

I felt someone tapping me on my shoulder, "Joe, don't you think it is about time that you came inside and lay down. You have been out here for hours, I know you must be hungry. I made some chili, I know you like that." My wife helped me back to the house. The chili was good and spicy, just the way I like it.

I went to the bedroom and laid down and before I knew it the kids were home from school, they were standing at the edge of the bed just staring at me when I awoke.

They all said at the same time, "Hi daddy how are you feeling."

"Better now since you three have come home." The kids were fascinated by the 22" scar across and down my chest and all the additional cut downs from the healed drain whole scars. They

had a great deal of fun using a ball point pen drawing on my chest and my back. I told them to draw whatever they wanted to draw. They played Tic Tac Toe, drew railroad tracts, practiced printing the alphabet or just about anything that crossed their minds. The time
seemed to past fast when they were having fun writing on my stomach and back.

They got a little rough sometimes and I said, "hey how about easing up. Hey you three knuckle-heads you are digging in pretty hard again with the point of the pen."

They just giggled, and said "we're sorry daddy,"

"Wait , there you go again." I heard my oldest son
Joe Joe say, "I told you he could feel it. We had better quit before we get in trouble." Giggle, Giggle, Giggle.

I asked them, "who turned on your giggle boxes. Your mother is calling you for dinner, you better hurry or I'm going to get there first and eat it all up."

"Ah, daddy you won't do that, will you? Last one to the table is a bullfrog." I didn't know that they could run so fast.

"Daddy, guess what? You're the bullfrog because you are the last one to the table."

There were only four houses in the section where we lived. We were isolated from everyone and the kids had to make do with whatever they could come up with. So, after my injury it was a relief to sell the house and move back to where civilization was in South Nashville.

While being off on Disability, I enrolled in a Vocational School chalking up 920 hours before quitting the Bookkeeping and Accounting School. I did not finish the Bookkeeping and Accounting Classes due to the fact that my education was cut short because I put in my request to return to the Police Department and I was approved.

Angel On My Shoulder

I didn't know if I would be able to get back in the grove after being off for so long.

Angel On My Shoulder

THE TRIAL

The day finally arrived, October 1, 1970 in Criminal Court with Judge Raymond Leathers presiding.

Tom Shriver the District Attorney and Albert Noe Assistant Attorney General were the Prosecutor's. The defendants Roy Allen and William McClain from Lewisburg, Tennessee with their Attorney the Public Defender James Havron for Roy Allen and William McClain's Attorney was David Vincent.

The selection of the Jury is a slow process. Picking a Person that would be beneficial to either side is difficult to say the least. All in all the Jury selection took all of the first day. During the selection the prospected Jurors were asked many questions by the Attorneys.

Our table faced the Judge and to our left is where the Jurors were seated. Adjacent to our table which was 90 degrees, sat the Public Defender James Haveron and to his right sat Roy Allen. Beside Roy was William McClain. Right from the start Roy would stare at me for long periods of time. I guess he was trying to intimidate me but all he was doing was just hurting his case. I would just stare back with a slight grin on my face. I would occasionally mime the words Bye Bye, while I was staring back at this thug that tried to kill me. I had a strong desire

to knock him out with a right hook. But I knew this could not happen, all the while I still had a deep contempt for these two Defendants.

that made me very uncomfortable due to the rigid composition of the brace. The first day ended with instructions that the Trial would resume the next day at 9 A.M.

After arriving home I could not remember anything about the trip to my house. There is a term in Psychology about this condition, but I can't remember the name. It is funny how the

Angel On My Shoulder

mind plays tricks on your memory. I guess with what all I had gone through up to this point would make you lose concentration.

The Jury selection was completed on the second day and a 1 hour Recess was ordered by Judge Leathers. After lunch I took the stand and told my horrific story.

Upon cross examination the Defense Lawyer did a thorough questioning. He asked questions about everything. How did I find the Auto in lighting time, how the cars were stopped, what was said, how many shots were fired. What the shooter looked like, why I did not wait for another car to arrive. What was I doing earlier, on and on and on. I believe I was on the stand for 2 hours.

The chain of evidence, the Detectives, Supervisors anything and everything was brought up and dissected to find any flaw in the Investigation. The suspects claimed that they were beaten up by the Police at Headquarters. Most Criminals use this excuse especially if a confession is entered into evidence.

A Forensic Expert from the FBI took the stand to explain how the gun was found next to Allen when he was caught the same night I was shot. He was found hiding in some bushes and the gun he used was within his arms reach. This gun was the one used to fire the cartridges that released the bullets taken from my torso. How the markings on the 32 cal. bullet matched the same markings from the barrel of the gun found with Allen. This test was made through Ballistics' Testing in the Laboratory.

Roy Allen continued to glare at me during this time. On several occasions I raised my notebook to block the view of the Jury and the Judge and I gave Allen the finger. He would tell his Lawyer, but by the time his Lawyer looked my way, I would be sitting with my hands lying flat on the table. I would continue to look at Allen and smile.

The Trial lasted four days. I believe, before the Jury began deliberating.

Angel On My Shoulder

I called my wife and told her what was happening and she could not understand why everything was taking so long. This is understandable for someone who is not familiar with the Court System. I left to grab a bite to eat and when I came back and I sat outside the courtroom reading the Newspaper. Several hours later we were told that the Jury had reached a Verdict.

Guilty was the Jury's answer with Roy Allen getting 3 to 21 years and he was charged with Assault with Intent to commit Murder, 1st Degree and with a Larceny case at the same time.

More than 25 Robberies were cleared up with the Arrest of the 2 subjects that shot me.

Although the victims did not get their money back, they did feel some relief from the arrests of the perpetuator's.

I believe that Allen was paroled after serving only 42 months. William McClain was charged with Intent to commit Murder, 1st Degree and Aider and Abettor. He received 4 years.

GOING BACK TO WORK

I was off seventeen and one half months of duty after getting shot and almost losing my life. When I returned to the West Station, I was eager to get back into things. But, I knew that this would probably take some time to really get back into the regular routine. I felt like a stranger at Roll Call. I had a lot to relearn again, new zone area's that had be revised, new Rules and Regulations, new personnel that I did not know. I was just going to have to take it
one day at a time and I didn't know if I was really ready to come back. I had a big knot in my stomach. I was hoping that it was just nerves. Being off sure did put a new perspective on things. I did not realize how much one can forget in such a short time. But, I'm not going to let this get me down. I'm going to put all I have into this and make something out of this job. I don't want to be just a Police Officer; I want to hold some rank within the Police Department. I know that it will take a while, but someday I'll be there.

A lot of new faces, the Officers that I did not know seemed to be staring at me. McEwen, the Lieutenant wants you to come to his Office for your assignment.

"Yes Sir," I answered. When I entered the Lieutenant's Office and sat down, I realized that I had caddied for him at McCabe Golf Course when I was a teenager, he looked at me and smiled and told me to have a seat. I thought what in the world have I done?

"Yes Sir, "I said and then I sat down. He asked me how I was doing. I told him that I was eager to get back to the job that I loved to do. That's fine but, the Police Department just wants to know how you will react to being back on the job so we are going

Angel On My Shoulder

to have you ride with a Sergeant for a couple of weeks. Yes Sir, "No Biggie just common sense, "he added.

"Yes Sir, was my reply. That's no problem and I don't mind it at all.

"OK Joe, the Sergeant will be right out to your car. We're glad to have you back." He added, "We could use the extra Arrests, if you know what I mean?"

"Yes Sir, I will surely do my best."

"Just be careful out there Joe."

I went outside and just sat in the Patrol Car waiting for the Sergeant. I reflected back on the past 17 ½ months, I had worked at a Truck Terminal for only a month, it was just to mundane, it reminded me of the days working at A&P Warehouse in Louisville, Kentucky.

I sold my 1934 Ford Coupe hot rod for $700.00. I hated to get rid of my hot rod, but I didn't have the money to buy the materials to build a three car carport on the rear of my house in Kingston Springs. I remember how hard it was cutting people's grass, they lived on the same street that I lived on. Still I missed being a Police Officer and the constant excitement that goes along with the job.

Upon discharge from the Navy, I worked as a Repo man, Order selector for a Clothing Warehouse and a runner in a Hospital (a runner is a person that deliver's medical supplies all over the Hospital.) But none of these jobs can't compare to the excitement as being a Police Officer. This job puts you in the middle of problems and excitement. Being a Police Officer made me feel good about myself.

I felt someone tap me on the shoulder, "Hey Joe are you ready to get started."

"I sure am Sergeant. "

"OK, then let's get going, I'm betting on this will be a good night."

Angel On My Shoulder

The Sergeant and I got along real well, I listened to everything that he had to say and then after a week I began working with a Police Officer.

Virgil and I were working in North Nashville. We were working the morning shift, from 11 PM to 7 AM. This was the worst of the three shifts and the most dangerous. These hours are where a lot of crime takes place and also the Bars let out at midnight and the drunks seem to be everywhere. If it is going to happen it will happen on the 11 PM to the 7 AM shift.

About 4:30 AM, we were patrolling the Charlotte Avenue area. When I spotted a 4 door with 4 black males inside the car. Two were in the front seat and two in the rear seat. It was a cool night in September. We passed each other again but, we were driving in opposite directions and I told my partner that's the same car that we saw an hour ago, they seem to be cruising the streets, it made me wonder what were they up to. I made a U-turn and before I could activate the emergency lights the Chevy sped off in a hurry. My partner Virgil radioed that we were after a Chevy with 4 black male subjects inside the car. We chased the suspects for two blocks, at this time he wasn't driving real fast. We were right on his tail when the driver drove his vehicle into a vacant area adjacent to the main road. All four doors opened at the same time and they started running towards the heavy undergrowth of the bushes, beer cans, broken glass and tall hedges. This all backed up to a tall concrete wall. I stopped and my partner exited from the Patrol Car, I told him that I was going to the end of the block wall to stop their escape.

At this point in time all four subjects disappeared into the heavy brush. The bushes partially hide all the Graffiti writing on the wall. I stopped the squad car about 20 feet from the wall; I radioed and gave the Dispatcher our location and that we needed backup. I got out and walked very slowly towards the concrete wall listening for some noise. I could not hear anything right away.

Angel On My Shoulder

I was listening for some crunching of the broken glass being walked on, or a snapping of a twig.

I heard a siren and I knew that additional help was on the way. I was still trying not to make a noise. I could hear some rustling bushes and I was trying to locate where the sound was coming from so that I could get a fix on the subjects. I squatted down and listened but the noise had stopped.

With my adrenaline pumping and a brief flash of my meeting the Grim Reaper crossed my mind. I thought, why am I remembering this now. Concentrate, just concentrate and don't lose site on what you are doing. The sweat was getting in my eyes, I wiped my eyes and I knew that I had to focus on those four subjects.

About this time two Police Officers came up to assist and they asked, where are the Suspects. I pointed in the direction where I had last heard some noise. I motioned to the Officer's to be quiet. The area was very dim and the only light we had was from a couple of street lights and our Police Car headlights. I had a 4-cell aluminum flashlight in my left hand.

In the distance I heard my partner yell, "Put your hands up, face the wall, you're under arrest."

I began walking towards the wall at a brisk pace and as I approached the concrete wall I bumped into a male black who was squatting down against the wall. He was holding a sawed off shotgun in his hands. He immediately dropped it and tried to kick it away as soon as he saw me. I was so startled that I hit him in the head with my flashlight knocking him down. He was wearing a stocking cap, a denim jacket and blue jeans. I grabbed his arm and cuffed his wrists behind his back. There was some struggle, but my instincts of making an arrest came back to me real quick. When I pulled the suspect to his feet he said, "It's a good thing for you that those two cops showed up when they did cause I was ready to kill you!"

Angel On My Shoulder

I replied, "OH YEAH, I've been there and you had better be glad that I didn't kill you when I saw you holding a sawed-off shotgun."

"What shotgun, you must be seeing things, I ain't got no shotgun.

I thought you said that you were ready to kill me. I kicked at the bottom of the bush and the shotgun fell on the ground. What do you call that a stick?

"But, but Officer, I don't know nothing about no shotgun, somebody else must of left it there.

My reply was, "Yeah, and I'm the Tooth Fairy" and we have
already been through all of this. You know if I were to have the shotgun dusted for fingerprints, I have a pretty guess that they will be your prints. No comment for the subject.

Halfway down the block I saw my partner Virgil walk out of the undergrowth with three suspects all handcuffed together with the one in the middle walking backwards.

"Hey Joe," he yelled this is the way you handcuff 3 thugs with only 2 pair of handcuffs." We both just laughed.
Yeah that is one for the books, I said.

The car turned out to be stolen earlier last night. There was also a Pistol under the passenger's front seat along with a bag of weed. Two of the suspects had 3 outstanding Warrants. Three of the suspects were juveniles and they were taken to Juvenile for processing. The fourth suspect was taken to Prisoner Processing downtown for processing. I parked behind the Police Station, opened the back door and ordered him to get out.

"Fuck you," he replied and he just sat there. I reached in to pull him from the back seat of the car and he leaned over and kicked me in the chest. Our uniforms at this time were a white shirt and a tie which I despised. I looked down at my shirt and saw a foot print right in the middle of my shirt. I reached across the seat

and grabbed him by the hair of his head and started to drag him out of the car, I was really struggling trying to get him out of the back seat of the car. My chest was really hurting, but I would not let him know this. It was all I could do to keep my composure; I could feel the sweat
going down my chest. I saw stars there for a while. I finally got him from the back seat and he was yelling very loud, HELP!! HELP!! Somebody help me!!

I asked him, do you think anyone is going to come to your rescue, well think again asshole. I spun him around and put my right
arm under his right arm and bent his wrist back causing him a lot of pain, it seemed to take the fight out of him. I guess he was hurting where I pulled his hair.

"I'm going to kill you," he yelled!

"Hey shit head you know I'm no fucking Easter Bunny and I am out here 45 hours a week so take your best shot dog breath." All in all this was a good stop. If that dirt bag had only known that where he kicked me in my chest area was exactly where they opened me up to repair the gunshots to my liver, he would have probably kept on fighting.

As we went inside to obtain a Warrant, this perp looked at me and said, "You will regret this."

I put a little more pressure on his wrist and he shut up for a while. You do know with that remark that you just made I can get another Warrant. So either you keep your mouth shut or another Warrant will be obtained. He came back with, just do what you gotta do, Mr. Officer.

He was charged with Fleeing and Eluding, Assault on a Police Officer, and 3 outstanding Warrants. All in all the cock roaches were off the streets.

Angel On My Shoulder

While in the Prisoner Processing area our Lieutenant came up and said, "What you guys did tonight is really good Police work, keep it up."

So to summarize this ordeal, 1 stolen car recovered, 2 weapons recovered, a bag of Marijuana.

Later on while we were driving back to our Zone. I was thinking, I almost got shot again, I do believe that the perp would have shot me, if I had hesitated just a second when I saw him. But, I guess when I hit him with my flashlight it sort of dazed him for a while.

Someone has to be watching over me, maybe an angel, I've had this feeling before and it seems like there is a warm feeling that I have when get into a tight situation.

A footnote to this story. The suspect that was about to shoot me was killed three weeks later over an argument in a pool hall. Karma is a bitch sometimes.

It was hard at first but things began to come back for me. On several occasions I would work by myself on the night shift. Whenever I had a lull time I'd go by the Vanderbilt ER and just thank everyone for saving my life. Even though some of the staff had changed. When they saw the name plate with Joe McEwen on it they asked, "Are you the Joe McEwen that took two shots in the top part of your liver." Yeah, that's me. They told me that the Doctor's and the Nurses had talked about how serious your wounds were.

I looked all around but I did not see Patsy. I asked one Nurses if she knew if Patsy was off tonight. She told me that she had only been there for two weeks and that she would see if any of the other Nurses knew her. She was gone about 15 minutes and when she came back, I was told that they thought she might be working at St. Thomas ER now. I thanked her and I went back on Patrol. Nothing seemed to be happening so I went to St. Thomas ER to see if anyone might know a Nurse by the name of Patsy was

Angel On My Shoulder

still working there. When I went in and I asked if anyone knew Patsy, I told them I did not know her last name. There was an older Nurse who came out to see me. She told me that Patsy had left about a year ago, but she didn't know where she went.

As I was walking out the door, the older Nurse said, wait a minute Officer are the one that got shot real bad?

I said yes, why? Patsy talked about you all the time. She even told me that she had never felt the love like she had with you.

Damn, I thought I wonder where she is? Patsy had told this Nurse that she had to leave Nursing because every time that she saw some-one come in the ER that was bleeding and in serious pain that she could not hold her composure. She did not tell the older Nurse what she was going to do, but she knew that she had to find

another profession because the pain and the memories of you, she could no longer handle.

Officer do you have a card or something with your phone number on it and if I find out where she is, I promise you that I will call you. Here is my card with my number on it. Thank you so much at least I have hopes of finding her now. Again, thank you so much for the information and I will be waiting for your call.

I got in my Patrol car feeling drained. I just sat there in a blank state of mind. The dispatcher then gave me a call to go help another Officer with a rowdy subject. On my to help the Officer, I just kept thinking I'll always have my memories of the time I spent with Patsy, my special Nurse and how she really boosted my recovery and especially how she made me feel.

I've got to get her out of my mind; she is probably with someone else now. I just feel drained.

I went to assist the Police Officer with a rowdy subject, but he had things under control and he said that I didn't have to stay. The subject finally realized that he was going to jail and there was nothing that he could do about it so he calmed down. He was just

Angel On My Shoulder

another Public Drunk who had too much joy juice and thought he was King Kong. The Officer said he would beat on his chest and tell him that he was the King of the Jungle. Well this King of the Jungle
was on his way to Jail. He'll stay there a few days, get good food, a good place to sleep and then when he hits the Streets again it will be De Ja Vu all over again. What a way to live.

        Several weeks went by and the Lieutenant told me that we've got 4 new Rookies just out of the Academy and I want one to ride with you this week. He stated that he knew he could count on me to show this new Rookie what is expected of him and the right way things are done. His name is Brad and when I told him that he was going to be your partner this week, he was very pleased. OK Joe go ahead and fall in Roll Call.

        "Yes Sir," I replied and off I went
for Roll Call.

        After Roll Call, Brad and I went outside and got into the Patrol Car and drove to the gas pumps. I told Brad to listen up. I have a few points to make. First, always do a good search and that includes to the crotch and crack area. I added a young Police Officer was murdered by a Juvenile just outside the Juvenile Hall. The Officer was shot in the head; he never knew what hit him. This murder could have been avoided with a thorough search. If anyone gives you a Prisoner always search them again before putting them into your vehicle.

        Whenever we stop a car and it seems as if the driver is going to be arrested, stand in the V opening. This is the area between the car and the door when opened. I will stand behind you or you stand behind me. I have never lost a prisoner, never lost my gun or badge, or had my car stolen. Okay?

        "Yes Sir" he replied. "You don't have to Sir me. We're equal partners, I responded back.

If I happen to get shot don't stop for me, get the Son of a Bitch and if the situation warrants, kill him! Remember if someone comes up dead with bullet holes in the palms of their hands or shotgun pellets in their back, somebody is in a heap of trouble. Also as soon as someone is arrested and cuffed, give them the Miranda Warning, no exceptions. If you fail to do this you will be challenged in Court. Don't ever handcuff a Prisoner to a box car on the Railroad Tracks while you are trying to locate another suspect or while you are looking for anything that you might have dropped during the chase. Several weeks ago someone handcuffed a person to a ladder on the side of a box car. He was about 100 yards away when he heard the Train starting up and pulling away. The Prisoner was screaming and the Police Officer covered 100 yards in 11 seconds flat. The Officer was trying to uncuff the man from the ladder while running beside the Train and the prisoner was screaming for help. The Officer was trying to insert the handcuff key into the hole on the handcuff. They Key Stone Cops have nothing on us.

I got out of my Patrol Car one morning at the boat docks and dropped my car keys into the Lake in about three feet of water. I went and borrowed a rod and reel from the Bait Shop and I hooked the key ring with the fish hook. Believe me Rookie, shit happens and if it hasn't happened it will.

I added, don't take someone's dignity from them. If they are polite be nice back, if they're a smart ass then toughen up a little. If we are in a fight and the arrested subject quits fighting, then the fight ends on our side also. Just use enough force to make the arrest, you are the one in charge. Don't do anything that would get you in trouble and believe me there is a lot of people that like complain on the Police.

Remember this part comes from the FBI: anyone worth shooting is worth killing. If they are not worth shooting then don't shoot them! A serious mistake can cost you your job, you can

even get sued or worse you can go to Prison. Don't bluff with a gun. I don't draw my gun often,
especially on misdemeanors. It's hard and dangerous to cuff someone with a weapon in your hand.

Remember rainy nights are good burglary times. The rain muffles a hammer or pry bar noises. I ride behind a lot of Businesses in my Zone and I stop a lot of cars, I make many arrests,
tow a lot of cars and keep vehicles with no Insurance or Improper Registration or Expired Tags off the Street and this keeps the Tow Trucks drivers busy and happy.

I know that this may seem like a lot of information, but believe me, what you learn by being out on the streets, there is something different every night. This is an asphalt jungle out here and you have to watch every move that you make.

You know Joe, it has been a pleasure to ride with you and I know that the rest of the week is going to help me out a lot. But, there is just one thing I want to ask you? OK, what is it. Well at the Academy they told us about how you were shot. Well, I should have waited for back up, but I didn't want those two thugs to get away. Just what did it feel like to be shot?

Well, have you ever had your hand burned on a stove or fire? No, I can't say that I have. Well, it's about one thousand times harder to imagine. It felt like hot pokers were sticking in me. It was hard to breathe because of the blood that was filling up my lungs. Brad, I just hope you don't ever have to go through something like that. Just remember when you are alone and you see something going down, call for back-up right away. But, back then we only had just two channels to work off of, not like it is today. You know Joe, you should be at the Academy teaching. Why is that Brad? You can explain things in plain terms so that someone can comprehend them fully. Well, maybe Someday, I

Angel On My Shoulder

would love to teach at the Academy, but for now I love working the streets.

The next shift the Lieutenant told me that Brad was really impressed with my tidbits.
He also told me that he thought you would make a good teacher at the Academy. Well, maybe I will someday, but I like what I am doing out on the streets. You two get out there on the streets and take down some bad guys. Sure thing, Lieutenant.

One night while working West Patrol the Lieutenant called me on the air and told me to meet him at the White Way parking lot. I often caddied for Lt. Edmondson at the McCabe Golf Course when I was a teenager. His nick name was Duke and he was very well liked. He pulled up beside my car and asked, "Joe, what do you want to do? Do you want me to pick you up on my detail or do you want to keep on rotating back and forth on nights?" I replied, "I'd like to work on your detail Lt."

He said we will work days starting the 1st of the month. You can keep your same partner and nothing will change except every third month you will be working days. I said, thank you very much and then he drove off. My partner said, this is a first I've never
heard of a Lt. asking a Police Officer if he wanted to be on his detail. My partner added, it is generally the other way around. I said, you don't understand. I used to caddy for him when he played golf with my dad, I carried both bags and I made twice as much money. I also got all the potato chips and cokes that I could hold. You know times were rough back then, but I always had a few bucks on me. Damn, Joe, is there anything you didn't do when you were growing up?

Yeah, I answered, "I didn't get as much pussy that I wanted."

"You know Joe, you are something else and I love to hear your stories."

Angel On My Shoulder

"Yeah, you know my life back then was hard,
but sometimes I look back and maybe it was that way for a reason."

Angel On My Shoulder

BOYS ON BICYCLES

I answered a call one day about a lady who needed to talk to someone. When I arrived, I knocked on the door and a little lady told me that there were several boys in the neighborhood and they were riding their bicycles through her flower beds. This little fragile
old lady was shivering. I could tell she was upset. I asked her if she lived alone? She replied, yes I do. Well, what time of day is this happening? It took her awhile to answer and then she
stated that it was on the weekends and around 4 PM on the weekdays. I asked her if they were doing this every day and she said no. Have these boys said anything to you and again she said, No! Ok, do you know where they live? No Officer I don't, since my husband died I have kept to myself. How long ago did your husband pass away? It has been 5 lonely years.

I asked her to show me the damage to her flower beds so we went outside and I could see the damage that these boys had made to her flower beds. You know Officer, my husband loved to plant flowers, but I never really cared about them until he was no longer with me and now it seems that when I see these flowers I feel can since that he is here.

Can you help me, Please! Don't worry; I'm going to help you. I will drive around the neighborhood and see if I can see these boys riding their bicycles. I work this area, so I will
keep an eye out for them.

I sat in my Patrol Car which was still parked in front of her house so I could fill out my paper work. I was thinking about her being so fragile. I forgot to ask her if she had any family that lived close. I won't bother her again today, but I will stop back by and check on her from time to time.

Angel On My Shoulder

I'll make a card and place it on the Bulletin Board at the Station so that the other two shifts will be aware of what is happening and just maybe they can catch these boys on their bicycles tearing up her flower bed.

After being on the inside of this ladies house it reminded me of a house that I lived in many years ago in Crofton, Kentucky.

You know it is odd that I would get a call about wanting to talk to an Officer and then after I left the house I start remembering things from the past. But I felt that this gave me some closure on the house burning and losing my dog. I haven't thought about this in a long time. I guess some things happen for a reason.

I was still sitting in the Patrol car just watching the traffic whiz by and glancing back at the log Cabin type house that I had just been in. Even the outside reminded me of the house that I lived in Kentucky. This is really weird, I thought.

After getting back to the Station I was still thinking about all the things that I had remembered from the past. I couldn't get over how much the house looked like the one we lived in Kentucky that burned to the ground.

I put the card on the bulletin board inside the Station, with all the information about the lady that was having trouble with some boys on their bicycles and riding through her flower beds. I hope that these young boys will be caught, given a good talking to especially by their parents and then this fragile little lady can have some piece of mind with her flowers and the memories of her husband.

Angel On My Shoulder

ON TO SCHOOL – DUMPSTER DIVE

I was enrolled in Aquinas Junior College while working for the Police Department in order to obtain a Degree in Criminal Justice. Randall Wyatt was my teacher in Evidence Class.

On the way to Aquinas I would check out some of the dumpsters at local businesses before going to classes. There was a large dumpster behind a cabinet shop near the Fairgrounds and it usually yielded a trove of cabinet doors, hardware, hinges, wood scraps, etc. The dumpster was huge, with a 8 foot depth and the side of the walls were smooth. I parked my pick up next to the dumpster and looked inside. It was empty except for numerous cabinet hinges that were on the floor of the dumpster. I lowered myself into the dumpster and picked up the 40 plus pairs of cabinet hinges and tossed them over the top of the dumpster into the bed of my truck.

I tried to get out of the dumpster but was unable to pull myself up from the 8 foot walls. It was also due to the fact that I had no leather gloves on, I had always worn them since I had put a big gash in my hand one day. This time I forgot to put them on. All I had was just bare hands and there were no toe holds on the smooth steel walls.

My classes started in about an hour and the sun was starting to set. Panic set in after I tried several times and failed. I thought what would happen to me when the workers came to work in the morning and they find me in this dumpster? I thought, here I am a Police Officer and I'm going through dumpsters. Oh well, it is what it is.

No one knew that I was here and my wife would be belching fire if I didn't come home. I looked at the end of the dumpster and noticed that the front of the container had a slope of

Angel On My Shoulder

45 Degrees, I thought this is doable. I tried the first time with no luck and then on the second time no luck. Ok, Joe you can do this, just stop and think. I finally succeeded to reach the top of the canister by running at full speed, stepping on the sloped floor front and leaping onto the corner and getting both arms over the rim of the dumpster, pulling myself up and over. Bruised arms and a bigger bruised ego, somewhat dirty, but successfully getting out and to school on time.

I was thinking to myself that this was my last trip inside in an 8' dumpster. I would look inside, but I never went back into one unless it was half full or I had another Officer with me. I knew this would be easier and it would give me an escape route.

When an opportunity presented itself my partner and I would dumpster dive if we had a real slow night and try to find some free items. On one particular night we filled up the back seat of our Patrol vehicle with items from a large Department Store dumpster.

There was Perfume, bric a brac and Women's shoes. There were a lot of returned kitchen items that were still in their boxes and miscellaneous merchandise. This was a good haul.

As luck would have it we received a call to transport a shoplifter from a 7 / 11 Store. When we arrived at the Store I explained our dilemma about our back seat being full. The manager told us to empty out our car at the rear of the store and come back later and pick up our treasures. After my partner and I had finished our shift we drove back to the store and placed our finds in the back of our pick-up trucks. My justification of this is I'm keeping stuff out of the land fill.

Police have perks, like other jobs in the Corporate World, but ours is on a much smaller scale. But it does help not having to pay for these items. It may seem wrong but if we didn't get them, someone else would. At this time our pay was hardly enough to survive for a family of four with only one person working.

Angel On My Shoulder

NEW ROOKIE

The Sergeant said, "McEwen I want to see you after Roll Call." I was thinking what have I done now? After Roll Call I walked over to the Sergeant and asked him what can I do for you? Joe, we have a new Rookie that is not working out. After anyone works with him one shift, they all tell me that they don't want him in their car anymore. He said, "check with me at the end of the shift and let me know what's going on."

I knew after the first call he's going to be trouble, not only does he have a little man's complex but an attitude also. I observed how he talks down to everyone and has a tendency to belittle the people that we are dealing with. This is a train wreck in Police work, I thought.

It had been a long night and a busy night, so about 5:30 AM, I said "let's go get some breakfast? '

We found a little Mom and Pop's Diner that was in our zone. When we entered the Diner the place was unusually crowded. The booths were filled and only one stool left at the counter.

The Rookie was ahead of me and walked up to a booth where a young couple was sitting. They had finished their meal and drinking coffee and talking. My partner walked to the end of their booth and snapped his fingers twice and made a jester with his hands with his thumb pointing upward for them to get up and leave. I couldn't believe what I had just witnessed. I grabbed the Rookie's sleeve and told him to go get in the car now! As soon as he moved away from the table I apologized to them and I said, "This will never happen again and I am so sorry that this happened." I went to the cashier and asked how much the tab was for the young couple sitting over there talking and drinking coffee, she told me how much and I paid it. I went back over to the table

Angel On My Shoulder

and told them that I had taken care of their tab and I apologized one more time. I added, we do not act like that and he won't be around long. I told them to have a good day and left.

When I got outside I looked back and they were tapping on the window and they gave me a thumb's up. I knew that I had defused the situation and hopefully left a good impression.

I went to the patrol car and sat in the driver' seat. I turned and looked at him and said, "What is your problem numb nuts?" Who the hell do you think you are? I added, you can't treat people this way especially in a Police Uniform.

He said, " I'm a Police Officer and where I came from up North, this is excepted behavior."

"You're not up North and I can see why. I put the car in drive and radioed Dispatch to put us out at the West Station. I then called for the Sergeant to meet me at the Station.

He said, "Joe what is the problem?"

I replied, "I'll tell when I get there."

My partner said, "What's wrong?"

I replied, "You are too damn dumb to understand." I added, "This is the last night that you will ever ride in a car with me. It might be the last night that you'll ever ride in a Police Car, if I have anything to do with it. I continued on towards the West Station in silence.

When we arrived the Sergeant was already inside waiting for us in the Lieutenant's Office. We went into the office, sat down and the Sergeant asked, "What's this all about?"

I began to explain what happened at the Restaurant. It was very crowded and the Rookie went up to a couple that was drinking coffee and he snapped his fingers and told them to get up. I was so embarrassed because I have eaten there many times and I knew most of the waitresses.

Angel On My Shoulder

As a good jester I paid for the couple's meal and they thanked me by saying Officer you didn't have to do that. The Sergeant said, "Joe you didn't have to do that."

"No, but I wanted to, this uniform and badge means something to me and I'm proud to serve the people of Nashville.

The Sergeant said, "Well Joe I can understand how you feel."

"You know that we are here to serve the people of Nashville and if we set a bad example, well then it doesn't look good for us."I added, "I want to bring him up on CUBO (Conduct Unbecoming an Officer)."

The Sergeant said I don't think it will have to go that far. He then looked at Officer Beard and asked, "Is this how it happened?"

The Officer replied, that he didn't think he had done anything wrong. The Sergeant then told the Rookie that you are relieved of duty, so get your ass out of here and go home. I'll talk to you tomorrow after roll call, but first leave your gun and badge on my desk and when you get home gather up all and I mean all of your Police issued uniforms and other gear and turn it in tomorrow here at the Station. Do you understand me?"

"Yes, Sergeant I understand you very well. " The Rookie left the room and I told the Sergeant this guy is a real misfit and has no business wearing a badge or carrying a gun. I don't understand how he ever Graduated from the Academy with the attitude he displays.I added, "he is worse than Barney Fife could ever be. I can see why all the other Officers that had ridden with him nicknamed him Weird Beard. ' I asked the Sergeant, "You know it's just about 30 minutes until shift change and is it OK if I go home, I am still fuming over this incident."

He said, "go ahead," I'll explain to the Lieutenant what happened, I'll see you tomorrow at roll call."

Angel On My Shoulder

The end of this story is we never saw or heard of the Rookie again. It seems that no one ever knew where he went or what happened to Officer Beard. Probably back up North. But at least he did drop off all of his uniforms and equipment real early the next morning before our shift arrived. He was truly a misfit and I hope that he finds something that he is good at. Yeah right!!

STOLEN CAR'S

   Our detail at the West Station were given a Reward for
making an arrest involving a Roller. A Roller is when you catch
someone driving a stolen Vehicle. All of the Police Officers on our
detail tried to get as many Rollers as possible. The Lieutenant
would Reward us with a day off for each Stolen Car in which an
arrest was made on the person driving the car. This encouraged the
Police Officer's to be on the lookout for a Stolen Car.
There were a lot of times that we just stopped a car for some minor
violation and the car would be stolen. I believe that there was
about three or four thousand cars stolen every year in Nashville,
this was about 10 per day.
   My first year back at the West Station after being off
wounded, I managed to get 7 Rollers in 8 months. One particular
case stands out in my mind in which a young male and female were
coming off of the Interstate exit ramp and almost clipped the front
of my Patrol Car in West Nashville. This car did not stop at the
Stop sign and he then took off real fast when he noticed that it was
a Police Car that he almost hit. I gave a very long chase and it
ended when he turned down a dead end street. The male who was
driving the car was going to try and run, but I caught him before he
got too far. I handcuffed him and placed him in the back of the
Patrol Car. When I went to get the female out of the passenger's
side of the vehicle, she threw up all over the inside panel of the
door of the stolen car and on the street also. I cuffed her and placed
her in the back seat of my Patrol
Car along with her boyfriend. He leaned over and gave her a big
long kiss on her lips. He said, "damn, did you throw up because
your breathe stinks?" She replied, "I told you I could not drink a
beer on an empty stomach." This really made me somewhat
nauseous.

   Angel On My Shoulder

I retraced the chase from where it began at the Exit ramp off the Interstate to where the car stopped and wrote him a ticket for every Stop Sign that he failed to stop. I wrote him a total of 12 Tickets. When I went to Traffic Court the Judge stated that I had unjustly ticketed him by loading him up with 12 Tickets. The only Ticket that he allowed was the violation where he almost struck the front of my Patrol Car at the Exit Ramp.

He was charged with the Grand Theft of an auto and this case was heard in General Sessions where he was bound over to the Grand Jury. The Penalty for this charge was time served and Court Costs. Not too bad for almost wrecking several cars and just barely missing several people who were on the side streets.

The young female was not charged with anything. I think throwing up was punishment enough. I just wonder if she ever rode with this thug any more. Later while working in the Green Hills Area I noticed a Volkswagen that was parked in the rear of the Shopping Center. This car had been in the same spot for several weeks.

I was off two days and when I returned to work the Volkswagen was still parked and it had not been moved. I ran the VIN number through NCIC and it did not come back stolen. There were no tags on the car, no spare tire and no keys, but the wires were hanging down
from under the dashboard. I wrote down the VIN number and received a listing of the owner of this Beetle. It was not listed as stolen and it was an out of town listing with no phone number.

The next day I mailed a letter to the address that was given from the listing. I told the owner how long this car had been parked and if everything was alright, then just disregard this letter. However if not and this car had been stolen to call me and I'll meet you at the Shopping
Center and fill out a recovery form.

Angel On My Shoulder

Well, 2 days after I mailed the letter I received a telephone call from some lady in Cookeville, Tn., who said that the car was hers and it was stolen.

I met her at the Shopping Center, and she brought a trailer to take the car back to Cookeville. I filled out a recovery report on the Beetle and she signed it, stating that she had taken possession of her car. She was real happy to get her car back. I could see tears in her eyes, she said that finding this was a miracle because she had already given up hope of ever seeing it again. She just kept thanking me for letting her know that her "Bug" had been found.

I went to Headquarters, to Auto Theft and they ran the VIN and it had not been reported stolen. Upon checking further we found out that the VIN number had been placed in the NCIC wrong. Just one number was wrong. Mistakes do happen, sometimes happy endings and sometimes not so happy.

On another occasion while on the 5 PM to 1AM shift, I told my partner to pull behind a car witch had no headlights on. The time was 9 PM. We were headed out West End just past Vanderbilt College when I him up to let him know that I was behind him. He sped away driving recklessly in and out of traffic and making a right turn into Centennial Park.

This was one of the nicest parks in Nashville, with the Parthenon in the middle of the park. A large lake with ducks that were always swimming around and always looking to be fed. There were always cars stopping to fed the ducks and just enjoy the peace and serenity. There was a place towards the back with a large garden where the flowers were changed from season to season. There had been many weddings performed here. There was a small bridge that went over a little stream and in the summer time on the lake area there were paddle boats that you could paddle around the lake.

Vanderbilt University was just across the street and the students would come over especially in the spring. They would bring a blanket and just lay there enjoying the lovely scenery.

At one time there was a very elaborate Christmas scene with Mary, Joseph and baby Jesus. There were also angels, the three Wise Men, shepherds, cattle and of course the lighting display that was very unusual and beautiful. You could see cars from surrounding Counties lined up waiting to see the Christmas display. It was put on by Harvey's Department Store which was in the Downtown area.

The road forked to the right just after the entering to the park. The driver lost control of the car and hit a large oak tree that was three feet in diameter. The car hit so hard that it wrapped the front end of the car around the tree. The driver of the car got out and began to run towards the main entrance of the Park. I bailed out of the Police Car and a foot chase ensued. I finally tackled him in a flower bed and handcuffed him.

We immediately called dispatch for an ambulance to come to our location. I told the dispatcher that the passenger was in bad shape. The passengers head smashed through the windshield cutting him severely on both sides of his face. His cheeks were cut open and exposing his molars on each side of his mouth.

I was in the process of filling out the paperwork when the ambulance arrived. They put him on a stretcher and put him in the back of the ambulance and off they went to the hospital. The driver of the car was probably holding onto the steering wheel before before the impact, thus saving him from a serious injury. He was saved from being hurt, but not from going to jail.

A call came out from the dispatcher that a car had just been stolen from a Hospital near Charlotte Avenue. The only damage to the three feet diameter tree was the bark was scuffed and the tree still stands today. The driver had no driver License and the

Angel On My Shoulder

stolen car was worth about $800.00 tops.

Unlike the cars of today the older cars were easy to hotwire. A wire from the starter, a wire from the plus side of the coil and a wire from the positive side of the battery. Put them all together and touch the battery or the solenoid and bingo the car is ready to roll.

After booking the driver with a stolen car charge, no driver's license and reckless driving we went to the Emergency Room, the Doctor was sewing up the passenger's face while we were standing there watching I told my partner, every time this dude goes to shave or looks in a mirror with a scar running from his mouth to his ear he'll remember tonight. It took over a 100 stitches to put his face back together.

The man's car that was stolen was a total loss.

Several weeks later my partner and I were on Clarksville Highway. This was on a winter night and snow was on the ground. We were just cruising along when all of a sudden a straight axel, closed box truck passed us at a high rate of speed. We did not know at this time that the truck was just stolen from a business in our zone.

We caught up with the truck and I pulled up beside it and a black male was driving. I yelled for him to pull over. He then took off at a high rate of speed with us in pursuit. He then turned left from Clarksville Highway and the left rear double tires lifted one foot off the pavement. He straightened out the truck and as I got close to him, I started to pull beside the suspect again when he cut us off again and almost causing me to wreck on the wet snowy street. I told my partner to call for backup.

We continued the chase and on several occasions the box truck almost turned over, but somehow he managed to recover. He turned left onto a street that was a dead end and I told my partner that we have him now. He ran the box truck past the dead end

Angel On My Shoulder

of the street into the snow covered field until the truck became bogged down. We stopped our unit on the asphalt. This guy is nuts or high on drugs. Damn, I thought this guy is a hell of a driver. My partner and I exited our Patrol Car.

I told my partner to get the shotgun. When I started to exit the car I saw the door on the truck open and the black male jumped from the cab and he had a long gun in his left hand and it was pointed upwards, he turned and ran away from the truck. I said to my partner "shoot him!" My partner then fired 4 rapid shots until his gun was empty.

I yelled, "he's out of range!" I aimed the spotlight from my vehicle on the suspect and I fired once. The suspect then wobbled and I fired again. He was a long way from the box truck when I fired my revolver again and I saw the suspect fall to the ground.

We ran to where the suspect was and I saw blood on his right shoulder and he was screaming, you shot me in the leg. He said call me an ambulance.

I said, "OK you're an ambulance." He then stated, "No I mean call me a real ambulance."

Ok, I replied again, "you are a real ambulance."

He started yelling for help and then I told him to lighten up that the ambulance was on the way.

He said, "you tried to kill me."

So what I replied, "You tried to kill us when you tried to run us off the road."

"Well then, what did you do with the gun you had in your left hand?" I asked.

"I ain't had no weapon."

"yeah and I'm the tooth fairy!"

I called for an ambulance and then I asked the suspect "why did you run?"

He said, "I just stole the truck and I don't have a Driver's License."

Angel On My Shoulder

"Let me get this right, stolen car, no driver's license, fleeing and eluding. Shall I go on or do you get the mess that you are in."

The suspect was transported to the Hospital where he was treated for wounds to his right shoulder and left ankle. We had recovered the box truck before it was reported stolen."

We looked extensively for the gun that he pointed at us, but to no avail because the grass and the weeds were knee high and it was covered with heavy snow.

He was charged with Assault w/Intent, Suspended License, Stolen Truck, Fleeing and Eluding and Reckless Driving. He received 1 year with Sentence Suspended, except 90 days to serve with credit given for jail time before his trial, plus Probation and Court Cost.

After this incident, my partner asked for a transfer back to his old job on the inside.

He said, "I'm terrified working with you, Joe. It is something all the time when you are on duty. There is a black cloud that follows you all night long," my partner said.

I told him, "it is what it is because I am one Crime Fighting Son of a Bitch." But you know, I do get the job done even though it is rough some times.

At the next Roll Call, the Lieutenant said, "Joe you now have another new partner."

"Who's that Lieutenant? "

"Well Joe, you will find out when you go to your Patrol Car, he'll be waiting for you.'

I couldn't wait to get to the car to see who was my new Rookie partner. When I got to my Patrol car and sat down, the new Rookie said, "I'll see some action now."

I replied, buckle up kid this might be a bumpy ride and I then laughed out loud. The Rookie soon found out that I was not just a do nothing Officer.

He said, "you know you sure do keep busy, I've

Angel On My Shoulder

never ridden with anyone like you Joe."

I think this is going to be an interesting night. And it was. We were very busy and We didn't even have time to stop and eat a meal until later on in our shift.

Oh well, time flies when you are working hard and having fun and getting the job done. I had rather stay busy because the time flies by faster and I'm usually out of one situation and into another and before you know it's time to get off.

Finding stolen cars is sometimes easy to spot, because the left or right rear windows is broken out, the wing window broken out on either of the front door, mostly on the passenger's side. The side of the door gasket is torn because of a Slim Jim was used or some other tool, a lot of time a windshield arm was a great tool for opening a locked door. I would take the ignition key out and see if it works on the door lock. A lot of times a blank ignition key was used to start the car. A flat head screwdriver was hammered into the switch and a pair of vice grips clamped around the screwdriver and forcing the ignition on to start the automobile. Oh course, when you walk up to issue someone a ticket and you see a screwdriver in the ignition it is a "No Brainer." I have seen where these idiots have tried to hide the screwdriver with a small towel placed over the steering column in hopes that we would not notice the obvious. DUH!!!

When giving a someone a ticket I would always take their Driver's License (if they had one) to match their signature on the ticket. Sometimes a driver has identification in the glove box which matched him to some degree and when they signed the ticket I would compare that signature with the one on their identification. On occasion if the Drivers License was stolen, they sometimes could not remember the name on the stolen Drivers License and they would sign the Ticket with a different name that was on the Drivers License that they would give to me. We're not dealing with Rocket Scientist, but some dummy with

Angel On My Shoulder

and 8th Grade education and an IQ lower than a rock. I never gave them their

Driver's License back until the ticket was signed and handed back to me, and I then matched the Ticket signature with the signature on the Driver's License. This was a procedure that I followed on every Traffic Ticket that I issued. Signatures don't lie.

Angel On My Shoulder

HELL TO PAY

I entered the West Station one evening and there was no one playing cards. Everyone was either sitting or standing around without a sound being made. You could hear a pin drop it so quiet.

I was asked, "Who Died?" One older Policeman motioned for me to come over where he was. He began to talk in a low. "Silly me," I asked, "what the hell's going on?"

"Joe just listen and do everything by the book, don't break any rules or regulations."

"OK," I replied, but "what the hell is going on?"

"Alright, I'll tell you thought he was better that than anyone else and he had an air of snobbishness about him.

"Okay fall in for Roll Call," the Sergeant barked.

Eventually we were called into the Captain's Office one by one, but no one owned up to spray painting his car.

I learned at an early part of my career that Police are sometimes very vindictive.

P.S. No one was ever caught and the subject was never mentioned again. The Captain was a bigger prick now than he ever was and we all wished that he would get transferred and he did get transferred very soon after this incident.

Angel On My Shoulder

TRAINING A ROOKIE

One night while working downtown, I was training a new Rookie. I told him several things to be aware of when arresting a drunk person. I spotted a drunk on the street that was sitting on a bench on Union Street.

I stopped my Patrol Car and walked back to the rear of my auto, letting the drunk know that I was going to supply him with a free meal and a good place to sleep.

When I told him to get up and turn around that he was under arrest for Public Drunk. In a flash he hit me with a full round house punch on my jaw bone. I saw stars, but I recovered quickly and began shoving the drunk onto the back of my car and handcuffed him. My Rookie partner stood frozen watching the whole thing go down. He had a stunned look on his face like what the hell just happened watching the whole thing unfold. I told him you never know how a drunk will react, when you tell them they are under arrest. But, at least he will get a meal and a warm bed to sleep on like I had stated earlier.

When we went before the Committing Magistrate, I told my side of the story. The Magistrate asked me why is the drunk still standing if he hit you. No reply your Honor, but there was just a lot of laughs in the court room. I thought to myself, I'm never going to
be able to live this one down. The Rookie just looked at me and grinned. I told him the next drunk is on you to arrest.

His Bond was set at $1,000.00. He wasn't too happy about that. But he did say you know the food ain't bad, and there is a good warm bed to sleep in instead of sleeping in a cardboard box, so what the Hell.

Angel On My Shoulder

We headed back out on the streets and the Rookie said, you know he hit you pretty hard, man you can take a punch. I told him, "I have been hit harder many times and this is just part of the job."

The next drunk we saw, I let the Rookie handle it. The scared look on his face was gone and it was all business to him. He did all the right things and he made a successful arrest without getting hit.

I said, "Right on my man, you learn fast."

"I had a good instructor," he replied. The Rookie said there is nothing like on the job training and I think I've got one of the best instructors in the department. I replied, thank you for the compliment, but I learn something new every day on this job. I added, no one ever knows what each call will bring.

Once when I had a another new Rookie in my Patrol Car I would drive to our Zone and find some deserted street, pull over to the curb, stop the car and turn off the Police Radio off. I would them turn towards the Rookie and say "I've just been shot, I'm lying out there on the street, so what do you do?" A lot of time the Rookie would ask me what would I do? I can't answer you because I'm lying in the street bleeding to death and I replied the first thing that you do is pick up the damn mike and call headquarters, Officer down and I need assistance.

I said and then what do you do? They would look at me with a blank look on their face and say I called for help. I replied, where they are going, start riding around in circles, where the hell are we, what is our location Rookie and what street are we on. If you don't know the street name then look for a building, a water tower or just anything that stands out or any kind of a landmark. Think back what street we were just driving on. At least that will put them within
20 blocks of where we are. The Rookie would reply, Yes Sir. I said don't Sir me because I am not a Supervisor, I work for a living.

Angel On My Shoulder

I flipped the Radio back on and eased away from the curb and started talking to the Rookie. I said let's go back a few minutes and let's say that you gave the correct location to the dispatcher and then you run up to me to see what you can do to help me. I don't need any help, get the son of a bitch that shot me and don't waste any time with me because I've been there and done that. An Ambulance will be on the way and there's really not a thing that you can do for me except keep an eye out for the shooter.

Remember, any man worth shooting is worth killing. If he isn't worth killing then don't shoot him. And when in doubt, DON'T. Nobody said that this job was going to be easy or a cake walk. There is not another job that I can think of that requires monumental decisions to be made in a matter of seconds for so little pay. You know that $620.00 doesn't go very far. That is why we all work an extra job.

I'm not trying to be hard on you, but you have a whole lot to learn and a whole lot of things thrown at you all at once, and a short time to grasp the situation. I would add are your arm pits kind of sweaty now? Then I would laugh.

Another thing after you write a Traffic Citation hold onto the Driver's License until the Violator signs the Ticket and hands it back to you. Take his Driver's License and place it above his signature on the Ticket Book and compare the signature's. This is to see if the shithead is using someone else's License. If so, then that means Jail time because they should not even be on the road and you don't know who this person really is. I have told this to many Rookies and I just hope that they remember it.

That's enough of this lesson and me being mean to you, so let's go get some coffee. I only want to help you as much as I can to understand the ins and outs of this unthankful job. We really haven't even started yet, but I will teach you everything that I know and then some.

Angel On My Shoulder

One more thing, I read in some book that 20 percent of the Police Officers are doing 80% of the work and 20% of the criminals are doing 80 percent of the crimes. So every time you arrest a dirt bag you have broken the cycle of Crime with this one subject. If we do this enough we can pull the crime statistics down, which is one of our main goals. I added, you can make this job a challenge and do what we are supposed to do or you can be a lazy ass and just answer your calls and write a few tickets at night and do not engage in aggressive Police work. I choose to work and get into as many situations as I can. I like coming to work but I also like going home in one piece. Also, I feel when a Criminal is arrested someone, whoever or where ever is not going to be a victim tonight. It gives me a good feeling about myself and this is why I wanted to be a Police Officer.

"Hey Joe," the Rookie said can we get a burger and fries with that coffee? That sounds OK, but only if it is half price. Flirt with the waitresses, because they are the ones that write you a ticket and they will usually give us a discount. But do not ever ask for a discount or half price because that is a big NO NO.

The Rookie thanked me for information and he said that he knew I wasn't too hard on him but just trying to make a point that I would remember. He also asked if he could ride with me again. He said that what he learned at the Academy is nothing like working the streets. No, but the Academy gives you the basics on Law and take down procedures.

If you really want to get down to it this job requires a lot of common sense and just remember what would a just and reasonable man do in any particular situation. Look for the License plate on the back of the cars to see if they are properly installed and current on the expiration date. The tags on a truck are usually beat up from a trailer hitch hitting against it. While usually tags on

Angel On My Shoulder

a car look fairly decent especially if there is no trailer hitch on the car.

Sunday morning is the best time to find someone if you are looking for them and be suspicious of one that is backed in a parking spot. This is because people are lazy and don't normally park this way. If you go up to a car and the female has her dress pulled up, she doesn't give a damn about you. She just wants to get out of getting a ticket. Women are dangerous and if you are not careful your penis will make a slave out of you because mine has me. Your marriage will be put to the test with this job. You better have an understanding wife or it will be a rough ride. Police are high in the Divorce category. If you have children, they are really the ones that suffer with emotional scars. If you are wondering how I know this, well it happened to me. Everything that I have explained to you, I've been there and done that. You have to use your basic instincts on your calls and just remember there are no two calls alike. Every call is different, you just have to be aware of your surroundings and don't be afraid to call for back-up if something doesn't feel right.

Angel On My Shoulder

HE FOUGHT THE LAW AND THE LAW WON (BAD FRIDAY)

My watch showed 3:30 PM. Just one more hour to go and I'd be home to a good hot relaxing bath and wash some of this crud off of me. It never ceased to amaze me how dirty a person could get just riding around in a car all day. It must be the dirty air in Nashville, I thought.

The weather had taken a turn for the worse on this November day as I eased my patrol car through the 4 P.M. traffic on 5th Ave North. I turned my Patrol Car right onto Deadrick and the radio was silent. But my thoughts of getting off at the regular time was interrupted. There was a description of a wanted male black in an armed robbery. "Attention all cars, Attention all cars, Suspect last seen running east on Broad, wearing a blue jacket, blue pants, medium afro, six foot, 180 lbs., the subject was involved in the Armed Robbery of Cantor's Furniture Store. The other suspect has been apprehended and is being held by car 12."

I eased my car south into traffic and pressed my foot on the accelerator and sped towards Public Square thinking that the suspect might head towards that direction in an effort to get lost in the midst of the Friday crowd leaving work and trying to get out of the city before traffic got jammed up.

OK, I'm looking for a scared male black, running, who can cover a lot of ground in just a matter of minutes. I hit heavy traffic on the South side of the Court House. People were getting off from work now and the streets were really getting crowded.

Everyone was in a hurry, wanting to get home to a cool beer or get ready for a Friday night date. Past the square I drove onto 3rd Avenue North one way heading South bound towards Broadway. I cursed at the increasing traffic. He could be long gone before I even get near the crime scene, if I didn't start making better time. Down 3rd Avenue I drove, bumper to bumper, tapping on my horn for the cars to let me

Angel On My Shoulder

through. I didn't want to use the siren, because I was afraid that it would alert the suspect if I was close to him. All the while my eyes darting back and forth scanning the sidewalks, buildings and streets looking for the suspect. Lots of people out, this was like looking for a needle in a haystack, I thought as I inched along. It seemed as though everyone was walking at

a fast pace, due to the cold winter air, all the while my eyes were searching for that one M/B who looked out of place.

The cars poured from the garages and their parking places in an endless stream. Where do all of these people work? I didn't think there was this many jobs in the whole town for this many people. How unsuspecting and pre occupied everyone looked not knowing what had just taken place just a few blocks south of them. No one was aware of the armed and dangerous criminal that was in their midst and I knew that my job was to keep these people safe.

Silently I realized how much I sometimes envied these people who lived a normal life and didn't have to work swing shifts, or deal with the characters that cops deal with on every shift. I continued to slowly drive south on a one way street. As I was approaching Church Street I spotted him. Around the corner he came onto 3rd Avenue, half walking,

half running, one male black dressed in blue pants and a blue jacket, tall, heavy build, medium afro. I could feel the adrenaline starting to flow as I followed him with my eyes. He had not spotted me yet. He was still walking up 3rd Avenue North. As we came abreast of each other our eyes met even though we were 10 feet apart from each other. I yelled,

"Come here you", I said, "I wanna talk to you." The suspect broke and started running up the street as I slammed the car into park and jammed my foot on the emergency brake. The patrol car moaned under the sudden stop. No time to check out now, he would be too far ahead of me by the time headquarters acknowledged my location. I shoved the door open and bailed out of the patrol car, slipping, but catching myself with my left hand on the car to keep from falling to the pavement. I started after the suspect, leaving the car idling and the car

Angel On My Shoulder

door open, I only had one thought in mind and that was to apprehend the suspect before he had a chance to possibly harm someone or escape. My right hand automatically went for my service revolver, getting a firm hold on the oversized grips.

The suspect was running between the crowded cars and up 3rd Avenue past surprised people. As he reached the sidewalk on the opposite side of the street he pulled a chrome plated pistol from beneath his coat and held it up in the air waiving it back and forth." The people began screaming as he ran past them. I had a flash back and thought, Oh My God, here I go again, thinking back when a male black, dressed in blue, shot me and left me to die in the street. However this time it is different, I can see the enemy and it won't be an ambush like it was when I was shot. Now he was the prey and I was the hunter and I was closing in on him. Sweat popped out on the back of my neck and my
armpits felt sticky. My hand tightened on the pistol handle.

I began yelling for the people to get out of the way as I was waving my arms frantically while running up 3rd Avenue after the suspect. As I passed several cars I was yelling for someone to get me some help
in hopes that one of them would call headquarters and tell them of my dilemma and my exact location.

People were frozen in their steps as we ran past, they did not know what to do as they were watching in astonishment of what was taking place before their eyes. The suspect then turned into an alley knocking a young lady down, sending her sprawling onto a dirty pavement. As I ran past her she was frantically trying to pull her dress down, it seemed too short to begin with and she was looking up at me in surprise as her eyes were widened with fear.

She said, "get that son of a bitch." I aimed my revolver at the suspect but I decided not to risk a shot at this time. Too many people on the street and I didn't want to take a chance of getting fired for an accidental shooting of a citizen. I was breathing heavily as I opened my mouth wide, sucking all the air in that I could. My legs were starting to

Angel On My Shoulder

burn and they felt like lead, I could hear my heart pounding faster and faster realizing that I was really out of shape. Just riding in a Patrol Car for 8 hours a day can get you pudgy and out of shape real fast.

The distance between me and the perp had narrowed. The suspect then turned into the entrance ramp of the Central Parking Garage and headed towards the Cashier's Cage. I began yelling for everyone to get out of the way as I was waving my arms right and left in hopes the crowd would clear so I might get a good shot at him, but no chance.

Everyone was caught by surprise and they just stood and stared in disbelief as we ran by. They were frozen with fear. The suspect abruptly turned left grabbing a well dressed man by the lapel of his coat with his left hand and sticking his pistol in the man's face and then he looked at me and screamed, "Get away from me or I'll kill him!" The terrified hostage was leaning away from the robber and you could see the fear in his facial expression as he was expecting to be shot at any second. Heaven only knows what this man was thinking.

Here he was getting ready to get in his car and head home to his wife, now all of a sudden he was facing death!!! The robber had a crazed, desperate look on his face as I now realized that this was a maddened animal that had to be stopped and would probably kill or be killed in the process. It was either subdue him, possibly injuring him or me getting killed in the process. I was breathing heavily as I stopped halfway up the ramp bringing my revolver up to eye level, cocking the hammer with my right thumb and my left hand onto my right wrist to steady my aim. If you hit the citizen, I'll be tried for involuntary manslaughter, I thought as my finger began to tighten on the trigger. I did not know if he would let his hostage go or kill him.

I was intending to shoot the male black subject in the head if I could get a clear shot without hitting his hostage. This shot to the head would be a precise shot coupled with the fact a head shot paralyzes all the motor nerves throughout the body making it impossible for this male black to pull the trigger of his pistol. I had no problem shooting this subject because he was holding a pistol the head of an innocent

Angel On My Shoulder

victim. This is a mad dog running wild on the streets of Nashville, thinking that he can do anything he wants too. I knew I had the confidence regarding firearms, due to the Police training, coupled with the fact that my firearm score was the highest in my recruit training class at the Police Academy.

Concentrate, concentrate, and look at the sights, not the target, clearance on both sides, steady, a little more pressure, squeeze slowly...watch the front sight and align it with the rear sight and make the suspect the secondary vision I thought and I'll hit him right between his eyes. My finger was on the trigger when the suspect suddenly broke and turned running towards Printer's Alley. Damn, just a split second more and I could have blown him away. I un-cocked my revolver and started towards the Cashier's Cage when I saw the suspect knock an elderly woman down sprawling her packages everywhere. She frantically tried to get up realizing the dangerous situation she was put in by this male black. I heard her mutter something about there is no place to hide
as I ran past her.

The hostage that the robber grabbed a few seconds earlier began yelling at the top of his lungs for everybody to hide. Some people fell down on the dirty ramp and covered their heads, others crammed through the exit doors, one man put his brief case over his head and still others backed against the wall in a rigid frozen position.

As the black male reached Printer's Alley, he turned left and immediately ducked down hiding behind a concrete wall. On top of the wall was a fence with heavy wire and a pipe frame that ran the length of the Parking Garage. I looked at the opening where the suspect had just turned left and he couldn't go north because I would see him through the opening. The inch and a half steel pipe was approximately 6 inches above the concrete wall. This is the area where I would have to aim for a clear shot at the suspect. I took a couple of deep breaths, starring at where the suspect ducked down. I was trying to slow my heart rate down a little bit. Slowly I saw and afro coming up from behind the concrete wall. I thought he is trying to find out where I am so he

Angel On My Shoulder

could shoot me. I cocked my 38 pistol and aimed towards the top part of the wall. I squeezed a shot off and it hit the brick wall on the other side of the alley. The sound was deafening in the parking garage.

I moved three steps to the right so I would not be in the same place where I fired my first shot. Thinking I shot too soon and too high. It is hard to aim at the concrete wall because it seems like I would be aiming too low. However, I reverted back to my training and visualized his head as my target and waited.

Where the hell is some help, surely someone called headquarters after seeing this entire ruckus. Unbeknownst to me, there was a Bonding Company employee who saw this melee and was behind me and coming up the ramp. When I faced Printers Alley the Bondsman came in behind me drawing his weapon and serving as a backup for me. I brought my revolver up to eye level, steadying it with my left hand, cocking the hammer with my thumb. Seconds ticked by and nothing happened. "Come out of there, you bastard," I yelled, "Or you'll never live to see tomorrow."

"Come get me you pig", was the reply.

My teeth were clinched tight and my lips pulled against my teeth as I had just about decided to charge the wall. Suddenly his head began to appear and he was pointing his pistol in my direction. I moved about three more feet sideways after I yelled at him. I was not where he had expected me to be. I watched the top part of his hair rise about the wall and his forehead starting to show as he inched himself up to see if he could see where I was standing. His revolver was in his right hand pointing in my direction. I cocked my gun and kept saying to myself wait, wait until you have more target to hit. As his eye-brows were beginning to show over the concrete wall I aimed the front sight at the top of the wall, but below the opening. I aligned the front sight with the rear sight of my pistol and squeezed a shot just as his eyebrows cleared the wall.

This is it Mac, I thought, a fight to the death, somebody is going to die today, what'll happen to my kids, how will my wife survive, damn why didn't I look the other way as he went past, you dumb ass, what

Angel On My Shoulder

are you trying to prove anyway? I could feel   water running down my back, my heart pounding wildly, those bullets hurt like hell, it burns like a red hot poker, they tear your guts apart, my wife will never under-

stand and never recover from me getting shot again or worse getting killed. Damn, what am I doing in another mess and with no back up.

Come on super vel, do your thing….1420 feet a second, hollow points can knock his brains out, spread out the size of a quarter as you hit him…. OK, I thought, just remember everything that was taught on the gun range. I squeezed the trigger and the sound was deafening, my ears began ringing, a deafening boom permeated the air from firing my Smith & Wesson .38 cal. revolver.

More loud screams and everyone was scurrying away from me. The suspect disappeared again and there was silence. You could hear a pin drop. It seemed as though time stood still. Seconds ticked by and still no movement, my ears were so loud that it was hard to concentrate. Now was decision making time, I thought.

Repeating again and again. Do I stand here and wait or do I approach the wall where he was hiding? He could be crouching down and moving towards Church Street or he could still be there waiting for me to make a move. At this time I did not know if I had hit him or not.

My armpits wet with perspiration, ears ringing, breathing heavy as I slowly moved towards the concrete wall. Several more steps, another deep breath, I looked over the wall and saw both legs stretched out. I grabbed the steel support and fired two quick rounds into the suspect, one in each lung as his body lurched with each shot.

I jumped over the handrail and staggered across the alley with my revolver on the subject. Blood flowed from his ears and mouth, a steady stream was coming from his nose as his eyes were half closed. I fell against the wall of the Brass Rail Club, sliding down in an exhausted state, my eyes still focused on where the subject was last seen. I was thinking how easy it could be me lying there, as it was once, but not today.

Angel On My Shoulder

I was breathing heavy but I kept my eyes on the subject all the while still pointing my revolver towards the out stretched suspect that was lying on the pavement. I could hear sirens and they seemed to be getting closer.

Someone came over to me and asked, Joe are you hit? No not this time, I replied. You know Joe, he's dead. Yeah, I figured he was. I thought to myself no long drawn out trial for this one. I started humming "I fought the Law and the Law won."

You know Joe, only you would say that. You know Detective, I yelled. Yes Joe what? You know I want a fucking raise. He just laughed and then he added, Dream On Bro, Dream On cause it isn't gonna happen.

I felt someone shaking me and I looked up and saw Sgt. Hoosier. "Are you all Mac?" he asked. My head nodded up and down and my chest was still heaving heavily, my eyes fixed on the robbers face in an unmoving glare.

Someone was shaking me again, put up your pistol Joe, he's not going to do anything; you got him right between the eyes. That was a hell of a shot. "Can't you stay out of trouble, Joe," Officer Pierce asked me as I began to get up and looking at the crowd of people around us. I looked at him and a big grin crossed my face. "Next time don't take so long in getting here?" I said as I watched the ambulance drivers pick up the robber and place him in the meat wagon. Another day of survival in this sewer I thought as I walked towards my patrol car and wondering how it would be the next time.

Now the deluge of paper work begins I thought, knowing I would spend the next several hours giving statements, signing supplements and being interviewed by Internal Internal Affairs, Supervisors and Detectives and trying to dodge the News Media. This paperwork had to be done right.

Cars were still bumper to bumper as I approached my patrol Car, got in, shut the door and released the emergency break, rolling towards the traffic light.

Angel On My Shoulder

Arriving at the Police Headquarters I went straight to C.I.D. where a secretary stopped me in the hall and said, "I have something that you can take to calm you down," she added, "remember Joe once the statements are finished and you have signed there's no changing your story. The incident is etched in stone as to the facts stated." She handed me a yellow pill which I put in my mouth and gulped down a glass of water.

"What was that I just took anyway, I asked the secretary?" She answered, "you don't want to know, just say it was an aspirin." Remember Joe these types of shootings where there is a fatality, it has to be within the guidelines or you are in a world of hurt. She further stated from what I've heard everything is alright, but you can't take any chances, you have to be very accurate in all phases of this incident. On each question that you are asked, take a second to think before you speak. Everything you say is taped, even if you are left alone in the room, don't say anything out loud or talk to yourself needlessly. There would be no going back the next day to change your story about this incident. As I approached the interview room my legs felt weak as if they were ready to collapse, hands slightly trembling, a big knot in my throat and my mind was racing throughout the whole ordeal that had taken place in Printer's Alley. The reality had finally set in.

It seemed that just a few short hours ago, I was supposed to be getting off duty and taking my kids to the movies, I had promised them a night out with their dad.

This was a nightmare, rehashing all the gory facts before, during and after the shootings. How can I ever explain this to my children, will their little minds be able to realize what has happened. Will I ever get over this? They say while something of this magnitude happens you can't really phantom the severity or the lingering repercussions of it for years to come.

Three hours later I left headquarters and headed home driving slower than usual. Upon arriving at my residence I stopped at the end of the drive and put my forehead on the steering wheel thinking about the ride home. I could not remember leaving headquarters or

Angel On My Shoulder

anything about the trip home. What a fucked up day I thought upon entering my house.

My wife was washing dishes as I stepped into the kitchen. Where the hell have hell have you been for the past three hours. Did you forget you were supposed to take the kids to the movies tonight and they wanted to go eat pizza. OR "did you have fun with some bitch you met?" "Did you tell her you're married with three kids?"

I just stood and looked at her while taking my Sam Brown utility belt off and draping it over the chair. I suppose your going to leave your gun there on the chair so the kids can see it. So what I thought after a night I've had, I'm not going to listen to this shit any more tonight.

I turned and faced my wife who was slamming pots and pans down as she was washing them. "If you had looked at the 6 o'clock news you would have seen yours truly on the tube," I said in a sarcastic manner. You know if you'd try doing the dishes every day instead of once a week, it might not take you so long to do them.

"What did you do arrest some prostitute and get caught fucking around, she scowled?"

NO, I replied, "I was in a gun fight at the Central Parking Garage that runs adjacent to Printer's Alley and I killed a man, an armed robber. You know, bang, bang, bang you're dead. Only this was for real and much to your sorrow, I won this one and I didn't die. So no Insurance money or Widow's Pension this month "Toots." Maybe next time, by the way you know the Grim Reaper is an old friend of mine."

Do you remember back in March of 1970, I danced with him then, and I'll dance with him again and again. He's with me every time I get into the Patrol car. Believe me, there will be a next time. Reaching into my shirt pocket and pulling out a business card, flipping it on the counter top and said, "Call that number and ask anyone who answers what time I left headquarters?" I'm going to take a shower, I'm sweaty, dirty and damn tired. I turned and went towards the bathroom leaving my wife standing in front of a sink and counter with dirty dishes stacked high, as usual, and she was totally silent with her mouth agape.

Angel On My Shoulder

Just another day in paradise I thought as I began to unbutton my shirt while on the way to the bathroom. I stopped by the children's bedroom and they were sound asleep, unaware of the happenings that involved their father a few hours earlier.

Bending down I kissed their little cheeks, saying softly good night and whispering to each one of them, daddy loves you and tomorrow night we will see a movie and eat pizza. I was thinking about the movie Walking Tall, this would be a good one to see again. I shut their door and headed towards the bathroom closing and locking the door behind me. I just wanted to take a hot shower and let the water beat down on my body which was tight from all the stress of today.

I started thinking about everything that had happened to me during this shift from hell. I am a damn good Police Officer on Duty I thought. I began humming the song for the second time tonight, "I FOUGHT THE LAW AND THE LAW WON."

Man I feel better now being back home with my children and to be alive and able to Serve and Protect another day and keep all the cock roaches at bay. Damn I feel great.

Several days later I received a phone call from an elderly lady that resided in the Edgehill area. She said, you are Joe McEwen aren't you? I said, "Yes I am."

Well I just wanted to thank you for killing the son of a bitch that robbed the Furniture Store. She went on to say that this man has been robbing the elderly for a long time. You know we get our Social Security Checks about the 5th of the month and this is when we go to the grocery store and as soon as we leave he robs us of the money we have left. Some of the elderly have been hurt real bad. I just wanted to thank you from the bottom of my heart for getting this thug off the streets. I know that we all feel a lot better and you have done the citizens of the Edgehill area a big favor and we feel safe now. I hate that someone has to die, but he was no good. Again, thank you and may God bless you Mr. McEwen.

Once again, I thought about when I got shot in 1970. Those two men were robbing old people after they got their Social Security

Angel On My Shoulder

checks. They would follow them home and rob them. You know I guess things like this will always happen. The older people are easy targets and easy prey. I guess our Society will never change.

Angel On My Shoulder

HOMEWARD BOUND!!

Drunks are a big problem in downtown Nashville. The Police spend a lot of time keeping them off the streets by arresting them and taking them to headquarters. One Police Officer got the bright idea to ship them out of town on a Greyhound Bus. An Officer's brother in law was a bus driver for Greyhound. One night he checked with his brother in law and found out that the bus did not have many riders. He pulled his paddy wagon next to the Bus, telling the 15 drunks to get on the bus and it was going to the Police Department. All the drunks entered the bus and to Florida they went. When the Bus arrived at the destination in Florida and the drunks, (Now sober) got off the bus and realized they weren't in Nashville because they saw the all the water.

The Florida Policeman asked the riders where they boarded the bus at? They told him in Nashville, Tennessee, the home of the Grand Ole Opry. The Police Department in Florida made a phone call to the Nashville Police Department and gave them the news about the Police Officers who were shipping the drunks out of state.

The Nashville Police Officers were reprimanded and told never to put any more drunks on a Bus that was headed out of town. The Officer's justification was, we thought we were doing the Jail a favor because of the overcrowding of drunks that were being arrested time and time again.

Not only were the drunks a problem, but drugs seemed to be growing at a fast pace. Once while I was working North Nashville, I would come in contact with some drug dealers. It is quite frustrating for a Police Officer to be unable to catch these dealers in the act.

It is rather hard when you drive a marked unit and try to sneak up on someone. There was one lookout who would stand outside of

Angel On My Shoulder

the building and when he saw me come around the corner in my marked unit he would whistle to warn his partner that the Police was nearby. One day I stopped my patrol car and motioned for him to come over to me. I said, do you know the last thing that you are going to hear on this planet before you die? He looked at me with a puzzled look on his face and replied, WHAT! I replied, "Well, asshole it is going to be the sound on me cocking my 38 cal. pistol before blowing your fucking brains out." I added, that's what is going to happen if I catch you right. With that I got back into my Patrol Car and drove off.

Every time that I was in the neighborhood I would drive by real slow where he was standing and with my right hand point my finger at him and indicate like I was firing my pistol at him.

Angel On My Shoulder

LOST GUNS

How about the Sergeant who lost three service revolvers in one month! It began with the Sergeant using a toilet at a gas station one night in Green Hills. He hung his utility belt on the back of the restroom door. He left forgetting his utility belt and realizing a couple of hours later that he didn't have his pistol on his waist. When he went back to the Gas Station, the back door of the restroom was bare, no gun and no utility belt to be found.

A couple of weeks later the same Sergeant stopped in the rear of a Shopping Mall to relieve himself. This time he left his utility belt in the driver's seat, but he took his pistol with him while he relieved himself. He had placed the gun on the trunk of the Police car forgetting to pick it up when he finished. He drove off and at dawn he remembered his pistol was not on his side, he returned to the mall only to find no pistol. Another pistol lost by the Sergeant. Hello!

One week later the Sergeant went into a convenient store for his free cup of Coffee and doughnuts, only to be confronted by an armed robber. Yes, the robber took the Sergeant's gun during the robbery. Well the Sergeant was transferred from Patrol to a desk job at headquarters answering the phone, where he eventually took his Pension.

He still holds the record for 3 Revolvers lost in one month.

Angel On My Shoulder

PURSUIT

I always worked a second job whenever I could plus go to school twice a week. Whenever I came to Roll Call I was very tired and worn out. After Roll Call I would sometimes give the Car keys to my Rookie partner that I was training so he could cruise over our zone while I took a short nap. I told Rickie to stay on the smooth roads and don't cross railroad tracks if he could help it. Years later Rick Lankford retired with the Rank of Captain.

I don't know how long I had dozed, but I was awakened by someone yelling and beating on my left arm. "Wake up Dammit, I've been chasing this Son of a Bitch all over our Sector." I looked ahead and saw the suspect's car swerve and hit a dip in the road at an intersection with sparks flying from the rear bumper.

I grabbed the mike and radioed that we are in pursuit of a vehicle. "What did he do?" I asked. Rickie said, "he sped away when I lit him up. There was not much traffic because it was 3 AM. "Hang back" I said and let him wreck. The suspect was about 2 blocks ahead of us when he turned right. A few seconds went by and we turned onto the street and it was empty. The car was nowhere.

"Stop!" I yelled. "Stop and turn the motor off." I said stay in the car and give dispatch our location. I walked to the front the Patrol Car to listen for any noise. Nothing but silence. No dogs barking and no lights on. I could hear metal popping from the heat of our Patrol Car.

I began walking down the right side of the street touching the hood of each car feeling for warmth. I would also look up every driveway for a car that was not parked correctly, most of the

Angel On My Shoulder

cars on the street were parked in their driveway and not on the grass I felt about 10 car hoods before I found one that was warm. I motioned for my partner to pull down and turn on the spotlight facing toward the vehicle. I looked inside the car and saw someone lying on the front floor of the automobile. The car door was locked and I ordered the suspect to open the door. He pretended like he was asleep and didn't hear me. I began rocking the car and hitting the roof making loud banging sounds. He rose up and opened the door and I stood between him and his car door giving him no room to escape. I immediately handcuffed him and advised him of his rights. He said, what have I done, I ain't did nothing wrong.

I said, let me guess, I bet you can't find your driver's license? How about this you don't have one? Is it suspended, revoked or you just couldn't pass the test? He replied, its, well you know its suspended Officer. And I bet you don't have any Insurance either? I added, I bet I know why you don't have any insurance? Let me see, oh you don't have a valid driver's license.

I yelled at Rickey, call a Tow Truck. Why you calling a Tow Truck? To tow your car that's why. What is your name numb nuts, Charles he replied. He asked can't you just leave my car here? I only live two blocks down the street. I said no because you should have stopped your car when you saw us behind you. He hissed and said, "you ain't got no right to tow my car!"

"Oh, yeah," was my answer. I said, "just watch me tow your

car, that is if it is your car." Well, it's my brother's car and he don't know I borrowed it. Oh, I see. So now your brother is going to be mad at you for taking his car. Officer, you don't know who my brother is, do you. Why do you think I would know who your brother is? Well he's not one that you would want to mess with. I told him that you should of said, I don't think our brother wants to mess with me. I just laughed, which pissed him off. You just wait

Angel On My Shoulder

till I tell my brother how you treated me. Go right ahead, you know where I work. I added, you need to start brushing your teeth more because you breath smells like hog shit. Ah man, you didn't have to say that, I got feelings. Yeah Right!

Free room and board awaits you at the Metro Hotel. Oh! you also get a good cold bologna sandwich with a bottle of water and maybe a stale bag of chips. "Oh yeah, " was his reply.

Now tell me why you were in the lying on the floor of the car. I was looking for UH, UH. What is UH UH, I asked. Well you see Officer I was looking for my keys. I don't think so because they are in the ignition. Uh, I thought I dropped them. Can't
you think of a better answer than that one. Officer, I'm telling you the truth. Yeah, and I'm the tooth fairy. When I came up to the car you were pretending to be asleep. No reply from the suspect, just a dumb look upon his face like, oh hell I've been caught.

I said, once again you should have stopped your car when you saw us behind you with our lights on."

He hissed, "You're real funny."

"Ha! Ha!" I said, "I try to be, now get into the Patrol Car." Free room and board awaits you.

End Result:

No Insurance, car impounded, 3 old warrants served on the suspect…. 1 State Warrant, no driver's license, 1 State Warrant for reckless driving, 1 State Warrant for fleeing and eluding.

And I said to myself, "Not bad for coming out of a deep sleep and you know another one bites the dust." Plus a bonus, I know the suspect now and I know the suspects brother's car and where he lives. Now when I see him out I'll have probable cause to pull him over and make an arrest and tow the car. I'll get Court Time.

Cha Ching!!

Angel On My Shoulder

NO LIQUOR LICENSE

When I worked the day shift, I spent quite a bit of time doing bar checks. What I was looking for was violations, that is hard liquor in a beer joint and that did not have a Liquor License.

Once a year Police are given tickets to the Policeman's Ball to sell. These tickets are given only to the Police that belong to the Policeman's Benefit. I could never imagine a Policeman not belonging to this Organization. The dues were a $1.00 a month and when you retired in good standing or on a disability Pension, the member would receive $100.00 for every year that they belonged to the Organization.

After twenty years a retiree received a lump sum of $2,000.00 tax free. The amount that was paid in after twenty years was $240.00. This is an unbelievable investment.

On one hot summer day I went into the Bar at 6th and Jefferson, when I entered I looked to the right and saw a patron leaning on the jukebox selecting records to be played. His shirt was out of his pants and in his right rear pocket I could plainly see the outline of what appeared to be a liquor bottle. This tavern had no hard Liquor License, just a Beer License. It is up to the owner or the bartender to see that no liquor enters the premises. I walked over to where the man was in front of the jukebox lifted his shirt and pulled out a half empty bottle of whiskey.

He turned around and when he saw that I was a Police Officer he just stood there. I walked over to the bar laid the half empty bottle of whiskey on the bar and asked the manager how many tickets to the Policeman's Ball did you say you wanted to purchase? He replied, how many do you have left? I said, I have fourteen left. He then said, I'll take then all. I put the tickets on the bar he handed me the money and I said have a nice day. I turned and walked out the door. I guess he figured that this was cheaper

Angel On My Shoulder

than me taking him before Beer Board for a violation of his License.

My partner and I were working one night and we would walk into a Tavern and not say a word. We would just stand against the wall by the jukebox. Very few people would even noticed us until I unplugged the jukebox. Then it was as quiet as a Funeral Home. Sometimes we could hear a handgun being dropped on the floor. We would shine our flashlights underneath the tables and on occasion we would pick up the weapon. Also pills wrapped in tinfoil, small baggies of marijuana or anything illegal. The small stuff we would throw into the storm drain and the pistols were turned into the property room. Of course, no one ever claimed ownership and they were destroyed at a later date. We never did
find any cocaine or heroin that was thrown on the floor.

If no patrons were blind running drunk I would walk over to the jukebox and say to the patron's you all have a blessed night. Then I would plug the jukebox back in and we would leave the premises.

Angel On My Shoulder

JUDGE BIRCH

I answered a call one day around 5 PM in my zone. This was a car wreck involving just one car. It was a late model minivan. When I arrived both suspects were still in the vehicle, they were still dazed from the collision with a light pole.

I opened the driver's door and asked anyone hurt? They both replied in unison "NO!" I asked how did this happen? It was the old mystery car in the road excuse. I should have guessed as much. I wish I had a dollar for every time I had heard this excuse. The front end of the mini van was a total mess. It was wrapped around the light pole; I don't know what kept the pole from breaking into. They seemed to have just minor cuts. I don't know how they survived this wreck.

 I asked the driver for his license. He replied, "He didn't have them and that they were suspended."

I said "What for? A wreck with no insurance." He nodded yes. I placed him in the back of my Patrol Car after advising him of his rights and handcuffed him. I told the passenger to stay seated and I'll be right back.

I went to the passenger side and noticed the passenger was hurriedly trying to put something under his seat. When I opened the door, I told the passenger to sit tight. I noticed that the glove box was open and clearly I could see a 32 caliber pistol which was partially covered by a piece of paper. This gun was within the reach of the passenger and thus making my search perfectly legal. I asked the passenger is this your pistol? No was his answer. I again asked, " whose gun is this?" No answer. I said OK, then you are under arrest and I'll just charge you both with possession of a pistol. But Officer, I didn't know it was in there! I then looked under his seat where I had seen him trying to put something under there when I walked up to the van. I asked, "what is that sticking out from under your seat?" I don't know what you are talking about. I just got into the car just a few minutes ago. Well let's see, oh what is this a

small baggie with white powder in it? I guess this is sugar in the baggie? I don't know sir, it's not mine, I never saw it before. You know when I was walking up to the side of this van I saw you bending over as if you were trying to put something under the seat. I was just sitting here Officer, I didn't do anything. Sure you did, was my reply. Do you think that I'm some kind of a dummy? No sir, was his answer. I cuffed the suspect and told him that he was under arrest and I then Mirandized him and placed him I the back seat of my car next to the driver of the wrecked Mini Van.

The vehicle was towed and both men were processed in the Booking Room, the driver was charged with having no driver's license, no insurance, and possession of a 32 caliber pistol and a small baggie of white powder. The passenger was charged with possession of a 32 caliber pistol and possession of a small baggie of white powder. The powder was tested and it was cocaine. So, this made the charges with possession of a controlled substance instead of just a small baggie of white powder.

Warrants were obtained after we appeared before of the Committing Magistrate at Police Headquarters.

Several weeks later I went to General Sessions Court for a Preliminary hearing. The is the first step prior to going before the Grand Jury for an Indictment in Criminal Court. I presented my case and their Lawyer hammered me about an illegal search.

I testified the search, because the glove box was within arm's reach of the passenger and it was open, thus making this search legal. I looked at the Judge Birch and he stated, I find probable cause to bind the suspects over to the Grand Jury.

After Court I stood in the hall next to General Sessions Court Room. There were several Police Officers present. We were talking about our arrests when Judge Birch emerged from the

Angel On My Shoulder

Court Room and walked up to us. He looked at me and said "Good Search Mac, keep up the good work."

"Yes Sir," I replied.

I had a big smile on my face as he walked away.

One of the Officers said to me, "Damn Joe, I never had a Judge tell me I did a good search!"

It is very rare that the Judge makes comments like this, but when he feels like an Officer goes by the rules of the Law and then he lets them know that they are doing good Police work. You know it feels good to have Judge Birch tell me this. He was always fair in Court. I do try to always go by the Rules even though sometimes you get a subject that doesn't want to cooperate and tries to weasel out of getting arrested.

I replied to these Officer's, "It is what it is!" More Court time and more money.

I had been in Judge Birch's Court Room on numerous occasions and he knew that I always followed the rules of the Law when arresting a subject. This is why the Judge had no problem with my testimony and handed down the correct ruling, at the Preliminary Hearing.

The second stage is testifying before the Grand Jury, which is quite easy because I did not have to contend with being cross examined by the defense Attorney. They do not have a say so in this phase of the Criminal Justice System. Cha Ching!!

SACK OF PILLS

While on Patrol one night I decided to look in the Alleys that ran beside the local Beer Joints. My partner and I were looking for anything that looked suspicious. As a rule we usually found an abandoned car or a few drunks which on an occasion were so drunk
that they would be fighting or that is trying to fight. As I pulled the Patrol car into the alley I spotted an abandoned car which was parked very close to the Beer Joint. There was enough room for another car to pass by. It was an old car which had seen better days. This was a clunker for sure.

My partner and I got out of the car and went to see if anyone was inside passed out. As we neared the old car we noticed two large black males standing in front of the car.

I stood to the side of the car and looked it over. The vinyl covering on the top of this automobile was in decent shape except for a rather large tear in the area beside the rear window
and the left rear window. The vinyl had a bulge underneath it and when I pulled upon the tear a bag of white pills fell out and I caught it with my right hand. There must have been at least two hundred or more pills in the bag. I looked at the two male suspects that was standing in front of this ragged car.

I asked them, "Is this your package or does it belong to the Pill Fairy?"

Both of them replied at the same time, "it's not mine. Officer we just got here." Sure you did, I wish I had a dollar for every time I had heard that excuse. Again, they stated that they had just gotten there. I felt of the hood of the car and it was still warm. I suppose neither of you saw the owner of this vehicle? No sir, like we said "we just got here and we were waiting for our friend to come pick us up."

Angel On My Shoulder

I told my partner to call for a Vice car so that we could turn in this sack of pills that I had found. The Vice Officers arrived shortly and we turned the pills over to them. The Vice Officer asked us about the two males subjects in front of the car. I told him that they said they had just arrived and they knew nothing about the pills. The Vice Officer said, Joe did you have on gloves when you picked up the sack of pills. I replied, I sure did. The second Vice Officer went to the front of the car and started talking to the 2 males. I said in a loud voice, you know since I had on gloves when I found the sack of pills you should be able to get fingerprints off the sack.

At this time the 2 males started running down the alley with myself and one of the Vice Officers in chase. We caught them in no time and they were handcuffed and we walked them back to the car. I asked them, why did you run? Uh, Uh, we didn't want to get blamed for the sack of pills.

One of the Officers said, Joe we got this now and thanks for your help. We walked back to our Patrol car and I told my partner that giving the evidence to the Vice Officers saved us a lot of time by not having to go to Headquarters and the turning the sack of pills into the property room for processing. After running a Record Check on the two suspects, I uncuffed them and told them no Warrants tonight fellows, maybe next time it might be a different ending.

I drove about two blocks and pulled the car over to the side of the street and began writing in my notebook the time and the 2 Vice Officers names that took possession of the sack of pills. My partner said, "you know Joe, I've learned more in just the short time we have been together tonight than I had amassed in a week while riding with another Officer's. I was told by several other older Officer's that you knew the rules and regulations and you followed everything by the book."

Angel On My Shoulder

"That's right; it's the only way to survive in this type of work. If you mess up, your ass is in a world of hurt. So always do it the right way and you won't have to worry about anything."

We headed back to the streets to Patrol our zone and I asked my partner do you want to eat Chicken or a hamburger and fries? Joe, you know the places in this zone better than I do so I'll let you pick. He answered, "I've changed my mind lets go pig out on a Pizza."

Ok, Pizza it is and we're off to the Pizza Parlor we went. We were about halfway to the Pizza place when we got another call. Looks like the Pizza will have to wait.

We had to go back up another Officer that was riding by himself and he was trying to arrest 2 subject's alone. By the time we had reached his location another Officer was nearby and the two suspects were already cuffed and in the back of the Patrol Car. The Officer who had put out the call for assistance said, "sorry about that Joe. I didn't have time to cancel the request. Thanks anyway."

We were on our way for the second time to get a Pizza. I told my partner see you can not predict what you will be doing from one minute to the next. Hell, there have been nights that I was so busy on answering calls that I didn't even get to eat. Always remember to bring you something to snack on and a cola in a little ice cooler. Like the Boy Scouts you have to be prepared. Joe, were you ever a Boy Scout? Yes, and I was in the Navy and on a ship and I stayed sea sick all the time unless I could see land and then I was OK. That was 4 years of Hell, but I did learn a lot about doing things the right way so you wouldn't have to do them over.

My partner said, "I like riding with you Joe, I hope we ride together again tomorrow night." Well, thank you. I have enjoyed working with you also. Let's head back to the West Station and check in for the night.

Angel On My Shoulder

STINKY ~ STINKY

My partner Tim Durham and I received a call one night about a disturbance and a disorderly male in our zone. We responded to the house and approached the front door which was open but it had a screen door that was closed. We looked inside and saw a small female looking from an open doorway just inside the main door. She looked frightened and pointed towards the stairs, with her right hand.

We started to open the screen door when a liquid with a putrid odor hit the screen, splattering all over us. I yelled, "Tim he's throwing piss on us."

Tim pulled open the screen door and we both charged in at the same time. We both weighed over 200 lbs. each and we became wedged in the door frame, trying to get through the opening. We looked quite comical struggling until we turned sideways and rushed towards the stairs. The suspect started running to another room but fell down because of the liquid on the hardwood floors at the top of the stairs.

We reached him before he could get up and fell on him at the same time. We knocked the wind out of him, so handcuffing him was no problem.

His wife was yelling for us to please don't hurt him. "OK, I replied just tell him to behave. She was yelling for us to please not to hurt him because he has a plate in his head. I said jokingly, "Is it China or Porcelain?"

"I don't consider that to be funny," she replied.

"You know, I don't consider having piss thrown on me funny either," I shouted back.

We transported him without incident to headquarters. He was subsequently fined $250.00 with 6 months' probation and Court costs.

Angel On My Shoulder

This was the first and last time that this will ever happen. Our shirts were soaked in this man's urine. We had to go through the rest of our shift with this awful smell. It was a cool night and we had the windows down, but the smell would not go away. We stopped at a Drug Store to get some spray but it made it worse. After this incident I always carried an extra shirt in the trunk of the Police Car.

When we turned our paper work in at the station, the Sergeant asked us where we had been. We told him what had happened and I don't think he believed us. But it did happen.

I always liked working with Tim, he was a great partner. We always had each others back and it seems like we always got into some kind of situation. We always had each other's back, no matter what. Tim Durham was fearless when it came to Police work. We went through the Training Academy together and upon Graduation we were both assigned at the West Station. When we rode solo, our Zone's always touched. This enabled us to back up each other when it was necessary and it usually was because we worked in the North Nashville area.

When I was off wounded for 1 year and a half, I returned to the West Station and I found myself working close to Tim's Zone. I then transferred to the South Station, Tim and I rarely ever saw each other while we were working. We were both transferred to the Training Academy but not at the same time as Instructors. Tim worked in the Firearms Section of the Academy and I worked in the Administrative Section which was dealing with the New Recruits and In-Service Training for the Police Officers.

We were both members of the original SWAT Team and we had been on many calls together and also at the Prison Riots in Nashville. Once again we always had each other's back. There was a very strong bond between the both of us and to this day we very close. I have known Tim Durham for 44 plus years and we have never had a disagreement.

Angel On My Shoulder

WAKE – UP

I remembered the time when Tim called me on the Police Radio to meet him near the Farmer's Market one night. There was a car which was parked in the parking lot with someone inside asleep. Tim stood on one side of the car and I was on the opposite side. We began rocking the Sedan back and forth and beating on the top of the car. The person inside did not budge one bit. After several minutes of trying to wake this subject up we were both getting tired and so we stopped. I told Tim, you know we have gotten our exercise for tonight. I also added, that this is the first time that I have never been able to awaken someone in a closed automobile.

I said, Hey Tim! Let's shoot a few rats behind the feed store. He replied "Suits me" and away we went…..to thin out the heard, so to speak. Against the Rules! Sure!! But what's life without an occasional Gamble?

Police work is the only job I can think of that the harder you work, the more apt you are to get into trouble. When a Policeman is complained on, they are automatically "Guilty" until proven innocent. People have a slanted opinion. If something is in print against a Law Enforcement Officer, the Public assumes it's the truth. I've always said, "believe nothing you hear and only half of what you see." This quotation came from my dad.

Even an honest mistake can sometimes result in an Officer being suspended without pay or worse, being fired.

Angel On My Shoulder

Life And Death

I started thinking about the time that Tim was working part time at Washington MFG Co. Clothing Outlet, on Nolensville Road. It was December 23rd and the time was 7:48P.M., which was almost closing time. Tim was wearing civilian clothing with a vest to conceal his 9mm pistol with 12 rounds. Tim had the safety on, with one in the chamber. All he had to do is pull the trigger.

Suddenly 2 masked men burst through the front door and one was carrying a pistol, which was a 2 shot 38 cal. Derringer. Tim felt if they found he was a Policeman there was a very good likely hood that he would be shot or killed. The two robbers were yelling and waving their arms.

Tim turned sideways with his right side away from the robbers, waving his left hand back and forth for distraction and telling them just wait a minute. OKAY – OKAY – Just calm down! The lead robber pointed his pistol right at Tim's head which was just about 18" away.

Tim was taking his right arm sliding it under his vest, reaching slowly for his 9mm pistol. In a split second Tim swung his pistol around and taking his right thumb, releasing the safety, squeezing the trigger with his index finger as he swung his 9mm to the front of the robber

shooting the first robber in the gut and he continued shooting him right up the middle and stopping at the robber's chest. I think he fired 4 rounds. The robber dropped like a sack of potatoes. The second robber began turning around after the first shot was fired and was heading

towards the front door. Tim turned his attention towards the second robber. In an instant the robber was out the front of the store with Tim firing through the plate glass as the robber in a flash disappeared around the side of the building.

Angel On My Shoulder

This second Bandit was hit in his elbow and once in his torso. He ran to their truck which was parked beside the building. All this took place in a few seconds, from start to finish.

The first robber that was shot died and the second robber was caught later. Most Police shootings are over in a matter of seconds, unlike TV where they seem to go on for an extended time, Hollywood style.

I also worked sometimes part time at the Washington Mfg. Co. Outlet, but on this night it was Tim who was working and he was always alert, especially at closing time.

Angel On My Shoulder

NEW STATION AND NEW TERRITORY

I went into the West Station one day and asked my Sergeant how much longer before the South Station opens up? He replied in about a month the transfers will start. I replied, I would like to go South and work on your detail. I added it will be so much closer to where I live. Sarge, I live be about 4 miles from the South Station. He said, I know how you work and I'll make you a Zone Commander in the Donelson area.

At the new South Station he added, that the Patrol Cars will be a take home vehicles Zone Commander. He said going to and from work and Court time this will not cost you a penny in gasoline.

The new South Station was a remodeled Doctor's Clinic on Nolensville Road. I will be able to drive from my house on Brewer Drive to the South Station in less than 15 minutes. I thought this would be so much better than the distance I have to drive to the West Station. Depending upon what shift I worked it usually took about 45 minutes to drive there, also the gas that it took would cease, because at the South Station I would have a take home Patrol car and this would be about a $25.00 a month raise.

I thought to myself this is really great if it really happens. I'll be closer to home and it would be less time on the road and a few extra bucks in my pocket each month.

The Sergeant told me the truth, as soon as the South Station was finished remodeling I was told to report to the South Station to start my new assignment.

I thought to myself, "Happy days are here again."

I really didn't realize that being so close to home saved me about an hour a day, which comes out to about 20 hours a month less on the road, and away from all the crazies.

Angel On My Shoulder

BONG TIME

One day when I came home, I told my two sons, Joe Joe and Eric to come with me to our shed, beside our house. Inside the shed I had placed 2 Bongs (A device for smoking Marijuana, Hashish and any other substance used to abuse drugs) these Bongs were Brass with flexible hoses and a wooden mouthpiece. Each one was about 2 feet tall.

I had Court the next day and I brought them home so I wouldn't have to go to all the trouble turning into the Property Room and checking them back out 12 hours later. This is against Rules and Regulations, but at the time it seemed like a good idea. The only one that knew about this was me and I surely wasn't going to tell on myself. I planned on using them in Court and then turning them in when my Court Case was heard.

I told Joe Joe and Eric that these bongs are a start of using drugs and ruining someone's life. I added, using something like this is the first stepping stone for more dangerous drugs. This leads you on a road that only spirals downward or in other words on a road to nowhere which is lined with heartache and trouble. Not only you but, to the people that love you. Like your family. You know that friends come and go, girlfriends come and go, but family is a
lifetime commitment. Drugs only leads to misery and death. The one thing that all drug users have in common, they don't live to a ripe old age, just like smoking cigarettes.
I also added, I better not ever catch either one of you using something like this. May it be large or small and you better not have one in your possession. My boys were 10 and 11 years at this time. I added, If I do catch either one of you with such a device like this, I will not whip you, I will beat you. Also if one gets caught then both of you will get punished. Do you understand me!

Angel On My Shoulder

Yes daddy we understand. Their heads moved up and down like Bobble Heads.

I thought to myself, I believe that I made a valid point. Sometimes fear is a wonderful persuasion.

You do understand you are not to touch these or tell any of your friends about them don't you. Yes daddy, yes we promise that we won't even touch them. They both nodded their heads. After they went to sleep I went out to the shed and got the 2 bongs and locked them in the trunk of my Police Car. The next morning they went running out the back door and when they came back in with a surprised look on their little faces. I asked, "What's the matter?"

Daddy we didn't do it, we promise. Do what, boys? We didn't move the 2 bongs that you had in the shed. Don't worry boys, I moved them last night. By the way, why did you go out there? Just to see them daddy, that's all. Go ahead and eat your breakfast and I'll take you to School. But, daddy can we just see them one more time. No, now eat you're breakfast. I will take you to School and then I have a 9AM Court Case on these two Bongs. My wife spoke up and said, you showed them some bongs, they are too little to realize what they are. I told her they need to know about things like this so they won't touch them or use them.

I'll see you boys tonight and we can eat Pizza and watch TV. Oh boy was their reply. Be good in School and we will talk when I get home.

I drove them to school and the whole time they were giggling. I sure do love these boys. They make coming home at night bearable. Oh, well I guess this is just going to be another day. I only hope my boys listen to me. I only want the best for them.

Angel On My Shoulder

SNAKES

I had a 55 gallon drum at the back of my property in which I used to burn trash. One time my 2 boys were with me while I was burning some trash. They put empty plastic bottles on a long stick and put it over the burning trash catching the bottle on fire. They were really surprised when they saw the different colors dripping down from the bottle as it was burning. I told both of them that they were never ever to do this when I wasn't around. I knew in a way that this went in one ear and out the other. After all they are just kids who had found a new way to occupy their time. They both answered, "OK dad." Those two boys could come up with more things to do. I just wonder if they will ever try this when I wasn't around.

Just a few weeks later they were playing in the back yard, I heard them yelling and I went outside to see what had happened. They were out of breath, because all I could hear out of their mouths was mumbling. OK, boys calm down and tell me what's wrong. Dad, there is a big snake back by our tree house. He's really big. Daddy go get your gun, I'm afraid that it will climb up the tree and get in our tree house.

I went inside and I got my revolver, as soon as they saw me with the gun in my hand their eyes lit up.

Eric said, "Oh boy daddy's going to shoot the snake now." After I found the snake, I could tell that it was a poisonous one because of the triangular shape of its head. I took aim and fired my revolver at the snake. They couldn't look at the snake because their eyes were fixed on my revolver.

I acted like, John Wayne by blowing my breath on the end of the gun. Their eyes were filled with awe. I got a stick to pick up the snake and then I put it into the drum where I burn trash. I went back inside to clean my gun and then I put it back upon the shelf in

Angel On My Shoulder

my bedroom closet. I could hear them playing and pretending that they were shooting a gun by saying Bang, Bang.

Angel On My Shoulder

ANOTHER CONFRONTATION

The days really grow shorter as fall approaches I thought while parking the 1970 yellow Maverick beside the side door of my home in South Nashville. Earlier my three children had already entered the car and sat down in the back seat. They were giggling and poking at each other. I told them to be quiet before their mother got in the car you know it makes her nervous when you act up in the car. OK, daddy was their reply and they giggled again. My wife got in the passenger's seat, shut the door and said "I'm already, so let's go.

You know daddy doesn't like us to be late." Oh, I surely don't want him to get mad at us for being late since we have been waiting on you to come out for the 30 minutes. Just shut up and let's go. "Yes my dear," was my laughing reply as I pulled out of the gravel drive and headed towards Nashville.

We headed to Joelton on the North side of Nashville to have dinner with my in-law's, this evening as we did several times a month. It was a long drive, about 30 miles one way. Three kids playing and teasing each other and a wife that was nagging about my driving.
Wow, what a trip this was going to be.

Upon reaching the Interstate I-65 N, I stayed in the right lane doing about 5 mph under the speed limit. Traffic was fairly light, as I headed North on I-65. For the past 2 miles I kept checking my rear view mirror as a vehicle seemed to be tailing me pretty close. At one time the Blue car behind me was so close that the headlights could not be seen. I started to slow down to about 40 MPH as the blue vehicle darted from behind me and pulled up beside my yellow Maverick and he then flipped me a bird as he sped by pulling in front and headed North on I-65.

The blue auto exited Trinity Lane which looped back under I-65 Bridge. I then turned onto Trinity Lane and headed west towards Whites Creek Pike. The blue car slowed down and pulled quickly to the right in front of a gas station.

Angel On My Shoulder

I said out loud this guy is looking for trouble; I'm stopping behind him because I don't want him behind me again. When both automobiles stopped I reached for my pistol which was beside me in the front seat. Just then the male black's driving the car opened his door quickly exited his car, turned and began to walk towards my Maverick. Traffic was heavy and it was getting dark. Passing cars illuminated the male black as he approached the front of my auto.

I quickly exited my vehicle, stepping back and closing the front door of my car. My 38 caliber pistol was in my right hand and behind my back as I took one step towards the male black and stopped. The male black had his left arm in a full arm cast from his bicep to his wrist with a 90 degree bend at the elbow, and his right arm behind his back. Cars were speeding by as we were facing each other. There was about eight steps between us. I then shouted, "Before you do something stupid, I am a Metro Police Officer with a loaded pistol in my right hand." I also added "you had better be damn careful what your next move will be, because it might be your last day on this planet." Easing my right hand from behind my back, with my elbow close to my side slightly exposing a department issued service revolver.

The suspect slowly exposed his right arm with a blue steel revolver in his in hand. The barrel was pointing directly down towards the asphalt. The male black said, "I is got's a permit to carry this gun Sir."

I then leveled my revolver at the suspect and yelled, "bullshit, put the gun on the pavement real slow and you'll live another day." You are under arrest for reckless driving and carrying a weapon. The suspect bent over and placed the weapon on the road at the rear of his vehicle. "Turn around shit head and put your right arm behind you back,

I ordered. The suspect obeyed my command and was facing towards his car, I stuck my service revolver into the front of my pants and stepped quickly to the suspect, grabbing the male blacks right hand and bending it behind his back. I then quickly glanced back and saw all three of my children with their heads sticking out of the driver's

Angel On My Shoulder

window, taking it all in. My wife was screaming uncontrollably when I yelled "shut the fuck up!"

I then picked up the suspects pistol from the pavement. I said to the suspect, "you probably thought I was some putz with his family tooling down the road," I added just remember Metro never sleeps and we are all over this town on duty and off duty.

As we approached the service station I yelled to a worker, call the Police and tell them Officer McEwen needs assistance now at this location.

"You're hurting my arm," the suspect said.

"How's this," I replied as more pressure was put upon the arrested man's arm.

We entered the office and I pushed the male black into a chair by the entrance. I told the suspect don't you move asshole or you'll be sorry.

Within minutes I heard the sirens as they came closer to the gas station. The first Officer on the scene asked me, damn I thought you had been shot again, "not this time," I replied. 'I do need you to handcuff this guy. I don't have any with me. I'm going to have to start carrying a set with me,' I replied.

The Officer told the suspect to stand up, but he then realized he could not cuff him because of the cast on the suspects arm which extended partially past his wrist.

"Let's see your license," I barked! The suspect retrieved his billfold from his right rear pocket and placed his billfold on the desk beside him. I opened his wallet and took the suspects license out, they were worn pretty bad. I guess he has shown them to more than one Police Officer. I said, you're under arrest for carrying a weapon and reckless driving for starters.

Would you like to try resisting too? No Sir was the reply. Pick up your wallet and and come with me for your free ride downtown.

Officer, the suspect said, "Can I leave my car here at the gas station?"

Angel On My Shoulder

"Not a chance tough guy. It's going to the tow in lot where it will

be nice and safe."

I handed the Driver's license to another Officer and I told him to see if which was near the office. Get in I ordered and opened the rear door on the left side of the police car. The suspect got into the back seat and so did I. I leaned real close to the suspect and said, "you fucked with the wrong guy this time you prick." I drew back my right arm to

hit the suspect in his left rib cage. Just in an instant the suspect pulled his left arm with the cast back to block the punch I threw. My knuckles hit the rock hard cast with a thud splitting my middle knuckle open. Without saying a word I grabbed the suspects hand pulling it forward and punched the suspect several times in his left side. I got out of the rear seat while the suspect was screaming for help. I slammed the door shut and put a handkerchief around my split finger.

"Hey Joe, the Officer yelled, "this guy has 17 outstanding warrants on him. This was a good collar tonight Joe.

"Yeah," I said, "you know it messed up tonight's dinner with my in-laws in Joelton."

I walked over to where my three children Joe Joe, Eric and Lisa were sitting in the rear seat of the Maverick. I opened the driver's door, got in and shut the door. I then turned towards my wife and said, I have to go to headquarters to process this guy and it's going to take some time. Dean turned to me and screamed, "I can't take this anymore, "I can't put up with this turmoil in our lives, I'm a nervous wreck whenever we go anywhere."

'If we go anywhere," I replied, "Dean why don't you stay home and the children and I will go without you." Oh sure, you'd like that wouldn't you!!"

"It would be a lot more peaceful," I replied.

Dean, I added do you realize I got a criminal off the streets with a pistol and 17 outstanding warrants? "But, but you could have been

Angel On My Shoulder

shot again only this time your kids would have witnessed the shooting," she yelled.

"Listen, calm down, just shut the fuck up and listen to me. I'm not going to get shot in a frontal face off. Maybe from the back but I'll never take a hit face to face with some low life scum. The only reason I didn't shoot him was because of you and the kids, with their heads hung out of the window watching everything. Dean this is what I do, all you got tonight was a little taste of what's going on in this town, day and night, rain or shine. This is what a Police Officer does, he protects. Now please calm down and wait for me in the audience section of night court with the kids. Night Court is very interesting and the reality of what life is sometimes like here in Nashville. Two hours later we all left headquarters and headed home. Why did I expose my kids to something like this? Although they did get to see first-hand how someone is taken down and arrested for a crime or in this case it was a stupid act upon this subject.

It is like this every day a Police Officer is out on the streets. I probably should have just let it go and drove on to Joelton for dinner, but may next time we'll make it or maybe not, you never know. Nothing really changes. Its sunshine one moment and you're down in the sewer the next moment. Oh well, it is what it is.

When we arrived at the house I took the children one at a time inside and placed them in their beds. While Dean was sitting on the toilet in silence. I looked at each one of my kids as I covered then up and whispered in their ears, "no one will ever hurt you when you are with me. hurt you when you are with me. I am a force to be reckoned with when you all are with me."

Dean had already shut the door to the bedroom, so I stretched out on the couch in the den. Another day in Paradise I thought. Things are not going well in this marriage. If only she could accept what I do and what will not change because this is my calling in life and I do it pretty damn good. I drifted off to sleep with the TV still playing. When I awoke the next morning, I saw all three children looking at me. They

Angel On My Shoulder

asked, "daddy why didn't you sleep in your bed. Not now kids, get ready for school and I'll fix your breakfast. OK daddy.

I was wondering what would happen after I took the children to school, I really didn't want to go back home and get into another argument with Dean. She has got to understand that I love what I am doing. I went to the driving range and hit a few balls and after that I sat down and drank a cola and had a bag of stale chips. I was feeling pretty good now, so I guess I'll head home. But when I got home it was the same old thing. I don't guess she will never understand that I love doing what I am doing and I'm not going to give it up because I know in my heart that one day I will hold a rank higher than just a Police Officer.

Angel On My Shoulder

HOME SWEET HOME

While working the Donelson area in the early 70's, I received a call that someone wanted to talk with an Officer.

Donelson was a growing community and there was very little crime happening there. This was a typical middle class section, with lots of Churches. The homes were a typical Three bedroom, two baths and mostly bricked homes with attached garages which most family's turned into a den.

The homeowner was standing outside his house when I arrived. After I got out of my Patrol Car I recognized the man, he was an old school chum from Father Ryan. He had a beard, weighing about 180 lbs., blue eyes and getting a little bald. I guess that comes with age or handed down genes from your father. He was a good athlete in school.

Hey Joe, "how are you doing?" Ok, I guess just working hard and trying to stay out of trouble. So what seems to be the problem? He told me that he and his son were not speaking and that he was living elsewhere. He then stated that his family was going on vacation the next week and would I drive by his house from time to time and check on things. He said that he feels like his son will break into his home while they are out of town. I told my school chum that I would pass the information on to the two other shifts. He added that he would prosecute anyone, including his own son that was caught burglarizing or stealing from his home while they were on vacation. Several days later after 12 PM, I drove by the residence and I saw a motorcycle parked behind the house. I parked my cruiser on the blind side of the house. I checked out with the dispatcher and gave my location. I also asked for a Supervisor to meet me at this location.

Angel On My Shoulder

I knocked on the rear door, but no answer. I knocked on the front door, no answer there either. I then went under the house VIA the crawl space and the air was stuffy and damp with a lot of spider webs near the opening, it was a dirt floor but it had plastic down for a vapor barrier. I waited in silence trying to hear any kind of talking or movement. I then heard whispering and the floor squeaking and then someone inside said "where did the Police Officer go?"

About this time I saw the Sergeant pulling into the driveway and I motioned for him to be quiet. I told him the situation about the homeowner wanted us to check on his house while he was on vacation, because of his son's behavior and who he was hanging around with.

The Sergeant then yelled for the suspects to come out. We will use forceful entry if You don't open the door now. I was standing at the corner of the front of the house, but I could see the front door and when I heard the sliding Patio door open, there were 2 teenagers who stepped outside. I ran towards the back of the house and the Sergeant had already caught one of the teenagers and had him handcuffed.

As I approached the other suspect started running at a fast pace trying to get away from me. I unbuckled my utility belt and let it fall to the ground and gave chase. "I shed about six pounds when I dropped my utility belt." The temperature was 90 degrees with no breeze at all. The suspect sprang over a four foot chain link fence and cleared the second fence as I was approaching the first fence. I was 37 years old at this time and my suspect was 17 years old.

The young male kept sprinting over chain link fences and the distance between us was increasing. Damn, I don't know how much longer I can keep up this pace, my heart was beating faster and faster.

Angel On My Shoulder

The 6th fence was cleared by the suspect without any trouble and it seemed as though he was starting to slow down some now, Thank God. I muscled myself over a fence and ran to the side of the last fence. The suspect was nowhere to be found. It was just like he had vanished, but I knew he had to be close by.

I knew that he was hiding because I could see up and down the street and the only thing that I saw were some men who were working across the street and I asked them, if they had seen anyone running this way? They said, "No." I turned my attention back to the brick house to my right. I thought the only place that there was to hide was under some low limbs from the Pine trees.

I looked down the street and saw my Sergeant approaching my location. He was in his marked unit with the other suspect in the rear seat.

I looked real close under the two Pine trees and saw the suspect lying with the pine needles over his legs. I grabbed his legs, pulled him out from under his hiding place and putting my hand around his belt so that he couldn't escape. I told him "You're under arrest for 2nd Degree Burglary and Fleeing and Eluding! The suspect said, "It's my house dumb ass!"

I replied, "You'll have to take that up with your dad!" He doesn't seem to like you very much anymore because of what he has told me about you hanging out with the wrong crowd and using drugs.

What were you doing here anyway? No reply! You know that he asked us to watch his house while he was away, because he was afraid that you would break in and take anything of value and then sell it so you could buy drugs. My dad wouldn't do that to me because I am his son.

Angel On My Shoulder

Oh yeah. Well the Mr. Smart guy, tell me why your dad would ask us to keep an eye Out on his house. My dad wouldn't do that because my mom wouldn't let him.

What about my motorcycle? What are you going to do with my motorcycle? Well, let's see. Since I am responsible for the cycle, I'm going to have it towed to the Tow In Lot where it will be nice and safe. Damn Officer, can't you just leave it at my dad's house. Sorry, I can't do that. I then added, so you can tell your punk ass friends that I am the Zone Commander for this district and I'm responsible for the safety of all these citizens and I plan to do just that. This is a good start and only the beginning. But, Officer, I was going to get some of my things out of the house. Sure you were, do you mind telling me about all the
stuff that is piled up by the sliding doors. Uh, that's my stuff.

You'll have to see your dad about it when you get out of Juvenile next week. If you are saying that the stuff at the sliding doors are yours, well from what I see it looks like things that you would have no use for. I suspect that these things are something that could be sold for drug money. I don't do drugs. Oh yeah, that's not what your dad said and I would believe him over you any day. You see your dad and I went to Father Ryan High School together and I know that he is a good guy.

It's all mine, I promise. Your promise doesn't mean anything to me and I'm sure that it won't mean anything to your dad. Come on man, give me a break. I said, OK, I'll give you a break. You can spend the next few days in jail with your other buddy waiting for someone to get you out.

Fuck you man was his reply. Boy those are some pretty strong words but not thank you. Now shut up and get in the back of the Patrol Car.

He spoke up again, "I know my rights." I do to and you don't have any. I slammed the door shut and we were off to

Angel On My Shoulder

Processing at Juvenile to get these two processed. They said that they were going to plead Not Guilty.

I got in touch with his father and he thanked me for taking care of this problem. I told him, if there is anything else I can do for you, just give me a call. I didn't hear from him until we went to court. They each received six months jail time, which was suspended, and Court Costs in which they had to pay. One year supervised probation with drug tests on a regular basis.

It really feels good to help out an old school buddy. Back then who would of ever thought that I would become a Police Officer. Back then in my life all I could think about was a good place to sleep and getting something to eat. Playing Golf was a big part of my life and I really enjoyed it a lot, that is when I wasn't having to caddy for my dad. I don't even think my dad ever went past the 8th Grade. He was a successful Golfer and his band kept him going, but as a father well what can I say, nothing really. Joining the Navy was a relief, at least I had three meals a day and a good place to sleep. Although I did stay sea sick the whole time that I could not see land. All in all it was worth it going into the Navy, I grew up real fast.

RAIN RAIN GO AWAY

Sometimes Police pull into some deserted places to catch some shut eye. The Police know where every deserted spot is in their Zone. It is against the rules, but like the old timers say, Rules are meant to get fired by, not to go by. It is only against the rules if you get caught.

One such night about 2 AM, I drove my Patrol Car to a wooded area to take a break, my head was splitting. The midnight shift is the only that you can get away with something like this. My partner said he was going to get into the back seat and stretched out. He rolled down the window and stretched out his legs on the open window sill and his feet were outside the car.

The radio was silent and it was peaceful as I was trying to shake this headache. My partner was snoring loudly when a light rain began to fall, then I drifted off to sleep. The rain continued for about 30 minutes soaking my partners legs from his knees down.

We received a call and I told him to get up we have got to go. He started complaining how wet his socks and pants were from the knees down. I promised not to tell anyone about this incident. Yeah, Right! We rolled down the two front windows and placed the heater on high to dry out the lower part of his pants and his socks. I laughed when I told him that tomorrow I would bring some plastic bags to put on his legs, he laughed and said , there's not going to be a next time. I said, you smell like an old wet dog.

We were dispatched to a stalled motorist and when we got there, my partner got out of the car and started walking and you could hear the sounds coming from his wet socks squishing his shoes. I don't think we will ever do this again. Well, at least not on a rainy night.

Angel On My Shoulder

SINGING IN THE RAIN

While working South Patrol on the 5 PM to 1 AM shift and after being dismissed from Roll Call, I went outside to my Patrol Car. I noticed that my right rear tire was flat and it had just started to drizzle rain. I went back inside the Station House and walked over to the Sergeant who was my immediate supervisor for the night. This Sergeant had a reputation of being a real horse's ass, because he was lacking in people skills and just plain human nature. I told him, Sarge I'll be a few minutes late in checking in because I have a flat tire and I am going to call the garage to have a truck sent out here and change my tire.

He said, go change it yourself. I said Sarge it is starting to rain out. He said haven't you been wet before and I don't think it will hurt you. I responded by saying, on your orders I will gladly change the tire getting my uniform wet and my hands nice and dirty and I will also began singing I'm singing in the rain. Don't you
remember that song , Sarge. This was one of Gene Kelly's signature songs and one of his famous movies.

I said all of these statements in a hateful tone. I turned and went outside opening my trunk and thus began the process of changing my flat tire. I thought to myself that he will pay dearly for this. After changing the tire and getting filthy and soaking wet I walked back into the Station and asked the Sergeant, do you have any other shitty job that you want me to do before presenting myself to the public looking like this. Not right now anyway, was his answer.

In Patrol we change shifts, the Sergeants would work different areas. The very next day, I had a different Sergeant which was in charge of my section. I worked extremely hard writing numerous tickets, making traffic arrests and answering all

Angel On My Shoulder

the calls and then having to fill out all of the paper work. About an hour before the Police Officers are due to change shifts, we meet the Sergeant at some pre-arranged location to give him all of our paperwork that we had done for the shift. This is known as turning in your mail.

Several nights later, I had the same Sergeant that had ordered me to change a flat tire in the rain. I wrote absolutely no tickets, and called the dispatcher on a private phone and told him that if any calls bordering my zone in which I was working to give it to another car, because I would be doing surveillance work. When it came time to turn in the mail, towards the end of the shift, I met with the Sergeant pulling beside him in my car and he said do you have any mail?

I said I have one report regarding a stolen wheelbarrow. He looked at me and said is this all? I replied, I'm a Crime Fighting Son of a Bitch, Sergeant.

He said, do you mean to tell me that you rode for eight hours and didn't see not one traffic violation.

I said that's right Sarge. I asked him, just how many have you written in the last year? He said it is not my job to write tickets.

I responded aren't you still a Police Officer? Could be because you spend too much time at the diner drinking coffee. I added, what happened when you made Sergeant, did you retire from
Police work?

He said, "Joe don't get smart with me."

I said, "What are you going to do - transfer me to Patrol too start changing everybody's tires. I put my car in drive and looked over at the Sergeant and said, I'm going out to look for violators, I won't bother to ride the alleys to see if anyone has burglarized the business establishments nor will I bother to go into the Bars and check the Liquor Violations or stop any scum bag in a beat up Chevy who would be looking for something to steal, I'll just sit off to the side of a stop sign and see if I can sandbag the citizens coming home from work. I ended by saying I'll see you tomorrow and I then drove off.

I followed this procedure every time that he was my Supervisor. The other Sergeants had nothing but praise for me due to the fact that I turned the most tickets, arrests and reports on my detail. You don't get mad, you get even. This went on until I was transferred to Crime Analysis at the South Station. I was transferred about four months later to the Training Academy This is a place that I really wanted to be.

TERROR ON MOTORCYCLES

One sunny day in the Fall of the year, I received a call about 3 individuals who were terrorizing a neighborhood near the Interstate in Donelson. These boys were riding their motorcycles through yards, flower beds, streets and just about anywhere their Bikes would take them.

One of streets in a subdivision was a dead end. This neighborhood was an established section which was quiet until today.

I parked my Patrol unit several houses back, got out of the vehicle and listened for the sound of the motorcycles.

I saw an older resident across the street standing on his front porch and he was pointing in a northern direction. I cut between two houses and approached a house to my left which had a daylight basement. The garage door was open and I saw the 3 young boys sitting on their motorcycles. They were just there talking, probably planning what their next move would be. The motorcycles were idling, sometimes they would rev them up trying to make the tires smoke. Just like they have seen in the movies. As I approached the garage the 3 suspects sped out of the basement and 2 of them went out a nearby driveway, one almost lost control of his motorcycle. The third suspect raced down the slight hill towards a creek. The other two cyclists turned right to what appeared to be leaving the area.

I focused my attention to the cyclist that went around the last house on the block next block next to the creek. I ran to the house where I last saw the lone cyclist and as I turned the corner running as fast I could, I tackled the biker and we tumbled about eight feet down the sloped yard. I landed on top of the juvenile and I felt something pop in my lower back when I hit the ground.

Angel On My Shoulder

I handcuffed the suspect and muscled him to my Patrol car shoving him into the backseat.

I radioed for a wrecker to come to my location and pick up the motorcycle. Then as usual the paperwork began on the juvenile. He was yelling at me the whole time that I would be sorry for arresting him. I told him that I was already sorry because I had hurt my back! He yelled back "I wish you had broken it."

After arriving home from my shift I received a phone call from the wrecker owner where the motorcycle was towed. Jack said, "the juvenile's father told him he was going to sue me for roughing up his son."

I told "Jack" that's OK because I'll have a suit for him also and that he would have to get in line like all the other irate parents, but he'll just have to wait, because there are several ahead of him. After going to Juvenile Court and getting a guilty Verdict, this was the last time I ever heard about his case. When the dad heard from the witnesses how his son and his two friends had torn up their yards and flowerbeds, he then realized that his son had lied to him about the whole situation.

I often wondered what happened when they got home. Some parents are oblivious to what their kids are doing while they are at work.

I filled out a 101 Form (Injury on Duty) for my back. My back continued to get worse and I finally had a operation for repair of a ruptured disc. I had instant relief and a full recovery, but I was still on light duty for several weeks until I got the OK from my Dr. that I could resume my regular duties.

One of the nurses at Baptist Hospital told me later, the Doctor who operated on me was shot by his wife and he was paralyzed from his waist down.

This was a bad ending of a bad story.

Angel On My Shoulder

MACE TIME

My partner Tim and I received a call in Donelson about a drunk and disorderly male at his residence. It was in the fall of the year and the air was a little cool and there was a lot of moisture on the grass.

As we pulled into the driveway the suspect was yelling obscenities and told us to come on up and get your asses whipped!

We both exited the Patrol car very fast and sprinted towards the suspect. I reached for my mace and held it in my right hand and extended it as we neared the suspect. The suspect immediately assumed a Boxing position with his fists clinched. When I came within 5 feet of him I aimed my mace towards his face and soaked his eyes with a long burst. Tim and I tackled the male and we all fell in his gravel driveway scratching his cheekbone during the melee.

We struggled briefly before he was handcuffed. His wife was standing nearby watching the whole incident. I told her we were going to General Hospital to have his eyes checked out. She said, "I'll follow you there."

While on the way to General Hospital, I began to write what happened in their
driveway on a notebook that I carried with me on my clipboard.

Tim took the suspect into the Emergency Room. His wife pulled into the parking lot shortly after we arrived. I asked her to come over to the rear of our Patrol Car. I handed her the summary that I had written and asked her to read it and does she agree with it. If you do agree, I need your signature at the bottom of the page. Can I have a copy of the report? You sure can. I told her that I had her address and as soon as it was processed that I would see that she gets a copy. I sent a copy of a report that I had written several days later. She seemed very concerned for her husband. I just

Angel On My Shoulder

hope this doesn't come back to bite me in the ass.

About this time the Sergeant arrived and walked up to where we were as she was in the process of signing the paper.

She turned and walked towards the ER. My Sergeant told me after she got out of hearing distance, "That's the way you do it Joe, C.Y.A." (This means Cover Your Ass.)

He said, "I'll talk to you guys later when I pick up the mail. I was thinking this job is so unpredictable. One minute cruising down the road and the next minute you're in a fight getting all wet and dirty.

With all being said this job is never a dull moment and from one day to the next things are never the same. For sure this job is not boring.

Angel On My Shoulder

MALAMUTE'S / BRUNO – BRUTUS – POPEYE

I was dispatched to a seedy Motel several miles out Murfreesboro Road just past Bell Road concerning a disturbance in Cabin # 5 which was behind the Office of the Motel. I pulled my squad car around back beside Cabin # 5. There were several junk cars which looked as if they had been abandoned, the grass was tall and there were beer bottles and trash was strewn around everywhere. Damn, I how can people live in a place like this. When I approached the door, I noticed that the paint on the cabin was peeling and needed a lot of work. While I was knocking on the door I heard a very loud and intense argument going on between two people inside. The male said, "shut up bitch," can't you hear someone is knocking on the door.

So what, she replied, "It's all your fault."

So now it is my fault and then I heard what appeared to be something that was knocked over. The door opened and a man stepped outside very quickly and closing the door behind him as if he had something to hide.

I asked, "what's going on inside?" I don't think that's any of your business Officer. Maybe not, but I can make it my business real quick. His hair was stringy, long and very dirty and he weighed about 175lbs., hazel eyes and needed a shave, dirty t-shirt, dirty blue jeans and barefooted. Typical makeup of an unemployed thug.

"What's going on," I asked.

"Nothing officer, just a husband and wife spat," he replied.

"I need to see your wife, now." I said. Just then the door opened and a young girl was standing in the doorway. I noticed a big red mark on her left cheek and she looked as if she had been crying. She was a small girl about 5', maybe a 100 lbs. soaking wet. All she had on was a man's large white t-shirt that was

Angel On My Shoulder

hanging down past her hips. I couldn't help but notice the large bruise on the lower part of her leg. She looked in her early 20's and was motioning for me to come in. I stepped inside, followed by her husband. I heard dogs barking and the sound was coming from the bathroom, the door was closed. The place was in very bad disarray, there were clothes strewn all of the floor, empty containers of empty beer and plates with uneaten food on them. This was a small place with a kitchenette, a living room and bathroom.

I looked at the girl who was visibly afraid, not from me as a cop but something else. The dogs were barking louder as we talked. The girl had red marks on her neck and the pocket on her t-shirt was torn.

I looked at the male and said, "What about it tough guy, do you like to bully women?" No was the answer given by this cowardly looking man. I could tell that he wanted me to leave, he was getting nervous and sweat was beginning to show on his face. The dogs were going crazy in the bathroom.

I asked, "How many dogs do you have in there?" Again no reply from either one of them. Do you know that no pets are allowed in this cabin's "Uh, Uh, they are mine, I just got them from the pound," was his answer.

"Open the door," I ordered and then I stepped back leaving plenty of room between the suspect and myself.

He asked, "what for?"

Because I said so, that's why. "Now open the door or I will," was my answer.

He opened the door and inside were 3 beautiful Malamute's with blue eyes and their tails were wagging, as if they were happy to see me. All three of them came to me quickly, I bent down on one knee and they were all over me. I have never seen dogs this happy to see someone.

Angel On My Shoulder

One of the dogs looked up at me wagging his tail and very excited, he would not leave my side. I asked this twerp, have you been mistreating these dogs?

"Hell no was his reply. I love these malamutes."
The perp yelled, "These are my dogs and you have no right to be here."

"Shut your pie hole tough guy."

"You can't talk to me this way," he shot back.

"Oh yeah, well I didn't just come here on my on, I was asked to come here by the owner of these Cabin's because she was afraid something might be happening with all the yelling and screaming going on. I looked at the girl and she nodded her head like she was trying to tell me, "Yes."

The suspect glared at me still insisting that the dogs were his. I could have bored a through this thug the way I was looking at him. The largest Malamute was at my feet, he sat beside me wagging his tail. I looked at the abused young woman and said, "are you scared of your husband?"

"He's not my husband officer." I noticed the male looking at the door and I moved into the doorway facing him. He again, told me to leave. I replied, Not until I find out what is going on."

At that time, I stood 6' 1" with my Trooper boots on and weighed 215 lbs. With the Police hat on it put me at 6' 3". I just looked at the suspect and smiled as I keyed my Radio for the dispatcher to get a complaint number. I did not want to leave this young girl in this environment, but at this time I had no choice. I winked at the girl as I was going out the door, but I stopped as he was trying to shut the door. I put my hand on the door and told this thug, if I have to come back here things will not be in your favor.

The girl looked very scared. I asked the girl, "can I take you anywhere."

She replied, "I'm OK." She looked at me and she seemed

to be very scared. I told the suspect if I do have to come back here again, "you will go to jail."

I probably should have called for backup when I arrived on the scene, but we were short-handed with several Officers out sick. I realized it would be useless to ask for assistance at this time since I did not have anything to charge this thug with.

I met the Sergeant and turned in my paperwork and headed home since this was the end of my shift.

It had just started to rain. I arrived home in about 20 minutes and pulled my car around back and sat there thinking about the call that I had just answered. I knew that this bum couldn't afford a thorough bred like the Malamutes, but at this time I had no way to prove that they were stolen.

I went inside the house and took off my wet shirt, draped it across a dining room chair and went into the den to read the Newspaper. My wife left a note that she had gone to the store and would be back shortly. I picked up the paper and turned to the want ads, I always look at the section under Lost and Found. I was startled when I saw an ad in big bold print. Lost or stolen, 3 Malamutes ¾ grown, blue eyes and their names are Brutus, Bruno and Popeye. I called the number that was listed on the ad and when a lady answered the phone. I explained who I was, I then I asked her how long these dogs have been missing. She said that she had filed a report Monday morning. So I guess they were stolen on Monday. Monday was my day off and I explained why I didn't know about the theft of these dogs earlier. I explained to the lady what had happened a couple of hours ago and she became very excited knowing that these dogs just might be hers. I asked where she lived? I told her that I would be at her house in about thirty minutes. I thought under the circumstances it would be best if we both went to the Cabin and I could bluff my way in.

Angel On My Shoulder

I knew that if this couple left we would probably never find these dogs and I could get by in Court because this was an emergency situation.

When I arrived at her house she showed me a picture of the three Malamutes. I told her that I had to make a positive ID in order to get back her dogs. I asked her "would she have any problem going with me to properly identify the dogs."

In an anxious voice she said, "Let's go."

As soon as she got into my Patrol Car, I immediately called for a backup and told the dispatcher that I was off duty and I was trying to recover three stolen Malamute dogs.

I told the lady that when we arrived at the Cabin to stay in the car. My backup arrived the same time that we did. The lady asked, "is this where you saw the three dogs?" I guess the the dogs heard her voice and they began barking very loud. I got out of the car and knocked on the door of the Cabin. He opened the door and said what do you want now? I told him that we needed to talk. He answered with, I don't want to talk with you. I told him that he did not have a choice. I added, "invite me in where it is dry or I'll pull you outside and we can talk in the rain. I'm already soaked so I don't give a damn, it's your call tough guy." He stepped back and we stepped inside.

I said, let's go in the kitchenette, I walked behind him into the kitchenette and I then grabbed his left arm and put some pressure on his wrist. I whispered in his ear, "either you tell me where you stole those three dogs or I'm going to break your fucking wrist!" The whole time I more pressure on his hand bending it back and causing him a great deal of pain. I asked him, "how long can you stand this because I have all night?"

He said, I took them from a house that was behind my grandmother's house. I always wanted a Malamute but I couldn't afford one." I replied, well I guess that isn't a good reason for

Angel On My Shoulder

stealing them, but at least they are going back to their owner now. I then asked "where are the bolt cutters?"

He said, "they are under the bed."

I looked under the bed and retrieved a very large bolt cutter. I asked him if this was the one he used to cut the lock off the chain link fence gate where the dogs were taken from.

He said, "yes." I handcuffed him and told the girl to let my backup inside the Cabin. I took the suspect and told my backup to hold on to him while I get the victim inside. I went to the door and motioned for her to come in. Which she gladly did.

I told the girl to open the bathroom door so that the victim could see the dogs. When the bathroom door was opened, the dogs went crazy, one started howling and they all ran over to her in frenzy. She kneeled down on the living room rug and began hugging all three of them as they was licking her in the face. I couldn't tell who was the happiest, the dogs or the victim. The lady looked at me with tears in her eyes and said, thank you so much because I never thought I would see my babies again.

I gave him the Miranda Warning and took him out to my backups car and put him in the back seat. I told him that he was under a rock and a hard place now with no place to hide. He responded with, "Fuck You!" Now you know that's not a nice thing to say. I'm a very sensitive person, was my response.

I went back inside and told my backup that I would meet him at headquarters. I'm going to charge him with Grand Larceny. I stated to my backup that I have to take the victim and her dogs home. I then turned to the girl and asked, "do you have a place to go tonight or do you want to stay here?" Your boyfriend could possibly make bond in a couple of hours and then he will be back here.

She said, "yes I do." I can call my brother to come and get me. She told me that as soon as her brother could get here, I'll be

Angel On My Shoulder

gone from here in thirty minutes or less. The girl looked at me and said, you know Officer you probably saved me from a beating tonight or maybe something worse. He blames me with everything that goes wrong.

She looked at the victim and told her that she was sorry for the trouble that we caused her. I tried to get him not to steal the dogs but my please fell on deaf ears. I opened the back door of my Patrol car and she got in first and the dogs jumped in right behind her. While in route to her home, I reminded her again to have a chip put in each one of these dogs. She said first thing in the morning, I am going to take them to their Vet and have them checked out and
let the Vet put a chip put in each one of them.

When I pulled into her driveway, I got out and opened the rear door and she said, to me thank you once again, you have saved me from a lot of sorrow. She added, if you are ever out this way and you want a cup of coffee or a glass of tea please feel free to knock on my door. I told her, "I might take you up on that someday." I wished her well and hoped that she had good news tomorrow when she took Brutus, Bruno and Popeye to the Vet. OK, what did I tell you to have the Vet do these beautiful dogs tomorrow.

She answered; "have the Vet put a chip in them."

The three dogs followed her all the way to the door and they all went inside. I know she will sleep good tonight.

After 4 hours of recovery of these dogs and all the paper work had been filled out and thug was put behind bars for stealing these beautiful dogs. I was on my way home for the second time. I had a great feeling of satisfaction in solving this case as I thought as I drove down I-24.

This is why I love this job so much. I made a person's life happy and whole again with the return of her dogs.

Angel On My Shoulder

Upon arriving home, I went in the bathroom closed the door and soaked in a hot tub of water for about an hour. I got into bed and went to sleep thinking about those 3 beautiful Malamutes and how happy their owner was to have them back home.

Later on the male subject never showed up for his court date. A Bench Warrant was issued for him and the was the last I heard about this case. I was just happy that the lady had gotten her dogs back.

LUCKY GUESS

One evening about 3 PM and I was driving through a parking lot at the corner of Nolensville Rd. and Harding Rd. As I drove past the rear entrance of a Restaurant I noticed two male whites loading up a small Motorcycle in the bed of a small Pick-Up Truck. I circled around the store and parked a couple hundred feet from the Truck, blending in with
the other automobiles. I no sooner stopped when the Pick-up Truck started to pull away and drive off. I thought to myself that these two guys were stealing one of the employees motorcycle. I caught up with truck; they got caught up in traffic. I wrote the license plate number of the truck and the motorcycle down in my notepad. I also took a picture of the truck and the motorcycle, I always take a camera with me where ever I go. The two suspects had not spotted me at this time merely because I was in my own personal car. I did not have my Police Walkie-Talkie with me nor did I have a cell phone (cell phones were not available at this time) I dropped back about 7 car lengths and followed the truck up Nolensville Rd.

They turned right near the South Station and then turned left two streets up. When I turned onto the street where I last saw them, I saw the truck going up a driveway of a house. I drove by and saw the address on the mailbox. I wrote the number down and headed back to the restaurant.

I went in the employee's only door and introduced myself to the first person I saw, telling them that I was a Policeman off duty and I asked , "does anybody that works here own a motorcycle that was parked out back." One of the personnel in the kitchen said, "I own one and it is parked out back." I explained to him what had happened and told him to call for a Zone Car to

Angel On My Shoulder

come and take a report on a stolen motorcycle. He was very upset about his
motorcycle at this time and I told him to relax, because I knew where the motorcycle was and explained to him that I had the license plate number of the truck and that I had taken a picture of the truck with the motorcycle in the back of his truck. I also knew where they live. I said the reason I didn't intervene was because I did not know if the motorcycle was stolen or not and I did not have a back-up. I also told him that when the Police arrived he would have to make a stolen report and I will tell him where to go to pick up the motorcycle.

When the Police arrived I told the Officer what had happened and the information about the incident and I also gave him the license plate number of the truck and the number of the house where the two suspects took the motorcycle. I advised the Officer that I did see the two white male's putting the motorcycle into the back of the truck and drive off. The Officer asked the employee if he could get off work so that he could ride with us to identify the motorcycle. His boss gave him permission to do so.

Just before we left the Officer said to me, "hey Joe, you recovered a stolen motorcycle before it was reported stolen." I'll see you at work tomorrow and you can tell me how everything went. I saw him the next day and he told me that he gave the motorcycle back to the owner and filled out a recover vehicle report, seized the two suspects truck and arrested those two dirt bags. They wanted to know how I knew where the motorcycle was and I told them, "A little birdie told me."

Joe, I only want to know how you come across so much when you are on your day off?

"I guess I'm just lucky," I replied. Lucky hell, there isn't another Police Officer on the force that gets the collars like you do. How many cars have you recovered?

Angel On My Shoulder

So far this year I have recovered 7 rollers (a roller is a stolen car with someone driving it). Our Lieutenant gives us a day off for every roller that we find. Damn Joe, "I wish I had your luck."

I asked the Officer, did you put me down as a witness so that I could get Court pay. Sure did Joe was his reply. I'll see you in court in 2 days from now. Thanks man, with these three kids of mine they stay hungry all the time. I feel your pain too, but I only have two kids to feed plus a wife that does nothing but watch TV. I told the Officer it costs to keep those little assholes puckered. You know Joe, I never thought about it like that and I'll keep it in mind andthat is a funny quote to remember.

I've got a 9:30 AM Court Docket at the Court House and you know the Judge doesn't like for us to be late. You better get going, see you later man, was my reply.

I was just whistling along thinking I do get into a lot of things. "I'm never off, I'm always looking for something out of the ordinary." I love ruining somebody's day. Plus Court Time….Cha Ching!

Angel On My Shoulder

SELLING SUNDAY NEWSPAPERS

I usually cut my aunt's yard every two weeks. I ran out of gas, so my son Joe Joe and I drove to 11ᵗʰ and Woodland to a Texaco Station to get some gas. Upon leaving I saw a male black selling Sunday Newspapers, he was standing in the middle of the street. My aunt did not get a Sunday paper, so I thought I would buy her one. This was the first time I had ever seen someone selling newspapers at this location. When I paid for the paper and went back to my truck and started to drive off I noticed the front page of the newspaper it was red stamped,
IF THIS NEWSPAPER WAS NOT PURCHASED FROM A NEWSPAPER STAND THEN IT IS STOLEN.

I parked my truck and told my son Joe Joe, to stay right here and I'll be right back. I took my Police portable radio and a pair of handcuffs and motioned for the male black to come to the curb. My Police Badge was in my left hand and when he approached I identified myself.

I told him that he was selling stolen newspapers. They're not stolen; I'm selling them for my uncle. OH yeah. You do know that these were stolen from the newspaper machine and this is how the newspaper carriers make their living.

He replied, "I didn't steal these. I told you I was selling them for my uncle."

I asked him, can you read? He said, yes I can read, I ain't no dummy. Well look at the front of the Newspaper you dumb ass and tell me what is in red letters.

Uh, Uh, I ain't got my glasses with me, Officer.

At this time I told him he was under arrest for theft, handcuffed him and called for a Zone Car on my radio to come to my location and transport him to Prisoner Processing. I was wearing bib overalls. When the Zone Car arrived, the Officer said,

Damn Joe give it a rest. I said not this time because the Newspaper printing gives a $100.00 Reward when someone is caught stealing Newspapers from their machines. Cha Ching!

Two hours later, Joe Joe and I pulled into my aunt's driveway with the gasoline and one Sunday Newspaper. My Aunt said, "where have you two been? I was getting worried about you."

I explained to my aunt what had happened, which resulted in me being gone so long. After finishing the yard and driving on the way home, I said to Joe Joe, this has been a good day. So far I have made $111.00 dollars. How did you get that figure dad? You see I got $11.00 for cutting my aunt's grass and a $100.00 Reward from Newspaper Printing, but it will take about a month for them to process it after I go to Court and this male black is found guilty of theft of Sunday Newspapers.

I told Joe Joe that I was going to give me $10.00 today, just for helping me.

About a month later, I received a check for the $100.00 from the Newspaper and after working my 8 hour shift I went home and I asked Joe Joe, where do you want to eat, he said how about Pizza dad? I said, that's fine with me. Go get Eric and Lisa and let's go.

I don't think Pizza had ever tasted so good. We had a great time.

On the way home they asked, can we do this every week daddy? I said the reason we had so much fun tonight was because I had gotten some extra money today and I wanted to share it with you. They all spoke up at the same time, Thank you daddy. This really made me feel good.

SNEAKIN DEACON

I was working a weekend night Security at a popular restaurant which had curb service in South Nashville. It was a local hangout for young people on the weekend that liked to cruise around the curb service in their cars and socialize. There were only 3 car hops working this night. One young girl came up to me and said, "Joe, the man in the Volkswagen at the end stall ordered a coke and he had his thing out of his pants just shining it around." She was visibly shaken and I told her to take the coke to him and look back at me and shake your head up and
down, if he still has his thing exposed or shake your head from side to side if he does not.

As she walked to the Volkswagen that was parked at the far end of the canopy and handed him the coke, he paid her. She turned and nodded her head up and down. I approached the vehicle on the left rear side, which was also a blind side of the suspects' car. I used the large
menu's sign for cover so I wouldn't be seen until the last second. I came up on him fast and from the left rear. As I approached, the driver saw me in his left door mirror and reached down to grab his pants. His left window was rolled down and I reached in, opened the door and I shouted, "Oh no you don't, you Son of a Bitch," and I dragged him out of the car with his pants down around his ankles. I made him lean against his vehicle as I handcuffed him. The car was a Volkswagen Beetle.

I advised him of his constitutional rights. I asked him, what was his occupation? He stated, that he was a Minister at a Church in Brentwood.

Just then another Police car drove up and the driver said, "Hey Joe, what do you have?"

Angel On My Shoulder

I replied, "I have a sneakin deacon" the Policeman said to the Minister, "you should be ashamed of yourself, Tsk, Tsk," no way you can enter the Pearly Gates acting like this."

The preacher said, "May I pull my pants up Officer?" I told him as soon as I free one arm you can. But don't try to do anything funny, because you are already in a lot of trouble. I left the handcuffs on his other wrist.

I asked, "What in the world is wrong with you, what is your problem numb nut?"

He said, "I'm sick and have low blood sugar and I needed a cola!" I replied back, "What were your intentions, to stick your pecker into a cola cup for a drink?" No reply from the preacher.

I called for a wrecker to tow the Volkswagen and drove the suspect to prisoner processing to get a warrant for lewd behavior involving a minor. The car hop was only 17 years old.

He asked if he could make a phone call, so I uncuffed one wrist so he could use the phone in the hall. I stood nearby and heard him say,

"Honey, I've sinned and acted like Jimmy Swaggert tonight." He continued, "can you come and bail me out?" He finished his phone call and was processed through the booking procedure.

Several weeks later I went to General Session Court for disposition of this case. The preacher testified that he became dizzy and drove into the restaurant to order a coke. He stated he removed his pants to have a bowl movement on the car seat. Of course the District Attorney made the preacher look like a complete fool during prosecution.

The Judge's ruling stated that in all of his years on the bench that this excuse was the most bizarre that had ever been told in the courtroom. He ordered a fine to be paid, 2 years probation and intense evaluation.

CASE CLOSED......

Angel On My Shoulder

INSTRUCTOR AT THE ACADEMY

I had always wanted to be an Instructor at the Academy after attending the In-Service Training each year for 1 week. I felt that I had a lot to offer the new Recruits as well and the Police Officers and higher rank also within the Department during their 1 week of training. During my time with the Police Department and while being on the streets I had been in quite a few ordeals and also experienced the right and wrong way to handle situations. To me this was the best place to gain experience. So, when I was asked to come to the Academy, I gladly accepted.

I knew that I had a lot to offer these new Recruits in preparing them to have knowledge of what they might encounter after completing their training. I told them how I had been shot 5 times and survived. I could relate to them on the do's and don'ts and that to keep in touch with your fellow Officers that worked around you. Each day I could tell which Recruits were listening and which ones were not. They learned to listen and take notes in my class.

I also assisted on the gun range as a Firearms Instructor. My duties included all phases of Firearms Training. This was a two week course and they seemed to enjoy this phase of their of their training. I guessed some of them had never fired a weapon before.

We had daily morning Inspections and after the first week, no one was ever late for class the second time.

Physical fitness was a big at the Academy. Exercise and running every day. Some did not complete the 22-week Course.

Many Recruits excelled in their Police Careers. I have listed a few of the successful Police Officer's that have exceled in rank within the Nashville Police Department.

Recruit Steve Anderson to Police Chief. Like many future hopefuls was a model Recruit. He was focused, smart, neat in

Angel On My Shoulder

appearance, eyes and ears open with goals for the future. Shortly after he Graduated from the Academy he taught Law to the new Recruits and In Service Training Officer's.

Deborah Faulkner advanced to Deputy Chief with the Police Department and then upon retirement she went to the State of Tennessee in charge of Tenn Care Fraud and now she holds the Title of Inspector General, State of Tennessee. Deborah was very articulate and very professional in her work. She was well liked as a Supervisor.

Retired Captain Bill Hamblin, went to Police Recruit School 6 months before me because it took me a while to move from Louisville, Ky. to Nashville. He was one of the most professional, knowledgeable, courageous, hard charging Police Officer that I have ever had the pleasure of knowing. He was a Criminal's worst nightmare. He knows all that there is to know about Police Work.

Retired Lt. Tim Durham, knew no fear and was as tough as wet leather. I always felt safe with Tim as my partner or with him while going on SWAT calls. I knew in my heart that Tim would take a bullet for me as necessary. He is the best in performing under life and death decisions.

Retired Robert Dodson as a Captain and he was my Training Officer upon my Graduation from the Academy and assigned at the West Station. He was always calm under pressure and it was a pleasure to be his partner.

Retired Captain Rickey Langford, was assigned to ride with me while he was a Rookie. We worked North Nashville and he gained a lot of Street experience while riding with me.

Retired Captain Kenneth Pence. Upon his retirement he became a Professor at Vanderbilt University. He was a brilliant Officer in which I was proud to have the pleasure of working alongside him at the Academy and on SWAT Calls. He was very instrumental in teaching me the proper way to rappel from a building and the correct way to tie various rope knots used during descending from buildings. It is my understanding that he has successfully written several Novels which have been published.

These are just a few of the Police Officers that I known and respected during my years with the Police Department. There were many more Officers that I had the honor of working with or had acquaintances with during my years with the Police Department. Some had been fired, many retired, some quit and some murdered. I carry a lot of memories and stories with me still 24/7. These are memories that I will always cherish.

This next man I have known for 60+ years. J. Randall Wyatt Jr., we were in High School together. He was also my Teacher at Aquinas Jr. College and as of this writing he is a Judge in DIV 2 Criminal Court. I have nothing but praise for this Ex Police Officer, Ex-Marine and a former Prosecuting Lawyer for the District Attorney's Office. He is a man with flawless character and Integrity. A well respected citizen throughout the Nashville Community an everywhere else. He almost died once in a Traffic Accident and he had a stainless steel rob placed in his upper leg. There were also broken facial bones and some of his teeth were knocked out. We stayed in touch for over 6 decades.

And last but not least, Retired Chief Joe D. Casey. He was the man in charge of a small Army of Police Officers. I received two Promotions during his tenure. Chief Casey was very popular among the rank and file and visited me many times during my stay at Vanderbilt Hospital after I was shot. I have very fond memories under his Command as a Major and Chief of Police.

Many times the Police Color Guard went to Police Headquarters and stood across the street in front of a Police Memorial. This was truly an Honor for me to serve as a Color Guard member.

Angel On My Shoulder

MAGNETIC ATTRACTION OF A POLICE OFFICER

Why are some women drawn to a Police Officer? Some women just like a man in uniform. The uniform signifies a lot of things namely, authority and power.

Many women after reaching their 25th birthday probably have had several relationships with men where they have been mistreated in one way or another.

Think about it, a woman meets a guy in a bar or wherever, she does not know anything about hi m except for what he is telling her. Men like to brag about what kind of a job they have or what kind of car they drive whether it is true or not, mostly not true. Men like to boast about their position in front of a woman that he is trying to hit on. Their driver's license could be suspended or revoked for DUI's, or just not paying tickets. A woman does not know that the man she just met had ever been arrested, just released from jail or prison, on parole or probation, or has a job, married, eking by, paying child support or going with someone else. He could be a dead beat or a strong user of drugs or a sex offender. On the negative side the list is endless not even counting the lies.

Now she meets a Police Officer. She knows he has a good job with benefits. Steady paycheck and He is of good moral character. He has got to have a valid license, because it is one of the requirements for Police to have these types of documents. She also knows that a Police Officer is a powerful person in the community. Police know Judges, Lawyers and a host of professional people that are in his network that maybe could be of service for him or someone else seeking a favor.

Police are known to upwardly motivated because many have a desire to get ahead and obtain supervisor status within the department.   A Policeman has a wealth of information at his disposal   and could possibly help someone that is in a bind. Women know   these things. Women are thinkers and planners.

Angel On My Shoulder

A woman feels she   can be safe with him especially from an ex-boyfriend that won't let go.

Being a Police Officer gives him a power that most men can never achieve. He is a person of statue and dignity who is always willing to help someone. But at the same time on duty or off duty a clear mind and is watching out for the unexpected. He is a person that knows many other Law Enforcement Officers. Every time a Policeman goes out he seems to know many people, most of them on a first name basis and he can also get free legal advice from Lawyers he knows.

Belonging to an FOP Camp, he pays dues which helps those children   in which otherwise would not get to enjoy going to a summer camp. This helps these kids enjoy their summer vacation and they learn valuable information from the leadership that is taught at the summer camp. There is a swimming pool for the kids to enjoy and for Police Officers and friends also.

By nature Police Officers are aggressive and not bashful.

Most approach women with the same forceful and out spoken and persistent attitude. They don't have to look for women, women will seek a Policeman out. Maybe it's the uniform or maybe it is just the job they do.

These women are everywhere, all sizes and shapes.

Most women who date a Police Officer may not realize that Police have a very poor success rate when it comes to marriage. In most instances women don't care if a man is single or married. Married today and divorced tomorrow.   If he has to pay child support from a previous marriage,   that's OK.   He'll just work extra jobs to provide for his children. Extra jobs are always available for off duty Officers. Most employers know that Officers are very dependable and also have the power to make an arrest if necessary.

In short a Police Officer is really a good catch.

Angel On My Shoulder

HAMBONE RANGE

I wanted my children to be proficient in using a gun or rifle. I had intense training at the Police Training Academy and also at the FBI with the SWAT Team and in the Navy. I know the importance of having the right skills in weaponry.

One spring morning I took all three of my children to the Gun Range at the State Prison in West Nashville. I had made arrangements with my close friend Tim Durham to meet us there at 10:00 A.M.

The Gun Range at the State Prison was called "Hambone Range" I don't know where the name came from, all I know is that is has been called "Hambone Range" for as long as I can remember.

Heading up the main road to the Prison Hambone Range was to the left rear of the walls. This is where we trained the Police Recruits before the new Gun Range was built at the Training Academy on Tucker Road.

When we arrived at the Prison you could not help but notice the 20 foot stone walls that surrounded the Castle. The Prison was a good distance away from the main entrance. When we arrived at the main entrance it gives one an eerie feeling just knowing that there were hundreds of men doing time for their crimes and waiting for their sentence to be completed behind the walls.

I told my children that every prisoner in here would do time for their Crime that they had committed by making poor choices in life. This was one of the few times that all three of my kids were totally silent. My oldest son asked me if this is where the men that shot you were. I replied, I think so. We turned left and then right to the Gun Range. I conveyed to my children that the prisoners inside were babies at one time and just think about where they are today.
Again there was total silence as we drove towards the Gun Range. I stopped my truck and we all got out and headed towards the Gun Range. My youngest son asked me if I had ever put anyone in this

Angel On My Shoulder

Prison. My reply, was no because I am not the one that sent them here. I have arrested numerous law violators and this is the final leg of their journey after their Trial. It is up to the Judge and Jury that hears their case and that is where a decision is made on the Criminals outcome as to whether they go to Prison or be exonerated for their crime.

I told my children that as an Instructor at the Academy I wanted to teach a person that had never held a gun in their life. The reason is because they have not developed any bad habits regarding firearms. Old habits die hard, I said.

Tim was right beside me as he was telling my children that when a novice puts their hand on a gun for the first time they become highly excitable. He emphasized the firearm safety over and over telling them to always keep the weapon pointed down range. They were told to raise their hand, if they have a question while they were holding a weapon. Lisa asked why? I told them that if you turn with a weapon in your hand towards someone, that you could accidentally

injury or kill someone. Also taught was the proper grip, sight alignment, trigger squeeze, breath control and the proper stance. These initial proper instructions will be engrained into their memory

and become natural movements to them if they ever have to pick up a pistol. I told them that Tim and myself are both certified NRA Firearms Instructor's and what we are teaching you is the proper handling of a weapon. I added Tim and I have both been in many dangerous situations during our time working for the Police Department in adjoining zones in North Nashville.

Firearm Safety has to be stressed and that a weapon is either pointed at the target or pointed downward in a safe direction. But once a young person is taught properly, it is like riding a bicycle for the first time you never forget what you have been taught. Good habits are like bad habits they die hard. Repetition equals proficiency.

Tim said that he could teach my kids how to shoot a weapon better than I could and that I could teach his kids better than he could. I could understand this, because I would probably

Angel On My Shoulder

be too lenient on my own kids. They seemed to listen to what Tim was telling them. They kept looking my way and I would motion for them to pay attention to what Tim was telling them.

I gave eye protection and ear plugs to all three children and after about 2 hours of firing .38 caliber ammunition all of my children became very proficient in a short amount of time and I was very proud of them. I also said, that Tim was an excellent marksman and like me he knows what to do when he is faced with an issue involving a person with a weapon.

They hugged Tim and thanked him for being there to show them how to handle a weapon. He said, well I know that your dad has shown you all of this before but it never hurts
to take another lesson on the proper use of a firearm and Tim said that he could tell in their eyes and the tone of their voice that they worshiped their dad very much.

I told all three of my children, I bet no one in their school has ever been to "Hambone Range" and shot live ammo. I added, that this will give you something to tell the other students on Monday when you go back to school. I also stressed the responsibility of a person behind the handle of a weapon. I especially repeated gun safety and that you should always treat every weapon as if it was loaded.

They were mostly silent all the way home. I guess they were processing what they had experienced today, and experience that they will carry with them throughout their lives.

Angel On My Shoulder

LUNCH TIME PURSUIT

Myself and two other instructors from the Police Academy were on our way back from lunch. We were headed West on Trinity Lane. I was driving a white station wagon from the Academy. We called it the White Blimp.

A car passed us on a double yellow at a high rate of speed. The Officer in the passenger seat had just been promoted to the rank of Sergeant. I turned on the siren and gave chase. We raced up one street and down another. I t was obvious that the suspect was very familiar with this area. He went down a long street and did a 360 degree turn and came directly towards us. The new Sergeant said, "So long stripes, hello Police Officer again." When the suspect
knew I would not swerve out of the way, he cut 90 degrees to his right. I hit his left rear quarter panel knocking him sideways into someone's yard. The dust boiled up over both cars as he sped across the front yard. The new Sergeant said that he would have the shortest promotion in Metro. He added, promoted one day and stripped of rank 3 hours later.

The chase continued for several more minutes. The suspects left rear quarter panel was caved in and rubbing the tire. He pulled into a gravel driveway, jumped out of the car with me right behind him. I tackled him just before he could open the side door of the house.

I cuffed him and yelled, what's wrong with you? Someone could have been killed or injured the way you were driving. This is not some race track you have been driving on, do you know how many violations you can be charged with? He replied, "I have warrants on me and my license is suspended." He added "I thought if I got inside my house you could not get me."

Angel On My Shoulder

I replied "WRONG". I said, "you're lucky we didn't shoot you or hit you head on".

This was 12:45 PM and after all the paper work was filled out we finally arrived back at the Academy at 3:15 PM. Hey Joe, the Lieutenant wants to see you and the Sergeant in his office right now.

You guys know you are not in Patrol anymore or am I missing something. If you want to go back to making arrests I can have you transferred today the Lieutenant said. I answered, I'll keep that in mind Lieutenant. I added, well it is time to go home now, I'll see you guys tomorrow.   The new Sergeant said, I had no control over this, I was in the passenger's seat and I was just hanging on.

REGISTRATION VIOLATION

Whenever a new class of Recruits began their training at the Academy, I would always go out to the parking lot and check the License Tags and see if the tags matched the automobile. I would always find one or two that were expired or the tags not registered
to the proper automobile or truck.

On this particular day another Sergeant was with me and we decided to run background checks on these new Recruits. Well much to our surprise 2 of the Recruits had a criminal record. Nothing serious, just bad checks which is fraud, and just misdemeanor's. However they both had mug shots that showed up on the screen of our computer. If a reporter ever found this out it would make headlines. We immediately informed the Lieutenant of our findings. He said that he would take the necessary steps to check this out.

Several days later we were called into the Lieutenant's office. He informed us that the Assistant Chief was furious that we were second guessing his personnel and their background procedures. He went on to say that we would have to apologize to the Assistant Chief and then we would not get suspended. I said "suspended for what?" I added, "if I get brought up on charges the Newspaper will love this story."

He told me in private that if I go to the Newspaper I would be fired eventually. Maybe not now but sometime in the near future for something else. I said "So Be It," but I won't go alone. We all three went to the Assistant Chief's office and apologized for doing
Investigation work outside our classifications.

Angel On My Shoulder

An Ironic ending of this story is the 2 Recruits were fired several weeks later on Academic Grades. Sometimes things do have a way of working out with the right ending.

Angel On My Shoulder

MAINTENANCE MAN OR COP

One a summer day at the Academy a 2 story 8' X 8' tower needed to be built, this was the third gun tower to be erected at the Training Academy. I was the only one that could lay block or I was the only one that volunteered to build it. The bottom half would be concrete block with a steel door and a metal frame. This was for an entrance to the storage area. It had a shingle roof on the second floor of the building. The top half was made with 2 X 4's with

plywood sheeting for the exterior surface and a glass front for the viewing area of the Range Master to orchestrate the target system. The wooden steps that went up to the second floor was made by the maintenance because he was a master carpenter. Not many people are skilled enough to use a framing square and mark off the step pattern onto the 2 X 12 board. By watching him make these steps, I learned the basics and how important it was to get the angles just right when making the step construction. This structure was a permanent fixture on the Gun Range.

A new Recruit Class started while I was building the tower. The second week of Recruit training would encompass firearms qualification along with a Remington 12 gauge pump shotgun proficiency. Every morning about 9 AM the Recruit class would line up in formation and march past where I was working, on their way to the big Gun Range at the top of a hill. I had on bib overalls, tennis shoes, a sweatband around my forehead and no shirt on. I was sweaty and dirty as they would pass I would Salute the class as they marched past me. I did this every time they started in the morning and finished in the afternoon. Sometimes and individual would finish early and stop on the way back to the Academy

Angel On My Shoulder

Academy and smoke a cigarette or just vent about the rigors of training. I asked "one Recruit what he thought about this place?" I never let it be known that I was a Lieutenant. He said, "the training was hard and challenging and he further stated he didn't like those Sons of Bitches as Firearms Instructors." I nodded and said "I understand." If my memory is correct this Recruits name was Sulfridge.

A couple of weeks later I was scheduled to teach 16 hours regarding Motorcycle Gangs in Nashville to the Class of Trainees. I was already in the classroom when the class entered. I was in a Police Uniform with the Lieutenant Bars on my collar. I called the Recruit over to the Podium. This is the Recruit that I had talked with earlier after he had finished his class on the gun range. He looked startled when he realized the man that he had been gripping too was not a maintenance man, but an Instructor and also a Lieutenant. I learned close to him and said, "I don't like those Sons of Bitches either." A large grin came over his face and I winked at him as he turned to go back to his seat.

Several Recruits told me everyone thought I was the maintenance man. My first 10 minutes of the class covered, the topic on things are not always as they seem and loose lips sink ships, and never judge who a person is or does just by the way they are dressed. These Recruits who thought I was a maintenance man could not believe that I was a Lieutenant. They told me that they had a lot of respect for me. The class was very attentive and they
seemed to take in all of the knowledge that I presented to them about the Motorcycle Gangs. All in all it was a great class.

While inspecting the New Recruits one morning, I looked at one Recruit's shoes. I asked him, "Did you polish your shoes last night?" "Yes Sir," was his reply. I retorted "what did you use, a Hershey candy bar?" "No Sir," was his reply. Well then what did you use? Well, it was some paste that I borrowed from my dad and it was kind of sticky, I tried to buff them out, but I don't guess it was good enough. Well, don't let this happen again. Yes Sir" was all he said and the next morning his shoes were shined to perfection.

Hair grooming was always a stickler with me. I stopped a Recruit one morning as he was coming in the front door and said, "I thought I told you to get a haircut yesterday!"

"Yes Sir" was his reply, "I just didn't have time." I told him well I'm making time now, go get a haircut now, high and tight and don't come back here until you have one. "Do you understand me?" "Yes Sir," was his reply. He left the Academy and never came back, I guess getting a haircut was too big of a deal for him. These Recruits just can't understand the importance in being given and Order and then following through with it.

I never had any trouble about the Recruits being on time to class; after the first couple of days. Punishment was harsh but effective. One female in particular always had an excuse, she would always smile at me when she entered the class room with a big smile on her face. I said, "Recruit Michelle" for being late today, I want a 5000 word composition on the Fourth Amendment regarding Search and Seizure before class tomorrow or you will be suspended and brought up on charges for Disobeying a Direct Order. That was the last time she was late and there were no more late entry's into the classroom ever again. I would tell the Recruits that I was never late and if I don't show up, I'm either in the Hospital or Dead.

When I retired I had 200 Sick Days that were built up, this was the maximum amount that you could have on the books..

Officer Chip Pearson and myself erected the first Gun Tower. It was only one story. This Gun Tower was a pipe structure. I used my own personal burning torches and welder because the Academy did not have any burning torches at this time. We obtained the steel pipe for the frame of the tower from the

Angel On My Shoulder

old Hospital building which had been vacant for some time. There was an abundance of pipes that we used. These pipes were used to carry steam to the radiators in the Hospital. They were wrapped in an asbestos covering, which at the time I did not realize how dangerous asbestos was. The pipes were cut down by using the torches. I used my Arc Welder to weld the structure together. This tower was built upon four eight inch wheels, which made it portable. The steel ladder was obtained from the roof of the old Hospital which was used to service the elevator. The sides of this steel gun tower was made from heavy vinyl with brass grommets on all four sides of the vinyl. This was held in place by lacing the vinyl to the pipe frame with ¼" rope. This tower could only be used when it was not raining because it would become saturated with water when raining. A third gun tower had to be built so that it could be used all year long.

Prior to the second gun tower being made Officer Kenny Barnes and myself welded fifty steel frames, these were used to hold the targets on the large gun range. The frames were made out of angle iron and each one was welded on all four corners. This was a tiring and mammoth job, but they had to be made. Once again I had to use my own Arc Welder, but I was glad to help.

The second Gun Tower, I built it also. I laid every concrete block structure and nailed the ¾" plywood to the floor joists to the ceiling of the first floor. The maintenance man built the steps going up to the second floor. The second story had an 8 foot ceiling and with plywood sides and the front had a glass for viewing. It had roll roofing on the top which would repel water. Shingles could not be used because the roof did not have enough pitch.

Angel On My Shoulder

MOVIE TIME

The air was damp as I exited my Datsun pickup truck, with my date. It was just two blocks to the movie theater as we walked slowly on the sidewalk facing traffic. I moved closest to the curb when we crossed the street after a brief wait for the traffic light to turn red.

Approaching midway up the block was a well-known landmark called "The Arcade" which runs from the 4th Avenue to 5th Avenue. It was lined with all types of businesses. At the corner of 5th and Arcade was a Walgreens Drug Store. I used to eat here when I was in High School and on my way home. All the stores were closed because it was Sunday. The streets were lined with parked cars, that were capitalizing on the free parking on Sunday by not having to feed the parking meter.

As we came closer to Walgreens there were 2 male blacks, leaning on corner post next to a popcorn machine, which was closed and locked. When we started to pass the black males, the larger male said, "I'd sure like to have me some of that, it would sure make my day and I bet hers too!" I should have kept on going, but my testosterone would not allow that to happen.

I took two steps, turned around facing the black males and told my date in a low voice to move against the wall and watch the smaller black male. I knew that she carried a Pistol in her purse. I then asked the black male, "Do you know why the streets are so deserted?" With no reply. I began to tell them that is was because assholes like you and your midget friend who go around insulting females at your leisure. The larger black male took two sliding steps to the middle of the sidewalk facing me, with his hands hanging loosely down by his side. I eyed my adversary who was about 6 foot tall, about 180 lbs., tight afro, baggy pants and a loose fitting jacket, early 20"s and very dangerous. My eyes were fixed on the black males hands just waiting for any sudden movement.

Angel On My Shoulder

The black male said in a menacing voice, "I'll take you out real quick!"

My right hand moved to the bottom of my cross draw leather holster which held my 38 caliber stainless steel, 6 shot revolver located on my left side.

"You and who else asshole, the only thing bad about you is your breath. Let's see how big a set of nuts you have cockroach. Hell let's dance," I replied! My left hand tilted the holster forward as my right hand went under my jacket, gripping the oversize grips, and gave my pistol a slight tug to clear it from the tension spring inside the holster that secures the weapon. The cylinder cleared the holster, as I moved my right foot 90 degrees to the right slightly turning my torso so only my left side was exposed to the suspect and not a full frontal body. Less target for him to hit, I thought as I leaned slightly on my left leg inching my pistol slowly out of the holster until only the tip of the barrel was left in the holster.

I glared at him and was still watching the suspects hands for any sign of movement.

"You're as close to death now as you ever will be in this life, ½ second from now ten toes up" I hissed. I added, "either do something or turn your black ass around and head back to North Nashville where you belong, and take this turd with you, referring to his friend which was

standing in the Arcade passage way."

The black male said, "you're Vice ain't you?"

"Never mind who I am, do it you chicken shit, do it, do it now! I was starting to drool slightly from the right corner of my mouth. Hell I thought my mouth was supposed to be dry, not wet.

This reminded me of the time I shot and killed a black male in the Central Parking Garage, after the black male had robbed a furniture store at gun point and held a man with his gun pointed at his head for some time until he let the man go. I am really in my element I thought, actually reveling in this situation. Another deep breath, half of it expelled, eyebrows raised and eyes wide open. The black male raised

Angel On My Shoulder

both hands up and mumbled, "AHHHH" and turned around and started walking North on 5th Avenue away from me. His friend followed close behind him.

I drew my weapon and stepped from the sidewalk behind a parked car, which gave me a good cover in the event the two males should spin around with a weapon. I was watching as the two suspects walked further and further down the deserted sidewalk and finally disappearing around the corner. I stayed in my position for several minutes, sighed a deep breath and told my date, it's time for a movie and some popcorn. We walked South on 5th Avenue looking back from time to time until we turned the corner and crossed the street to the movie theater. My date seemed to be very tense and I said, relax, "everything
is under control."

She asked me, "is this what your life is like every day?" Well, I just grinned and said, "I do have some exciting moments from time to time." Would you have shot him Joe," she asked. Oh yeah "was my reply, 4 quick rounds in the chest and then I'd save the last 2 for the turd that was near you," I added. Only if either one had pulled out a pistol or advanced towards you.

My date said, it would have surely made the local News and probably Paul Harvey's Radio program also.

Angel On My Shoulder

180 DEGREE TURN

One evening we worked late at the Police Academy and all of the Instructors took turns on a Driving course on evasive maneuvers in our Police Cars. It was hard, but I have done this one several times before and I had remembered all the ends and outs of the tactic.

When I arrived home I told my oldest son Joe Joe to come with me and let me show you how to do a 180 degree rear to forward turn. We drove to a vacant parking lot at his High School. A short distance from my house.

I drove to the edge of the asphalt and stopped the car. I told Joe Joe to buckle up and brace yourself because this was going to be ride that you will never forget!

I put the car in reverse and began backing up at a high rate of speed. When we reached 30 MPH going backwards, I shifted the transmission selector into neutral, cut the wheel sharply slamming on the brakes (all at the same time) as we were spinning around I
slammed the gear selector into drive and pushed the accelerator to the floor. We spun around and sped off in the opposite direction, barely slowing down. This is what we call a 180 degree turn.

I told Joe you must be certain that the tires are aired up or the tires will roll off the rims. Joe Joe asked, "Why didn't we turn over Dad?" I replied, "It's the low center of gravity for this car. If it was an SUV a rollover is very possible, so don't ever try doing this in a SUV." As a matter of fact, don't you ever do this at all? It takes a lot of experience to be able
to complete this maneuver. Joe Joe said, "Dad you don't have to worry about me doing this because I haven't been trained like you have, boy it's great to be with you and learn things
that I would never ever learn on my own or from someone else."

Angel On My Shoulder

I pulled onto the main street and headed home. Joe Joe sat there in silence, processing to what he had just witnessed.

I silently reflected back to the night of March 6, 1970 and wondered what man would have taken my place by now, if I had not made it that night. Women with children will not stay single for very long if someone asks them to marry, even if the man looks like a bulldog.

Life is strange and life goes on.

BACKWARDS ESCAPE

During football season my two sons and I would walk from our house to the 7-11 Market which was on the corner of Shacklett and Tusculum Road. This was just two houses away from my house. We wanted to buy a few colas to have while we watched a Football Game on TV. While inside the store I saw a car drive in the front of the store and he began circling around the gas pumps spinning his tires and driving in a very reckless manner. A football game at the Antioch High School had just ended and there was a lot of traffic in this area.

I stepped outside and ran towards the speeding car, but the auto then started backing up onto Tusculum Road and he continued backing down the street towards Blue Hole Road. I managed to reach the left front fender of the car trying to get through the opened window to grab the driver. As I neared his door he cut the front wheels towards me trying to hit me. I stepped aside while the driver backed onto Blue Hole Road and started to speed away. I managed
to get close enough to the vehicle to obtain the License number. I wrote it on the palm of my hand with a ball point pen. I always carried a pen with me.

I felt the driver was a student at Antioch, and came from the football game. We went home and I called Headquarters and got a listing on the License plate number. The following Monday I went to Antioch High School to the Principals Office. I was in my Police Uniform. I asked the principal if he had a student by the name that I showed him from the listing that I had obtained from Friday night. He replied, that he knew the person and that he would call him to his Office. I had my Ticket book with me and I explained to the Principal the reason that I was there and what had happened last Friday night after the Football game. I told him how he recklessly

Angel On My Shoulder

drove his vehicle around the gas pumps and then started backing down Tusculum in a dangerous manner. The Principal said he had no problem in having this young man come to his office. From the tone of the Principal's voice I could tell that he had trouble with this young man before. I sat beside the Principal's desk waiting for this young man to appear.

About 5 minutes passed and in walked the young man that was driving recklessly last Friday night. I said, "do you remember me?" No, was his reply. Well I am the person that you t ried to run over last Friday night on Tusculum Roads at the 7-11 Market. I replied, "Young man" I said, you're lucky that I don't arrest you for attempted assault with an automobile which would be on a State Warrant.

I'm giving you a break because it's almost time to finish my shift, so I'm giving you a Reckless Driving Ticket this time and you need to start driving more responsible before you kill somebody with that 4000 lb. weapon that you are in control of. I added, " You better have a Drivers License or you are going to Juvenile." Yes Sir, he said and he sat down handing me his License. I wrote him a ticket. I gave him the copy of his ticket and he turned and walked away. The ticket was paid before the Court Date.

I thanked the Principal for allowing me to see this young man. The Principal said it was no problem Officer. He also added, you know this might scare this young man to think next time before he does something stupid like this.

Angel On My Shoulder

TWO ROLLS OF QUARTERS

I was told to come to the Lieutenant's office one day after lunch.

"Yes Sir," I answered when I stepped inside the Lt's office.

"Sit down" he said. "Sergeant there's 2 rolls of quarters missing from my desk.

"So what's that got to do with me, I asked?" The Lieutenant answered the only personnel that's been in this office is the Recruits signing their evaluations.

I looked the Lieutenant in the eye and said, "How dare you accuse my Recruits of theft."

"Well then where are my quarters?" He quipped.

"I don't know, but I will find out before we go home today. "Good Luck!" He shouted back.

I had a hunch what happened and went outside through the back door of the gym. One of the maintenance men had his old truck backed into a parking spot. I thought he has never parked that way before. For some reason, I opened the truck door and looked in the glove box and there were the missing 2 rolls of quarters.

I took the quarters and marched into the Lieutenant's office and slammed them down on his desk top. Here's your missing quarters Boss! "Guess where they were?" I asked. I saw a surprised look on his face. "They were in your maintenance man's glove box. How about that?" I added; "Don't ever accuse my recruits of misconduct again unless you have solid proof. Okay!" The next morning we went into the Director of Training office and summoned the maintenance man to come to the office.

The two rolls of quarters were placed on top of the desk in front of an empty seat which was for the maintenance man. When he sat down looking at the quarters in front of him there was a look of disbelief on his face. He responded, "I was only funning." I was

going to put them back.

My Boss looked at him and said, "I have no choice but to let you go, due to the evidence that was presented to me by Sergeant McEwen." Go to Personnel and sign some papers and leave the premises. But before you leave give me all the keys that you

have pertaining to the Training Academy right now. The maintenance man complied and put all the keys on his desk and then he left the Academy.

I looked at the Lieutenant and said, another one bites the dust.

"CASE CLOSED."

Angel On My Shoulder

ACADEMY – SWAT RAPPELLING

Several times during the year the Metro Swat Team would train other nearby SWAT Agencies concerning maneuvers about tactical situations. One Class was involved in rappelling from the roof of the old Hospital Building on the Police Academy grounds. This was a vacated building of many years and was in serious need of being razed. Paint peeling from the inside and outside walls, puddles of water inside, broken window panes and other trash scattered on every floor. A couple of our Swat Team members would be on the roof with the guests that were going to rappel. We would teach them how to make a rope harness and how to tie a bowline knot and then tie it off of some stationary object on the roof. The remainder of the line would be thrown over making sure that it was long enough to touch the ground so that another SWAT member would be holding on to this rope as a safety measure.

This was called "On Belay." This is a safety measure in the event that the Trainee lost their grip with their right hand and started to free fall which would result in injury or possibly death.

Captain Ross had one rope and I had another for the second person that was rappelling. The person on the roof would yell loudly, "On Rappel." The person on the ground would answer by yelling, "On Belay." This was to insure that the safety measures had been taken by the team.

One of the Swat member's that we were teaching leaned backwards 45 degrees and stepped off the roof and onto the wall to start his descent. He lost the grip of the rope with his right hand and began a free fall towards the concrete below, which was 45 feet. Captain Ross immediately began backing up and pulling on the rope which stopped the downward motion of the rappelling SWAT member. The member was eased to the ground and he then went

Angel On My Shoulder

back upon the roof for a second try. This maneuver was carried out successfully with all the of class and it went without incident. The young man that had failed the first time successfully made it on his second try. I really was amazed with his determination on his second try and I told him that I knew you could do it, he told me that he was really nervous on the first try, but that he didn't come here to fail. We all realized how important the person on the ground was needed to have a safe rappelling class without any injury.

If Capt. Ross had not been on the ground, on belay, the member would have sustained at the very least serious injury and could of possibly killed him when hitting the landing upside down on the concrete. Someone was watching over him, I alone know the feeling very well.

Capt. Ross was gung how about SWAT Training. We went to Fort Campbell in Kentucky. This was on the Army Base. This was a huge base and we rode 25 minutes to get to our Training area. There were 12 members of the Swat Team that attended. It was extremely cold and all I had on long underwear sweater, pants, insulated coveralls and a sleeping bag to top it off. I slept inside a Van which was out of the wind and I still froze my ass off.

One night about midnight, Capt. Ross and another Swat Team member began drinking and they were setting on a steel bridge which spanned over the creek. They started throwing grenade simulator's into the creek and the explosion was deafening. I got up and rolled the window down and told them to go to sleep. It was quiet for about 10 minutes and they threw one of the grenade simulator's where I was sleeping. It sounded like a bomb had went off. The noise stopped when they ran out of the grenade's.

The next morning at breakfast, I told the entire Team that if I ever come back up here again, I hope all my kids get cancer and

Angel On My Shoulder

die. Because this is my last fucking trip up here. All of them started laughing.

This was not my cup of tea. I didn't enjoy it at all. I didn't like to train for SWAT or practice hitting Golf Balls, but I was damn good at both of them.

Angel On My Shoulder

VIGILANTE TASK FORCE

One afternoon at the Police Training Academy, a Supervisor approached me and said, Joe come outside with me, I have something to talk to you about. He asked, had ever heard about a Vigilantly Task Force or Death Squad in some South American Countries or in the Panama Canal area? I replied, "I hope this isn't going where I think this is. I heard that it was composed of several Police Officers in some Southern Countries who took the law into their own hands when an injustice had been done against the citizens and the Police through the Court System." I added, "they would execute a criminal that had been released from custody after being found Not Guilty of a very serious crime." He asked me what I thought about this. I replied with, well the way I see it, that is one way of reducing Crime, especially those Career
Criminals who seem to be getting a break and put back into Society. But at the same time, this is terribly wrong. We were not hired and trained to be assassins. What the Court System does is not our part of the Justice System.

He said, "Joe how many Officer's do you think would go along with this?" I said "do you mean something like a Magnum Force?" He replied, 'Yeah that's what I mean." Well I think it would take about four or five devoted Officers to this type of ordeal to do the job right. You know that the personnel would be very limited for this type of vigilante posse.

I replied, "do you realize that in this day and time when someone is killed there are hundreds of ways of getting caught." The biggest problem would be when one of the team gets drunk and starts flapping their tongue and what could happen. In my opinion, the biggest weakness that a human being has is wanting to brag or confide with another person. This is why it would never

Angel On My Shoulder

work, or it might for a while plus this just isn't right. This to me would be a recipe for disaster and the assassins could spend the rest of their life behind bars. Trying to avoid getting killed from another inmate would be very difficult if not impossible.

I asked my Supervisor, "have you asked anyone else about doing this type of vigilante action? He replied, maybe. But as of now it is hard to trust anybody of this type of request.

Joe, I wanted to talk with you and find out what your thoughts would be before taking the next step. Joe, he added "I just wanted your opinion."

Looking at my Supervisor eye to eye I told him do not travel down this road boss. Are you sure you really want to start up a Vigilante Task Force? The Supervisor gave no reply to this question.

I further stated to him, that this conversation between you and I never happened. I added, "this conversation is over for me and I have work to do inside." I turned and walked back into the Academy and thought to myself, what in the Hell is he thinking?

This haunted me for several months every time that I would come face to face with this Supervisor. There is no way in hell that this would work. It might have worked in some of the Foreign Countries, but not in this Department. Especially in this day and time. There are just too many Newspaper Reporters and TV News men roaming the streets. All it would take is for one small leak to get out and then everything and everyone involved would be in one Hell of a mess with no way out. Plus it's just not right.

In later years, I found out that he had talked with another Officer about the Vigilante Task Force that he was considering starting up. He also stated to this Officer that he had contacts with a higher authority and he really wanted this to become a reality.

This is the first time that I have ever mentioned this conversation which had taken place between my and myself to anyone.

Angel On My Shoulder

It wasn't too long after this when the Supervisor (the one who asked me what I thought about his idea of the Vigilante Task Force) died.

Angel On My Shoulder

FBI SWAT SCHOOL

During the late 1970's five members of the SWAT Team were authorized to participate in a Training Exercise at Quantico, Virginia at the FBI Academy. There were numerous other SWAT Teams from the Eastern States. Our members were Lt. John Ross, Sgt. Kenny Barnes, Sgt. Kenneth Pence, Sgt. Tim Durham and myself Sgt. Joe T. McEwen. The weather was brutal, 10 inches of snow with the 20 degree temperature for 5 days.

We were taught how to enter a second floor from the outside, with no ladders. Only by using a human pyramid to reach the second floor window. Room entrance, stairway safety and how to safely alight from the roof top of a building. Hostage negotiation, prisoner control, rear guard protection during movement and of course firearms training. We had one of the best scores on the gun range and running man targets. Sgt. Kenny Barnes posted the highest score that was ever recorded on the night firing at the FBI School. After the firearms qualifications our team gained a lot of respect from the other teams. We recorded top scores at the SWAT School.

And last but not least, strenuous exercising in the gym. We would follow the Instructor while carrying a medicine ball and jogging around and around the swimming pool until we were ready to drop from exhaustion.

Then we would go outside and rappel from a 60 foot tower several times to gain proficiency in dropping from the tower platform from the vertical wall 6 stories high. None of us had any trouble sleeping at night and we were glad to see Friday come.

We learned about plague build-up in our arteries and high blood pressure which goes hand and hand with Police work. The Instructor told us that most Police Personnel on the average live

Angel On My Shoulder

3 years after retirement. That bit of information really cheered us up.

We all came away after a week of training a much better Team than we were when we first arrived on Monday. Our faces were chapped and our muscles were sore, but it was well worth the discomfort.

After returning to the Training Academy we shared our training with the other Instructors.

Although I missed the Graduation of this Recruit Class. The Recruits gave me a present of a snub nose nickel plated 38 caliber revolver. This was about 37 years ago and I still to this day have this pistol and it has never been fired. This was a once in a life time present that these young men and women gave to me. My name and Social Security number was engraved onto the pistol.

This pistol will be handed down from generation to generation within the McEwen Family.

In May of 1981, some of the members of the advanced SWAT Team went to Fort Campbell, Kentucky for a Seminar on SWAT Training. The Metropolitan Police Academy staff and the department's M.U.S.T. team conducted this Seminar.

At approximately 2200 hours a member of the Murfreesboro S.W.A.T. fell off a cliff and landed on a hard rock surface, and sustained severe injuries. Myself, along with other team members, effected a rescue. The rescue included administering first aid, putting him on a stretcher, and scaling a 22 foot cliff, utilizing ropes and other rescue gear. The rescue was hampered by total darkness and slippery footing because of recent rains.

Later we were Awarded a Certificate of Commendation by Chief Joe D. Casey and Mayor Richard Fulton.

WHO FIRED THAT SHOT?

When the SWAT team was first organized we were not at all fully trained or had very little training at all. In fact the first team composed of personnel assigned to the Training Academy. Many times members were not available because they were teaching a class, on the gun range, giving tests, etc. Whatever personnel were available the team went on calls ill prepared and lacking knowledge of highly dangerous and intense situations. I fact we probably looked like an off shoot of the Keystone Cops. Particularly the time I charged a front door and hit it knocking it off the hinges. Crashing on the barricaded suspect who was peeping out of the small window in the top of the door. This is shear insanity and stupidity in these types of situations. On that particular case everything worked out OK, as we were very lucky on this occasion.

The SWAT team's transportation consisted of a windowless cargo van. We were all piled into the van like the Keystone Cops. On a couple of occasions a member was left at the academy where he was still getting dressed. Another was left on the front steps as we drove off because we didn't hear him due to the fact everyone was whooping and hollering like a bunch of mad dogs going after a free meal. This was close to a mob mentality.

Excitement ran high and mistakes were made. It did not take long for the department to realize that it needed a unit for someone who was barricaded in a house or whatever and the right equipment, proper training in all areas and individual transportation soon followed.

At one time before everyone received cars. I jumped into the rear of the van and plopped down on a storage box. When I sat down hard a pistol went off. The noise was deafening and it's a miracle that someone did not get shot. I got up and saw that a pistol was on the storage box where I had just sat down on. Someone had laid their gun on the box while the SWAT Team members were loading up. Situations like this caused the team to slow down and not go crazy on a call which is important as a these situations. Extensive training began at the Training Academy Grounds, the FBI Academy in Quantico, Virginia and Fort Campbell, Kentucky.

We had extensive training in weaponry. In firearms we had to fire an M-16 with open sights in a prone position from 50 and maybe a 100 yards. The pattern had to be grouped in an area the size of a coffee saucer. Of course the snipers had to fire a lot further, because they had scopes. These long shots were done at the Prison Gun Range with was called Hambone Range. We had to learn how to dismantle an M-16 and a Smith & Wesson 9 millimeter automatic. We learned how to rappel efficiently from 40 feet at the Police Academy and from the tower at the FBI Academy in Quantico, Virginia.   I along with another Sergeant Kenny Barnes made the steel two man battering ram. We learned proper door entry,   how to move at night without being detected. On one occasion we actually went through a subdivision without being noticed. In other words we were learning all phases of SWAT Tactics.

Updated equipment, new members soon followed, and the SWAT team became a highly skilled, professional, force as good as any team in the country.

I was only on the team for five years, but it was an interesting five years. I asked for permission to be dropped from the SWAT Team Roster because I felt using my own automobile to go the Training Academy where the primary staging for the SWAT Team took place. To me this was inappropriate with a town the size of Nashville and coupled with the fact that the

Safety Coordinator (Lt. Stone) told me personally that if I was involved in a wreck going to the Training Academy for a SWAT call that it probably would not be covered under Metro's Policy. Shortly after my resignation from SWAT, cars were given to the members of SWAT.

GOLF BAG CAPER

In the late 70's at the Training Academy, we came to work one morning and a Superior Officer told us that he was practicing Golf the last evening at the Physical Agility field. This was a huge area and a great place to practice hitting balls. He said that he walked about 150 yards to retrieve some of the golf balls that he had been hitting and he noticed that a car pulled up real close to his golf bag and the passenger which was a male black got out of the car and grabbed his golf bag and threw it in the back seat of the car and drove away.

This was a golf bag with a complete set of Irons, Woods, Wedge and putter. Plus a watch and a an expensive ring which was in one of the pockets on the golf bag.

Months later I was going behind the Academy in a deserted area to cut up a fallen tree for wood, that I needed for my fireplace at home. I did everything I could to save money because times were hard and every penny counted. The sage grass was knee high and
it was a very dense terrain in the area where the tree had fallen. I was always on the lookout for snakes. This was a good place for the snakes to hide. I had seen several black snakes around in this area. They probably hated me as much as I was terrified of them.

I looked around for a good place to stand while cutting up the tree. I looked to my left and I saw something round, that the grass had grown over this object. I walked closer to this object and taking my foot, I pushed back some of the weeds and then I noticed it was a
golf bag with clubs inside the bag. I picked up the golf bag and then I surmised that these were the clubs that were probably stolen months earlier.

Angel On My Shoulder

I immediately drove my vehicle back to the Academy with the clubs in the bed of my truck. I went into one of the offices where several employees were just sitting and talking, when they saw me with the golf bag they just looked at me in amazement. I stood the bag upright in the middle of the floor. I pulled a couple of the clubs out of the bag and the grips had been removed from the Irons and Woods. The previous grips were leather wrapped.

I asked where the Supervisor was and I was told that he was in the gym working out. Another Lieutenant in an adjoining office became very nervous and did not seem too pleased at what I had discovered at the top of the hill. I heard him say, "Ah Shit!"

I went to the gym and told the Supervisor that I had found his clubs and they were in his Secretary's office. His face showed surprise and his eyes widened and he asked "me what did you say?" We went back to the office and I took out several clubs from the bag. I said, they not only stole your golf bag, they had to come back on the grounds, drive behind the Police Academy and up a narrow rocky road, one way in and one way out on the road to the top of the hill and behind the gun range and the only exit from where the golf clubs were found is one way back behind the Academy and just past the maintenance man's house and out the main entrance.

You know they removed all of your grips from your clubs and then hid your golf bag up by the barn. How about that!!

The Supervisor replied, "was my ring or my watch in the bag?" I replied, I didn't look in any of the zippered pouches. He unzipped the small pouch and looked inside. I knew there would not be any jewelry or anything else in the zippered pouch. Everyone that was in the room sat silently and just watched as he took the bag and walked into his office and shut the door.

This incident was never mentioned again.

Angel On My Shoulder

SWAT CALL

One SWAT call which lasted 11 hours and this was one for the books. The call was shots fired from a house within a nice subdivision.

The SWAT arrived and set up a perimeter, on the side and back of the house. My partner and I were to the side of the house and behind a very large tree. This was a ranch style house with a daylight basement. We believed that there was only one white male which was barricaded inside the house with an unknown amount of weapons.

The command post was set up in the front and on the street. It was roughly 100+ feet from the house.

Within an hour the News media arrived and the start of the circus had begun. The suspect fired a round into the command post, while the negotiators tried to talk to the nut inside the house on the phone.

As the sun started to set my partner and I were told to pull the electric meter so the suspect would not be able to see the evening news. Both my partner and I had M-16 carbines. As we approached the house dogs started barking from inside the house. I cut the seal and unscrewed the clamp that holds the meter to the base. My partner was watching the upstairs windows when I yanked the meter from the meter base. We both ran from the house back
to our station, which was behind a large tree. The sun set and the TV news stories ended and the house was in total darkness. I turned on our night scope and watched the rear door. There was a boat and trailer parked close to the house. I told my partner to notify everyone that the suspect was beside the boat.

The suspect went back inside the basement. My partner and I were given orders to replace the electric meter. I was thinking boy

Angel On My Shoulder

is this a dangerous move or what? We crept back to the house being extra quiet so the dogs would not start barking.

This was the part of being on SWAT that is very dangerous. My partner and I were under the side windows of the house and if the suspect knew what was going on he certainly had an advantage over us. He already has shown that he is not afraid to fire his weapon coupled with the fact he had dogs and a high ground advantage. We had to use a flashlight in order for me to look at the meter lugs so we could replace them in the proper location. My partner and I were both sweating profusely. We could have easily been shot in the head from the second story window if he knew what we were doing. I put my left hand on the back of my partners bullet proof vest walking backwards looking at the two side windows with my M-16 shoulder height. There was a bullet in the chamber with the safety off.

We made it back to our post without incident. The time was about 11 AM and we had been here for about 9 hours. Another shot was fired from the house and someone on the radio yelled fire. I stood up and shot 3 or 4 rounds through the side windows just as the suspect stepped out of the house and began advancing towards the command post with his weapon pointed towards the trailer. My partner and I ran up the slope to the side of the house trying to see the suspect through the dense hedge, along with trees and tall growth of weeds and grass that served as a boundary of the house.

As the suspect neared the command post with his weapon pointed straight ahead, another SWAT member was inside the command post and was leaning out of an opening. The suspect advanced within 10 feet of the News media and the command post. The SWAT team member fired one shot hitting the suspect in the leg and he went down. He was then rushed by several Police Officer's.

Angel On My Shoulder

He was placed on a stretcher and lifted into the ambulance along with Medic personnel, the hostage negotiator and other Police personnel and the ambulance left for the hospital.

I told my partner this won't be the end of this, we'll be back here again someday. SWAT team members gathered up all their equipment and headed for the Training Academy for debriefing of this incident. I arrived home about 2 AM, took a long hot shower and went to bed trying to get some sleep, no way because I was too keyed up so I sat and watched television until it was time to go to work.

As Lyndon B. Johnson said, "A man's got to do what's he's got to do."

This is a true meaning if you really love you what you are doing you will never work a day in your life. Somehow this job gives me a feeling that I can make a difference, hopefully I did.

READY - AIM – FIRE

Every year the entire Police Department sworn
personnel spends a week at the Training Academy for In Service
Training. During this time qualifying with weapons is included in
the curriculum. Also the Recruits go through a strenuous regiment
of firearms safety.

One day the 12 gauge Pump Remington shotgun was used
for a refresher course. One old head, a Lieutenant (over 20 years
on the Force) was given the 12 gauge to fire upon a target on the
Gun Range. One of the Instructors, Officer K. Pence tried
correcting
the Lieutenant on how he was holding the shotgun by placing his
head too close to the butt of the shotgun.

The Lieutenant said, "Look Sonny I was using a shotgun
before you were in the first grade!"

"Okay Lieutenant, get ready to fire," the Instructor replied.
The 12 gauge shotgun really kicks or recoils when the trigger is
pulled.

The shotgun kicked hitting the (Know it all Lieutenant)
giving him one big bloody nose. It's hard to teach and old dog new
tricks. To this day he has never admitted that he had done anything
wrong. Somehow you can't cure stupid!

Police are supposed to be an expert with firearms, RIGHT?
Well somewhat. Police are required to qualify each year with their
pistol to hone their skills in weaponry, RIGHT? Well somewhat.

It would be interesting to know how many firearms are
accidentally fired and just how many Policemen accidentally shoot
themselves? The count would be highly inaccurate because
of the cover ups regarding stupidity.
Let's see, how about the time someone at the Training Academy
was teaching a course in firearms safety and the proper trigger
squeeze. He was a Sergeant and had been on for a long, long time. I

was teaching a class in the next room. There were about forty Policemen in the class when the Sergeant (with 30 + years of service) pointed the pistol at a wall and said, "Watch the hammer fall." That's right a loaded round was left in the pistol and when he pulled the trigger the bullet hit the concrete wall. Rumor has it that when the class went on break some Joker placed a live round in the cylinder. When the Sergeant picked up the pistol to continue the Fire Arm Safety, he assumed that the cylinder was empty. OOPS! I wonder why so many Police are hard of hearing and have ringing in their ears? It just happened to be a concrete wall that he hit thank goodness.

While at a Pistol Tournament someone on the Pistol team started practicing fast draws while watching himself in the mirror. The gun went off shattering the mirror and the bullet ended up in the empty adjoining room.

Four Instructors were sitting at their desks at a temporary office. One Instructor began dry firing his revolver. Dry firing is when you (supposedly empty the weapon) and practice sight picture and trigger squeeze. This makes a person at the grip end more proficient in the use of their service revolver. Yeah Right! Anyway, the hammer hits on an empty cylinder when the trigger is squeezed. However if the Training Instructor forgot to remember the basic safety procedure to unload the pistol, a loud, deafening noise permeates the air as the bullet is expelled through the barrel and lodged into a wall. Would you speak louder, I cannot seem to hear you!!!

Everyone around the incident had instant tinnitus for life. We were all laughing but, the noise was still permeating in our ears while the plastered wall showed a three inch crater where the bullet hit.

Physical Agility was another curriculum that the Recruits had to master. This would build up their strength to perform in tight situations after they graduated from the Academy. This too was an important part of their training.

Angel On My Shoulder

TRAINING ACADEMY ENLIGHTMENT

I had been at the Training Academy for a couple of years. The Instructors that were at the Academy had become good friends with one another. On one such day, I was called into the Lieutenant's Office. I said, "what's up boss?" Close the door Joe and sit down I have something I've been wanting to talk to you about. When you were wounded, you did receive some money, didn't you? Yes, "I did was my reply." If you don't want me to know just say you had rather not talk about it. No, Lieutenant, I was very appreciative that I had received anything.

He said, "you do know that First American Bank opened an account to receive donations on your behalf?"

I said, yes the Captain gave me a check that included donations from the Police Officers and anyone else that wanted to chip in. He said "would you mind telling me how much money you received?" I said, "the check was for $3,000.00." The Lieutenant said "was this the first installment or was this everything." No, that was the total amount. He leaned forward and put both elbows on his desk and said, Nashville has a population of

about four hundred thousand and at a nickel per person you would have received at least $20,000.00.

The Police Officers were giving $5, $10 and $20 dollars every time a hat was passed while you were in the hospital. A lot of money was donated by the Police Officers and the rest of the Department. The reason that I am telling you this is because the person in charge of collecting the money was bragging while In-Service that he had a lot of money in CD's which was drawing double digit interest and that he would take the interest and open another account, thus drawing interest on interest. Joe, this guy who handled the money was like putting the fox in charge of

Angel On My Shoulder

guarding the henhouse.   I have never liked this guy and I like him even less now after finding out that the amount that you received was ridiculously low. Of course, there is nothing that can be done about this now but, you just keep this in mind and the next time you see him, you just might see him in a different light. "I know I will and if I ever get a chance to break it off in him, I will." Replied the Lieutenant. I told the Lieutenant "that this is very upsetting to me, now because I had to sell my house because my disability check was only $308.00 a month."

He told me not to let this bother me and that he didn't mean to open up any old wounds, but I felt that you should know about this. He told me that he had been thinking about this for a long time and it had really been bothering him. Joe, I could tell by your conversation here at the Academy that you did not have much extra money, because you worked extra jobs and cut grass on the side.

When I arrived home that night, I did not remember the drive at all. The only thing I remembered was pulling into my driveway. I sat in my car and thought about what had taken place today and I decided that it is what it is.

Angel On My Shoulder

ROLE PLAYING WITH RECRUITS

During Recruit training many classes were involved in role playing with the Instructor's being the bad guy. We would start the class out by deploying several Recruits to the old Hospital Building to answer a call about a man with a gun. I would be on the
roof overlooking the entrance which was two floors down. As the Recruits neared the entrance very slowly and cautiously, I would dump three gallons of water from the roof on them as they reached the doorway entrance. This taught the Recruits to look up if the building was more than one story tall and beware of all the surroundings around them. They had to learn to focus on everything and not just what was in front of them.

I would tell them that this would be real and not like the stories that have been seen on the television. They would laugh; I told them that I didn't think it was funny, after all your life is on the line with every call that you may receive. After this was done a couple of times they became more aware of what was going on above their heads and everything around them.

I would then hide on the second floor in some trash scattered room. We were all using blank cartridges in our guns. The only time I ever lost the gun battle was to a Recruit named James Buck. He utilized all the tactics that he had been taught and he caught me by surprise.

It is a real eerie feeling to see the barrel of a gun pointed towards me and the bright orange flash coming from his revolver. Officer Buck turned out to be an excellent Police Officer, which I knew that he would.

The Recruits always looked forward to the two weeks on the Gun Range. It gave them hands on training, they were becoming proficient in weaponry. This training will stay with them the rest of their lives even if they left the Police Department.

The Recruits went out to the State Prison just off of 51st in West Nashville for firearm's training and role playing on traffic stops using Police Cars as props. The firearms that we used were Smith & Wesson 6 shot revolvers. The shot gun was a Remington 870 pump.

Automatics did not come into use for several years. I personally do not like automatics, because they are harder to master and have been known to jam on rare occasions. An automatic you have to remember to charge a bullet in the chamber and take off the safety.

A revolver or a wheel gun there is no safety, you pick it up and pull the trigger. It will fire every time and it is impossible to jam.

To this day I still favor a wheel gun even though they do not have the fire power that an automatic has with twice the rounds in the magazine. When the speed loaders came onto the market for revolvers it made reloading a lot faster.

At lunch time we would eat inside the Prison with a few of the Prisoners. While we we're standing in line to have the food dumped on our metal tray, one Convict said, they don't look like much to me! I answered by saying, "OK Big Guy, who put your ass in here, the Salvation Army or some Cop?" I don't think you volunteered to do time for your crime.

I was told not to eat any mashed potatoes because you would not know what kind of liquid could mixed in with the potatoes. All I ate was carrots, green beans, bread and milk carton that was sealed. No spuds for me!

The firearms training was top notch as all of the Teachers were Certified in NRA Firearms Instructors. Many of the Instructors carried a Distinguished Expert Bar above their

Angel On My Shoulder

left shirt pocket on their uniform, I wore mine with Pride because in order to obtain one a Person has to shoot 5 Perfect Scores of 300. All of the Instructors at the Training Academy could not only talk the talk, but we could walk the walk.

Once myself and four other Swat Team members went to the FBI Academy in Quantico, Virginia and received intense training in all phases of tactical situations.

JUMPING JACKS

Many times when the Recruit class had physical training exercise at the end of the day, I would sometimes lead them in different phases of exercises. I loved to test their agility.

One particular day I told the class that we were going to have a contest on how many Jumping Jacks that we all could perform.

At 100 we stopped for thirty seconds for a rest period. Thirty seconds had passed and we started again, some of the Recruits were stopping due to muscle fatigue. At 200 we stopped again for 30 seconds. My legs were killing me but I wouldn't let on that I was hurting. 80% of the class were out of this exercise at this time, they were just sitting on the floor and panting real hard.

I decided to finish up and go as far as my legs would function. There was about 6 or 8 recruits still standing and participating with me. At this time I was 45 years old and the Recruits were young people somewhere below 25 years old. Twenty years makes a lot of difference, but I was still going to be the last man standing.

I kept going until we reached 534 Jumping Jacks and I knew the diehards would not stop. I did not want to quit, but I had to stop at 534 mainly because my legs were starting to burn and cramp real bad. They all clapped as I sat down on the floor with them. One Recruit, Alan Herald looked at me the whole time with a smile on his face. I knew he was a true die hard and would not stop. I could tell t hat this young man was going to be an excellent
recruit. My legs were killing me but I did not let on that they were really hurting. Alan was one of a few Recruit's that lasted through the 534 Jumping Jacks exercise. I waited until all the

Recruits had left and then I got up and how I made it to my truck, I'll never know. My legs were cramping and filled with pain with every step I took.

When I got home I had trouble getting out of the my truck and how I made it up the stairs to the second floor was beyond me. I sat in a hot soaking tub for an hour. I was beginning to wonder how I was going to get out of the tub, but I managed. It was all I could do to get out of bed the next morning. I never told the Recruits how hard this was on me.

The Recruit Class gave me a trophy at their Graduation. It was titled "Jumping Jack Mac." It is one of my favorite Trophies and I still have it today displayed on a shelf in the Bonus Room of my home. Every time I look at it I think of Session 5, Police Recruit Class.

They are so proud when their Badge is pinned on their shirt. To Graduate from the class is a very high honor. We usually end up with about 15% to 20% of the applicants who do not graduate for one reason or another.

These hopefuls were a great bunch of recruits, and I had the Honor of being involved with them in their 6 month Journey, which was very hard at times if not, almost impossible.
These young men and women poured their heart and soul's out for me as we made the journey together side by side one day at a time.

The next 6 months of being a Rookie Police Officer is hard also. Even though they have learned a lot at the Academy, when they hit the streets it's a whole new experience. I know this first hand. I thought I was invincible until I took 5 shots and almost lost my life. I made this known to the Recruits while they were at the Academy.

In looking back, probably my most satisfying and memorable times at the Academy was when I was in charge of a Recruit Class. Watching these young men and women develop

Angel On My Shoulder

from a civilian to a trained Professional Police Officer is a priceless journey.

Few Police are given this opportunity. I am so grateful to be working with these fine young men and women. It is truly and honor to be a part of their time at the Academy.

Previously when I was working Patrol, there was always something different every day, but it was satisfying and different. But the satisfaction that I received from being an Instructor at the Academy was second to none.

Angel On My Shoulder

ANOTHER DAY AT THE TRAINING ACADEMY

I was called to the Lieutenant's Office one day and was told to delivered an envelope (8 X 11 brown interdepartmental) downtown to a Captain and no one else. I hand delivered this envelope to him only. I said, "Yes Sir" and I left. While going to my destination I pulled into a Restaurant parking lot and started to look inside the packet to see what was so important.

The contents contained numerous pages of questions and answers that seemed what would be used for a Promotional Exam. I closed the packet by looping the string around the red paper washers on the back of this large brown envelope so it would look like I had never opened it. I then delivered the envelope to the Captain.

When I arrived back at the Academy I opened the car door to get out and glanced down at the floor and saw a gun barrel sticking out several inches from under the driver's seat, it appeared to be a large weapon and it turned out to be a 45 caliber Tommy Gun with a silencer attached. I pulled it halfway out to look at it.

I took my handkerchief and wiped the gun, so that my fingerprints would not be on the gun where I had touched it. I did not want my fingerprints on a Tommy gun with a silencer. I slid it back under the car seat. "Damn," I thought to myself, "why would the Lieutenant need this under his car seat?" Because when this weapon is fired with a silencer attached all you hear is a clicking noise. A weapon that is not normally used in Police Work. Thinking that is for him to know and for me to never to find out.

I went into the Lieutenant's office and told him that the packet was delivered to the Captain downtown. I also asked him, "did you know that you left a weapon under your car seat?" He looked surprised and replied that he had it for protection. He also added "Forget what you saw, Okay". I nodded and placed his car keys on his desk and went to my office to try and process what I

Angel On My Shoulder

had just witnessed. Damn, I wish he had asked someone else to run his errands for him. I guess he picked me because I didn't have any Recruit classes assigned for today and he trusted me to do this for him. Oh well, it may work out to my benefit later on down the road. You never know!!!!

Angel On My Shoulder

KING OF THE GYPSIES

I would frequent a night club on Nolensville Road almost every weekend. I knew the doorman and the owner. The doorman would always let me and my date in for free because he knew if anything happened, that I would be there to help them. During the course of the night I would go to the entrance to talk to the doorman and just breathe some fresh air that would come through when the front door opened. I would sit on a display stand at the entrance.

Once while sitting and talking a burly big male came and sat beside me. I nodded hello. He responded, "Do you know who I am?" I replied "No and I don't really care." He said in a loud voice, "I'm king of the gypsies." "Good for you," I responded. He reached for his billfold in his right rear pocket. I thought to myself, I wonder where this is going?

He flipped open his wallet and showed me a silver badge which was about half the size of a real one. He said, "How about this?"

It was obvious he was drunk, his breath reeked of alcohol. I reached into my front pants pocket and took out my badge and my Identification which was in my wallet. I opened it up and displayed a gold Lieutenant's Badge about three times larger than his and I said, "Do you see this badge?" Yeah it's the same design as mine was his reply. Yes, but mine's gold and you know what else, "I asked?" What else in a burly voice was his reply? This badge can arrest your ass and put you in jail and yours can't. I added, your badge is something like a courtesy badge that is given out to some friend of the Mayor or Councilman.

To a real Police Officer your puny badge doesn't mean shit, they are a dime a dozen. Because if it meant anything you would have an ID card and that you don't have. He put his billfold back

Angel On My Shoulder

into his rear pocket and walked back into the club. I asked the doorman if he flashes the Badge when he comes in through the door. Sometimes he'll say that he is here on official business and we will waive the cover charge but it won't ever happen again.

I added he has no Police power or commission or anything, he couldn't even use if trouble broke out. The only business that he has in here is Monkey Business. I told the doorman he's the type of guy that would mooch his way in buy one beer and milk it for three hours. I also added, I bet he's the type that will get up and walk past an empty table with the drinks still on it and pick up a full beer bottle.

Sometimes you just have to show these drunks that they are not as brave as they think they are and call their bluff. I wasn't about to lose this one. If he made a spectacle of his self then I would arrest him for being a drunk Gypsy, and it would have ruined my night with filling out paperwork and taking him to headquarters for booking.

I'm going back inside; just give me a holler if he tries anything else. Sure Joe, thanks for having my back. It is always a pleasure to see you come here. By the way, I saw you dancing in there, pretty good dancer for a Cop and your date is a good looker too. Where did you find her? That's a long story and she has got a lot of miles. No need to explain anymore Joe, just go back in and have a good time tonight.

Angel On My Shoulder

STRANGER AT MY DOOR

One night while I was working Security at Washington Manufacturing Company, on Nolensville Road, my oldest son Joe Joe called and said, "Dad someone is trying to open the back door."

I immediately called Dispatch on my Walkie Talkie and told Headquarters this is Lt. McEwen and I'm at work, my boys are home alone. I told Dispatch the Zone car knows where I live and I've got one of my boys on the land line.

Dispatch said, that 2 cars are near Hickory Hollow and they will be there in a matter of seconds. I told Joe Joe to get my 2 Revolver's from behind the Bar in the den and I'll hold on until you come back. In less than 12 seconds he was back on the phone with me. Joe Joe said, "Dad I gave Eric a Pistol and I have the butt of my gun resting on the counter top pointing right at the rear door just like you showed us how to do.

I said, "Get Eric to unlock the rear door and then stand behind you. If the Burglar comes into the house shoot him in the T Zone, empty the gun on him." I could hear sirens nearing the house, "Joe Joe, when the Zone Car pulls into the driveway tell Eric to open the front door." Whatever you do don't take your eyes off the rear door! "Gotcha Dad," he answered.

Within seconds a Policeman told me, "everything is ok here Joe!"

One of the Police Officers told Joe Joe and Eric to put the gun on the counter top. He added it won't do you any good with an empty gun with the cartridges lying on the counter.
Joe Joe replied, "The gun is fully loaded and the bullets on the counter top are extra if we need them.

Tim Durham was one of the Police Officers that answered the call and told the other Police Officer that McEwen and I have

Angel On My Shoulder

trained these boys well in firearm safety and shooting and they are both excellent marksman. Neither one of them is afraid of anything.

I told Joe to put the gun's on the den coffee table and I'll see you guys in a couple of hours. When I got home, I told both of my boys how proud I was of them. They said, dad we did just what you showed us to do. The Police that came to the house said that you were on the walkie-talkie with them the whole time, so that they could tell you what was going on. I'm proud of you two, now get to bed you've got school tomorrow. I could tell that they weren't ready for bed so we ordered a Pizza and just laid back and watched TV for a while. It didn't take long for the Pizza to disappear and I only had 1 slice. That's OK, these boys will be grown and out of the house before too long. I have to cherish every moment I can with them.

Once again, I just want you to know how proud I am of you. You both kept your cool and didn't panic. Ok, boys off to bed this old man is tired and tomorrow is going to be here before you know it. Do we really have to go to school tomorrow? Joe Joe the oldest spoke up,I can't wait to tell the guys at school what happened tonight, Eric added, "me too".

One more things boys, when someone comes through our door breaking in, they are coming in to hurt someone. They are not there to audition for the head tambourine player for the Salvation Army. I added, if someone is worth shooting they are worth killing! If they are not worth killing don't shoot them or bluff with a gun.

Angel On My Shoulder

STOLEN BICYCLE

After working my 8 hour shift in an unmarked unit, I was headed home just to relax. This had been a really rough day. Upon arriving at my home, I saw my oldest son standing bythe back door. He had a look on his face as if he had done something wrong.

He walked towards my Police Car and said, "dad, I have to tell you something." My bicycle was stolen today. "From where I asked?"

"School," was his answer.

That is why I did not want you to take your bicycle to school. "Get in and let's see if we can find out anything," I said. We headed to the School and began asking questions." Do you have any idea who took your bicycle Joe Joe? He gave me the name of a student in his class that showed a lot of interest in his bicycle, insisting that he wanted to ride it during lunch time.

We went to this student's house and I knocked on the front door. The parents of the suspect were still at work and have not arrived home yet. The student insisted that he did not see or have Joe's bicycle. I responded by telling him that I have 2 girls that saw you riding a red bicycle from school. I told him all I wanted was the bicycle and I would not arrest him for theft.

He then told me the bicycle was in the garage behind the house. All three of us walked to the garage and retrieved the bicycle that was under a tarp.

As I was pushing the bicycle to my Patrol Car the boys dad pulled into the driveway and asked "What's going on?" I replied " I am picking up my sons bicycle that your boy stole from the school."

"How can you be sure my son took the bicycle," he asked. Well several reasons, First, 2 girls saw your boy riding this bicycle from school. Second, I purchased this bicycle from J. C.Penny last

Angel On My Shoulder

month and I have the receipt. Third, he admitted to stealing the bicycle. I added," if you don't think this enough evidence, I can arrest Junior now and take him to Juvenile and we can all go before a Juvenile Judge for a hearing at a later day. I can leave with the bicycle now and this problem is resolved. But I can tell you one thing that when I leave this bicycle goes with me. This is my son's bicycle, I paid $80.00 for it, I have the receipt. I need an answer right now as I unsnapped my handcuff case and held the handcuffs in my right hand. The homeowner said, "Take the bicycle and let's forget this never happened." I can assure you Officer that this will never, never happen again. He then looked at his son and said, Get in the house, NOW!"

As we left I could hear the father screaming at his son in the house. The boy probably wished he had gone to Juvenile now. Oh well, it is what it is. When we arrived home, I asked my son, and what are you not going to do tomorrow? I know dad, I'm not going to take my bicycle to school. Good boy, now let's get inside, I'm hungry or have you boys eaten everything in the fridge again. No, dad there's a little bit left. How about Pizza, no way I'm sick of Pizza. Let's go to Shoney's and pig out on the All You Can Eat Bar. Sounds good to me, so off we went to Shoney's and we did Pig Out.

When we got back home we chained the bicycle to a secure post in the back yard. I ran the chain through the front wheel instead of the frame. The next day the wheel was still chained to the post and the rest of the bike was gone. We never recovered the Bicycle.

Angel On My Shoulder

PARTTIME WORK

At the Training Academy were worked Monday through Friday. So on the weekends I worked Security at Shoney's Restaurant located on Nolensville Road and Harding earning extra money.

This was a favorite spot for the young people to gather and hang out on the weekends. The curb service was beside the Restaurant under a huge steel canopy. Each car space had a large menu attached to the canopy posts. When the car stalls became full the arriving cars would drive around and around the area in an endless circle. It was nicknamed "Circling the Wagons."

It was my job to hold down the noise, stop any alcohol on the premises and when the traffic became bumper to bumper I would direct the circling cars out of the curb service area and onto Harding Road. A Police Officer came to talk to me and we drank some coffee. This Officer was James Long, he was killed in a car wreck a couple of years later.

One car had 2 male teenagers in the front seat. When I told them to leave they developed an attitude. When they drove onto Harding they gave us the finger and started yelling "Fuck You Pig." Jim and I started running towards Nolensville Road to try and block off their route. Their automobile slowed down because of the heavy traffic which enabled us to catch their car on the entrance ramp to Nolensville Road from Harding. I got to the car first and did a stupid move. I ran in front of the automobile to block their escape. I yelled at the occupants of the car that they were under arrest for disorderly conduct.

The drive gunned the motor and the car rocked left and right from the torqueing of the motor when the accelerator was pushed forward. I drew my weapon pointing it upright and yelled "Don't you do it!" "Don't you do it!"

Angel On My Shoulder

The passenger the screamed "Run over the pig!" "Just run over him!"

Jim arrived at the car and kicked the door on the passenger's side, and yanked it open with his left hand. He pulled the passenger out and turned the ignition off. I then ran to the driver's side and pulled the driver out onto the street. They both continued to yell
obscenities towards us and acted like they were going to spit on us.

James took them to the side entrance of Shoney's and I drove their auto to a parking lot next to Shoney's. I called for a transport car to take these two juveniles to Juvenile for
processing. To make a long story short, they were found guilty and fined $200.00 each and they were both placed on Probation.

CUTTING GRASS

My oldest son Joe Joe and I were cutting grass for my Aunt who resides in East Nashville near Shelby Park.

This is where I lived with my dad when I was young. We stayed in the basement, because my dad did not have the money for us to live in a place of our own at this time.

This place brought back a lot of memories both good and bad. This was a two bedroom home on a curve on Oakhill Drive which ran into Shelby Golf Course where I use to play golf in my younger years, almost every day.

While we were in the front yard talking a car stopped in front of the house and a white male was violently thrown from the vehicle onto the street and then the car sped off. I ran to my truck which was about fifteen feet away and grabbed my service revolver and as my son and I approached the screaming male. I had no idea what was happening.

He claimed he was hitch hiking and was given a ride by the two male whites in the car that sped off. He claimed that these two males had severely beaten him before taking his $40.00 that he had in his wallet and then threw him out of the car. The boy said that he had just gotten paid for helping a friend with some yard work and these two guys gave him a ride were across the street where he had been working.

I told my aunt to call the Police and tell them that Lt. McEwen needs assistance and send an ambulance. We helped the victim to my aunt's yard and waited for an ambulance and a Patrol car to arrive. It seemed like forever before the ambulance arrived, but it actuality it was only a matter of minutes. The Police arrived shortly after the

Angel On My Shoulder

ambulance. After a brief few minutes of taking the victim's vitals they put him in the back of the ambulance and left for the Emergency Room. Before the ambulance left the young boy thanked me for helping him. I told him that I was a Lieutenant with the Police Department and that I was glad that I was here to help you. I asked, is there anyone he

wanted me to and let them know about this incident. He replied, no but thank you very much Officer. I'll call someone after I get to the Hospital. The ambulance driver said, "Joe we have to go, this boy needs to be looked at now."

I filled out a supplement report pertaining to the incident and also giving a description of the car. It was a 4 door faded red Chevrolet with a cracked windshield and

no hubcaps. I did not get a chance to get the license tag because it all happened so fast. We finished cutting the yard and went home to South Nashville. My son said,

"Dad you can't even cut grass without something happening." Well, Joe Joe that's the way life is sometimes, when it rains it pours. Just another day and another incident to report. This young man did not deserve to be beaten, they could have just taken his money without beating him up and throwing him out of the car.

This young man contacted me several weeks later at work and he said that the Detectives had caught the 2 boys that had taken his money and thrown him out of the car.

He also told me that his injuries were healing and again he wanted to thank me and my son for helping him. I told him that if he wanted to testify about what I had witnessed to just give me a call. It was good to hear that his injuries were minor and healing well.

My oldest son Joe Joe, said that I was his Hero. I guess it was good for my son to witness this incident, they know I will help anybody anytime if they are in trouble. I try to set a good example for my kids.

Angel On My Shoulder

By being in Law Enforcement you never know what you might get involved in and I'm not afraid to offer my assistance to anyone who needs help.

Angel On My Shoulder

POLICEMEN CAN ALWAYS SCREW UP

How about the time that two Motorcycle Officer used the Departments cycles and rode to Gatlinburg with their girlfriends sitting on behind them on the bikes. This was a weekend of R & R. No one saw them, not the News Media, Supervisors or a Politician.

These motorcycles were Police Department issue. I was told they used black electrician's tape to cover up the Departments lettering and numbers. They left Friday evening and returned Sunday afternoon. This is not a shit house rumor because one of the guys did tell me the same story on more than one occasion. He died several years later in an Automobile accident.

Now here's a good one. How about the time a Detective was having an extra marital affair with a Motorcycle Officer's wife. The Traffic Policeman saw the Detective's Corvette parked in his driveway one day. He took the garden hose and put the end of it in
the Corvette's window, turned on the water and drove off. They were divorced shortly after that. The Detective had a heart attack a few years later and unfortunately he did not survive.

Whenever tourists see a couple of Police Cruisers or Motorcycles parked at a Restaurant, they think the food is excellent because the Police are eating there. NOT TRUE, The reason the Police are eating there is because, the   is half price or free to Law Enforcement Officers. I believe that Police would eat just about anything if it was FREE. The fried foods that the Police indulge in are certainly not good for you.

That is why most Officers have blockages in their arties, with all the greasy foods, doughnut's, pizza, hamburgers and fries and whatever else is free or half price. I know from experience on this subject because four years after retiring from the Police Department, I had a Stent placed in my left circumflex heart artery that had a 90% blockage. But, the food sure was good. I would order a sack of Krystal hamburgers and eat the whole dozen at a time and when I went over to my girlfriend, Patsy's house, I'd pass a lot of gas that ran her out of the bedroom gasping for breath. I also had the same results when I ate 3 big Beefy sandwiches prior to going home. I would raise the cover over her head and pop out another one. Damn, Joe it sounds like you are lighting firecrackers. She told me one more time and you sleep on the couch. I bet she really didn't mean it, because she would come back to bed and we would cuddle up.

Little did I know, that later in life all the stress and excitement of this job along with the greasy and fatty foods, would cause me to have a triple by-pass. I had 5 arteries that were blocked 90 per cent, but the Doctor tandemed two of them (Whatever that means).

This was a rough operation. This was really an ordeal to go through and at times I didn't think I was going to get over it, but I did. At one point I told Patsy to please just let me die.
I think I was in the Hospital 7 or 8 days, but I'm not sure. Patsy stayed with me the whole time and never went home. She brought enough clothes to last a week so that she would always be by my side.

Those greasy burgers with cheese and onions sure did taste good. OUCH!!!

We have changed our eating habits. I'm getting a little older now, but I am still a fighter and I know that there are things I need to do for my family.

It is hard to change ones eating habits, but if you want to live longer it is worth it. As for doughnuts, pies, french-fries, juicy hamburgers it is a thing of the past, especially the doughnuts.

Angel On My Shoulder

POISON IVY

We lived in Antioch and there was a 7/11 store 2 doors up from us on a corner lot. One night Joe Joe, my oldest son and I drove into the parking lot of the 7/11 to purchase some Poison Ivy Lotion. The kids at Antioch called this place the "OK Corral."

When we entered the store they man told us they were just robbed by 2 white males that drove off in an older Chevy with 4 doors and the car had no hubcaps. I was driving my personal car, which was a Chevy Vega Station Wagon. I headed north on Tusculum Rd. and right onto Nolensville Rd.

I drove towards town and as we passed Harding, I noticed a black Chevy with 4 white males inside turning right onto Nolensville Rd. I pulled in behind them, I was in my personal car, no radio and no emergency lights. I was thinking that this was a big mistake if anything goes wrong. The car pulled into a driveway and I pulled in behind them. I gave my pistol to Joe Joe and said if I get shot, start shooting. Just as one of the suspects got out of the car Joe Joe yelled, dad I go to school with those guys.

I walked up to the car showing my Badge and telling the young men who I was. I explained what had happened and they said they had just eaten at IHOP and was headed home. I quickly glanced down at the wheels and the hubcaps were on the tires, so I knew that this was not the car. We shook hands and I wished them the best in their upcoming ball game this weekend.

I got back into my car and told Joe, I made a really bad decision. I said, "these mistakes will get a person killed."

Well Joe Joe I said, "Back to the store for that lotion again."

Angel On My Shoulder

STOLEN TROPHIES

One afternoon, my Aunt who lives on Oakhill Drive in East Nashville called and she seemed very upset. I told her to calm down and tell me what happened. I knew something was wrong, but she wasn't making any sense. She was so upset. When she finally calmed down enough, she asked me if I would come by after work. I asked her if she was alright, she replied it isn't me. Then I got to wondering if something had happened to my dad. He lived in the basement of her house. My aunt said, I really do hope that you can come by, because I need some suggestions about something. OK, I said I'll be there as soon as I get off from work. I was working at the Training Academy at the time and I had a class to teach.

When I arrived at my Aunt's house she told me that her house had been burglarized. She said that the Police had just left and she told them what had happened and that they had given me a complaint number. I told her not to worry; I'll get you a copy of it. She said (brother, that is what I was called me when I was young and I am still called Brother by most members of my family).

I asked her what was stolen. She then told me that Joe's trophies were stolen along with other items. Joe is my Aunt Annette's brother and she loved him dearly. She seemed to be his

protector. This is also my father and he was responsible for me playing Golf. My Aunt added that dad's upright Golf Trophies were not taken, but the ones which were the silver trays are the ones that were taken. I asked her, how did they get in. She said through the basement door. I went downstairs to check on the door and I secured it for her with a piece of plywood that was in her storage area of the basement. They had broken out a small pane in

Angel On My Shoulder

the door so that they could just reach in and open the door.

I told her this Wednesday night would be a good night for the thieves to strike again, because it's Church night. I told her that we would park our cars several houses down and she would leave the porch light on to give the appearance that no one was home.

I said, you and dad can sit in the den and do not turn, I mean do not turn on the TV, Radio or any lights. I explained to her that another Lieutenant would be with me and we would be sitting on the steps that led down to the basement just waiting for the burglar or burglar's to enter. You know that they will probably come through the basement door just like before. The basement door was at the back of the house and there was nothing but dense growth of bushes and trees that lined the back of her yard. I remember every inch of it, I had cut her yard many, many times and I knew where every hole was.

On Wednesday another Lieutenant and I went to my Aunt's house and we moved the cars down the street and walked back to my Aunt's house. We walked around back and went through the basement door. We locked the door from inside. It seemed like forever that we were just sitting on those steps. I asked my partner, does this seem familiar? How so, Joe? You know, like when we went on stake outs while in Patrol.

The house was totally dark and my dad and Aunt were upstairs being real quiet. I was armed with a .38 cal. revolver and I think that Bill had the same firepower. We just sat there waiting. We had handcuffs, flashlight and High Hopes for a capture. 9:30 P.M. came and we decided to call it quits. We moved the automobiles back and left. The burglars had either realized that was nothing else to get or they were scared off by who knows what.

Angel On My Shoulder

About one week later the South Station called and notified me that a tray with Joe McEwen's name engraved on the Tray was found inside a dumpster behind the South Station.

This was the only item that was ever found. There are several Apartment Buildings behind the South Station, but anyone could have thrown the Tray in there.

Criminals are very mobile when it comes to crime. Automobiles make anywhere accessible to criminal activity. I always expressed to a New Rookie to constantly check cars for any violation, making a Traffic stop is so important and when you have to apprehending someone you always need to be alert of your surroundings. I also instilled into them that you never know who a person is and you have to be alert on every call.

Angel On My Shoulder

EVALUATIONS GIVEN TO McEWEN

WHILE HE WAS AT THE TRAINING ACADEMY

These Evaluations were given to Joe McEwen by his ranking Superior's while he was at the Training Academy.

1-1-1975 to 1-1- 1976 / Officer Joe McEwen has executed his Police Instructor duties without constant direct Supervision. He never hesitates to work past his regular working hours when it is necessary. His personal relations with his fellow workers are without criticism.

Officer McEwen is a loyal, dedicated Police Officer and a credit tour Department. He never complains about his work load regardless of its size. He is an example that all young Officers can look up to and set their standards by.   **Rated by Lt. S. Peach

1-1-1976 to 1-1- 1977 / Officer McEwen is one of the most dedicated Officers in the Metro Police Department. He would be outstanding in any position given to him by the Chief. There will never be anyone more dedicated to serving mankind than Officer McEwen.

**Rated by Lt. Dozier

1-1-1977 to 1-7-1978 / Sergeant McEwen is the type Officer who supervises by setting the example. An example exemplary performance. His years of street experience prove an invaluable aid for him to draw upon instructing both Recruit and In-Service Personnel. The example he sets for Recruit

Angel On My Shoulder

Trainees is without doubt of extremely high quality and often results in "Hero Worship" by the Recruits. He is not afraid of hard work and his dedication to his Department and this Academy is of an unquestionable high caliber. I am proud to have Sgt. McEwen work with me at the Academy. **Rated by Lt. John Ross

1-1-1978 to 1-1-1979 / Sergeant McEwen has continued to perform in the exemplary manner of his last evaluation period. He has instructed both In-Service and Recruit level training programs and has demonstrated his superior qualities by receiving the highest marks from student critiques. He has supervised the Recruit Classes and has done an outstanding job. His performance on the M.U.S.T. team under trying circumstances has proven to be of the very highest quality. I am indeed fortunate to have such an employee under my supervision.   **Rated by Lt. John Ross

1-1-1979 to 1-1-1980 / Sergeant McEwen has continued to perform in an exceptional manner during this evaluation period. During this period, he has supervised a Recruit Class and instructed In-Service training. His attitude, performance and work out-put exemplified him as a true professional. His willingness to take on additional tasks and assignments and his resultant performance are among his strongest traits. He has continued his professional development by attending a 40 hour seminar on Officer survival given by Northwestern University. He continues to perform street police work at every possible chance even though he is assigned to an administrative job. He is a real asset to this Academy and to this Department, showing a high degree of professionalism by example. **Rated by Lt. John Ross

1-1-1980 to 1-1-1981 / Sergeant McEwen has performed in an exceptional manner during this evaluation period. He has been Operations Sergeant for a Recruit class and has instructed   in both Recruit and In-Service Training. His attitude concerning

Angel On My Shoulder

getting the job done in the most professional manner, no matter what effort is called for, is this man's strongest point. His ability

to maintain rapport with the respect of the street Police Officer of this Department allows the Academy to maintain a good image and working relationship with all other divisions of the

Department. He is indeed a credit to the Department, and the Academy, demonstrating the highest degree of professionalism. **Rated by Lt. John Ross

7-1-1982 to1-1- 1983 / Upon Lieutenant McEwen's promotion, he was assigned the responsibility of overseeing contemporary research into innovative programs at the Police Academy.

He has had significant input in this area. He is currently conducting research into Motorcycle gangs and their criminal behavior

patterns for presentation to In-Service and other training programs

next year. He continues to be a valuable instructor, with excellent rapport with all ranks and levels within the Department. He

cheerfully and diligently takes on any assignment given him.

He is a credit to the superior Officer ranks of the Department. **Rated by Lt. John Ross

7-1-1982 to 7-1-1983 / Lieutenant McEwen continues to do an excellent Job instructing personnel of this Department during their training. He undertakes each assignment with a personal commitment to produce a professional quality work product.

**Rated by Capt. John Ross

Angel On My Shoulder

CHANGE IS GOOD

After being at the Training Academy for 11 years, I felt a need for a change. I had talked with Foster Hite and he wanted to leave Traffic and go to the Vice Section. Foster stated that he was tired of riding a motorcycle. I went to see Captain Ross and I discussed this move with him. The Captain did not want me to leave because, he said that he needed someone like me to rely on. He added, you are one of the men here at the Training Academy that I can tell what needs to be done and I don't have to follow behind you to see that my orders were obeyed. Joe, as you know Supervisors don't like to lose personnel like you. I know that I can trust you with anything. You will be hard to replace. I'll see what can be done in the next few months.

At this time my marriage was going downhill and I definitely needed a change. I talked with Foster and he said that he would ask around and see if he could get us transferred to CID.

Joe, if I can get there and you follow or you go first and I follow maybe we can get the Biker Unit going full time. This had always been a goal of mine and Fosters. Even while I was at the Training Academy, Foster would give me a call if he had stopped some Bikers and asked me did I have information on this particular bunch? Sometimes if I was not busy at the Academy, I would get a camera and go meet him and take pictures and help him run the VIN numbers and run backgrounds on the suspects.

When I left the Training Academy on December 1, 1985 the personnel at the Training Academy gave me a going away party. They also presented me with a nice Plaque thanking me for my dedicated Service at the Academy from 1974 to 1985. This plaque hangs on my wall in my home along with all the other Awards that I have received over the years with the Police Department. There

Angel On My Shoulder

was plenty of food. We all just talked about the things that we had accomplished at the Academy and the good times that we had.

Foster and I got transferred to CID in the Auto Theft Division. We were there only a Short time when we were transferred to the Vice Section. Vice is where we were put into the Gambling and Prostitution Section. We started with just the two of us and soon we had a third man by the name of Steve Garton. We worked well together and the Arrest's started adding up.

During a two year period the three of us had made 3,210 arrests. We gave the Assistant Chief what he wanted and that was results.

Angel On My Shoulder

Crofton, Kentucky   1948   I was just 12 years old when
my Cocker Spaniel dog died in a house fire. He always
stayed by my side.

Angel On My Shoulder

NAVY   BOOT CAMP, Great Lakes, Illinois.

Angel On My Shoulder

BEACH AT NORFOLK, VA
I WAS 20 YEARS OLD

Angel On My Shoulder

Empire

State Building

New York 1953

Observation

Angel On My Shoulder

At the Training Academy I was showing the recruits how to run with the 100 lb sack of sand over their shoulder. A lot of it is leverage and upper body strength. It took them a while to master the skill.

Angel On My Shoulder

TRAINING ACADEMY -The Color Guard in front of Police Headquarters.

Left to right –Sgt. R. Briggance –Sgt. Joe McEwen Jr. –Officer Tim Durham – Officer K. Pence –Officer K. Barnes –Sgt. J. Manning –Officer P. Sutton –Lt. Tom Dozier

Angel On My Shoulder

TRAINING ACADEMY

Academy and going to CID

Party given to McEwen, leaving the

Auto Theft

Angel On My Shoulder

VICE -A Motorcycle Officer on Interstate 24 for Improper Placement of License Tag. I checked his arms for Tattoos. He was from Miami, Florida. He wanted to know how to get to a
certain Chapter House. He was surprised to find out that I knew where it was?

Angel On My Shoulder

A working girl

Angel On My Shoulder

VICE   Complaint about a Massage Parlor.
They had all their papers, etc. I wrote them a
ticket for failure to display signs.

Angel On My Shoulder

TRAINING ACADEMY
Trophy given to Officer McEwen by the Recruit Class
OFFICER JOE "JUMPING JACK MAC" McEWEN
FOR MOST JUMPING JACKS DURING
ONE P.T. SESSION   534
SESSION 5

Angel On My Shoulder

Angel On My Shoulder

VICE   ATF Raid on a Chapter House They asked me if I wanted to come, I said YES.

VICE   I received a call about a Booth at a Carnival.

Angel On My Shoulder

Meeting Evel Knievel in Clearwater, Florida

Angel On My Shoulder

PURPLE HEART AWARD - February 27, 2002 – Metropolitan Police

Department -Nashville, Tn. Left to Right: Acting Chief of Police Deborah Faulkner over Uniformed Services. My Wife Patsy and Retired Lt. Joe T. McEwen Jr.

Angel On My Shoulder

TRA AWARD

Angel On My Shoulder

Retired Lt. Joe T. McEwen Jr., talking with
Chief of Police Steve Anderson

and Judge J. Randall Wyatt Jr. at the TRA
Award Ceremony.

Angel On My Shoulder

The 2011
Theodore Roosevelt Association
Police Award
September 1, 2011

My wife, Patsy and myself at the Theodore Roosevelt Award. This is truly an emotional day for me as I accepted this Award. There were a lot of old friends there and each one had a favorite story to tell.

My oldest son Joe McEwen III, made a speech for me to receive the Theodore Roosevelt Association Police Award. Behind him was Mr. David Davoudpour

and my wife Patsy.

Angel On My Shoulder

CID / AUTO THEFT TO VICE

Foster and myself were finally transferred to CID in the Auto Theft Division at Headquarters. This was totally different for us; Foster usually just roamed the streets looking for violators and I was an Instructor at the Training Academy.

We felt like we were being used anytime someone wasn't available to do some mundane task or didn't want to and since we were the new kids on the block we caught all the shit details.

On one particular slow day and we were in the Office at 7:15 AM, just talking with our feet upon the desk. The Captain came into the Office and asked, do you put your feet on the furniture at home? No disrespect Captain, but I do and I piss in the sink if it is not full of dishes. He said, "OK smart ass you two go to Louisville to pick up a prisoner in the Jefferson County Jail."

Approximately at 1:15 PM we were in our Office talking when the Captain came in, and said in a hateful tone, "I'm not paying you assholes overtime to go to Louisville and bring a prisoner back." Some of the guys in the Office started laughing out loud. The Captain said, "what is so damn funny?" I looked at the Captain and told him that the Prisoner was in our Jail and if you don't mind, we would like to go get a bite to eat before our next assignment.

"You can't drive to Louisville and back in 4 hours." I replied, "Well you can if you drive the way we drive!"

We didn't tell him that we drove fast and we also got on the CB and talked to the truck driver's on the way there and that we were on our way to pick up a Prisoner for killing a truck driver.

Angel On My Shoulder

The responses from the Truck Driver's was always 10 – 4 Good Buddy and have a safe trip and they cleared the way for us whenever they could.

The Captain said "get out of here and I'll see you tomorrow." The next few days he was rather cool toward us. We just went out and rode the streets and made some arrests and we didn't have to listen to his sarcastic remarks. The Captain never asked us to Transport another prisoner.

My partner had talked to an Asst. Chief about going to Vice. I did not know about this until my partner came to me and said, Hey Joe guess what? I said I have no idea what you are talking about. You know I told you I was going to see the Asst. Chief about going to Vice. Yeah so what. Well I talked to him and I think we have a pretty good chance of going up there. Damn, how did you pull this off? I'll never tell. But we have to be quite about this until it is final. OK, by me. I can keep my mouth shut. Yeah right was my partners reply.

The very next week the Captain in CID came to us and said get your stuff together you two have been transferred to VICE. You're somebody else's problem now. It was hard to keep a straight face, but we did. We told him how we hated to leave CID. I know he didn't believe us and why should he. He made it sound like it was all his doings. NOT SO.

After going upstairs to the Vice Section we felt like we could breathe. Everyone worked together and seemed like one big unit. Thank God for small favors. This was the start of something big. We made a name for ourselves. After roll call we would hit the streets and in no time we were on our way to the Booking Room with someone that we had arrested. After going to Booking and filling out all of the paper work then we would hit the streets again for another arrest.

Angel On My Shoulder

They seem to come easy on some nights and again some of these girls like to fight, in hopes that they could get away. Their need for a fix is very strong and few of these women could ever break these bonds from the lure of the drugs and fast money.

But they always went to Jail. Our Moto was "You not get away." I had one girl who had on a denim jacket one night when I placed her under arrest. I grabbed the jacket lapel and she did a 180 and peeled out of her jacket in a split second, dragging me out the passenger's door. She was caught and when I look at these females, I think of overtime. Cha Ching!

The Prostitutes were not our only target. On day after getting to work, I got a call from a citizen about a complaint at a Carnival. She stated that there was something fishy going on.

I asked her to explain, she said that she didn't know what was going on but she did see a man give one of the booth operators a small sack. She stated that it was probably money inside.

I told her that we would look into it and I thanked her for calling. I told Foster about the conversation that I had with this woman and he said, "Ok let's go." Foster was never one to sit still, he had to be in the thick of things. We went to the Carnival and just observed some of the booths. We did not see anything suspicious and after talking with one of the booth operators we decided that this was just a lady that had been watching too many TV shows.

I heard one Assistant Chief say that when those men go out, you know someone is going to Jail. They are like a Force to be reckoned with. They have drive and they do their job well. I have no problem with them. They also make the Supervisor look good with all statistics they turn in. They do their paperwork and keep a running list of all of their arrests. Sometimes they get a double bubble when someone has outstanding Warrants. I don't know

Angel On My Shoulder

where they get their energy, but they always seem upbeat and ready to hit the streets.

It wasn't long after being in Vice that the other Officer's had a nickname for our very very effective Prostitution Squad. It was called the "Pussy Posse".

Angel On My Shoulder

PATSY

I kept thinking about my special nurse, Patsy wondering if we would ever cross paths again. My wife and I had gotten a divorce and I had all three children to take care of. Taking them to school, picking them up in the afternoon, washing clothes and fixing meals was a grind especially while I was working 40 plus hours a week. I am a fighter and I won't be beaten down.

I knew that there is more to life than just going to work, taking care of my kids. But, I am their dad and they depend on me to be there for them.

I was working at Headquarters now and I usually stopped at Shoney's on some mornings to just relax a bit and drink a cup of coffee before going to work. As I was leaving I saw, yeah right, I saw Patsy. She was by herself eating breakfast. I sat down at her table and just looked her in the eyes and asked her, do you remember me? She said of course I do Mighty Mouse. Patsy where have you been? I have been trying to find you for the longest. Well, I couldn't be a nurse any longer, when someone came into the ER all bloody and hurt real bad,

I would think about you Mighty Mouse and I couldn't do it anymore, it hurt too badly. I had given you my phone number and my address. I guess you lost it.

Patsy said that she had moved back in with her mom and dad for a while, but she felt too cramped in her parents' house and that she really wanted some freedom. So, she got a small house that she could really relax in after getting off from work. I just wanted to be by myself, she said. I told her that "I could understand that."

Angel On My Shoulder

Have you got time to talk for a while Joe or do you have to go to work now? Oh yeah, I have time to talk. What have you been doing Patsy? Well, I started working for Castner-Knott at Rivergate Mall, just as a sales clerk and then I was made a Manager over 6 departments. It kept me busy alright, but it was so far to drive and I was working 60 to 75 hours a week on a fixed salary that didn't go too far. It was rough. I was then transferred to Harding Mall where I worked for 3 more years. The first day that I worked there my 1956 Chevy was stolen from the back parking lot and it was never recovered. My dad had reworked the entire car from front to back and had it painted Candy Apple Red. So it was a Total Loss for both of us. I had always wanted a 1956 Chevy that was painted Candy Apple Red. Well at least I had it for one day.

The Police Officer that took the report said, that a man named Rabbit had probably taken it. The Officer also stated that Rabbit had been known to take a lot of cars from this area.

I could not please the Store Manager, he was a little guy, and well he sort of looked like Danny DeVito. He was always finding some kind of a lame excuse with my work. It was hard having 6 departments and trying to keep the track all the inventory and all the paper work was required of me.

Stop Patsy, stop just a minute. You still look like the woman that made my recovery go by fast and to this day I can't get you out of my mind. Damn it's good to finally see you.

It's good to see you too Mighty Mouse, I often wondered how your recovery came out. Did you ever have the bullet taken out. Yeah, Dr. Foster took it out three months after I left the Hospital. It started hurting real bad. He told me that he only made a 10" scar this time. Do you remember the 22" scar I had and that someone would and rub Vitamin E on it? I sure do, so what was the outcome of the long scar. Well, I still have it and I guess I always

Angel On My Shoulder

will. It is a good reminder of what you shouldn't do as a Police Officer. What's that Joe, she asked? I responded saying, you wait for back-up before you go gung ho.

As much as I would love to stay, I've got to get to work. Give me your number and I'll give you a call. You know Patsy, I never noticed your uniform until now. She replied, I work in Central Records on the day shift. I really like it, it's a little hectic sometimes, but I had rather stay busy. It makes the time go by faster. I'll give you a call. See you later Mighty Mouse. I love the sound of that name you gave to me Patsy, but I have got to go. See ya later.

Driving to the Headquarters, I just couldn't tell her that I had remarried. But the only reason I got married again was I needed some help with my three kids, but at the same time I acquired 2 more boys.

Only if I had tried harder to find her. She really made me feel good about myself. Oh well you never know what the future will bring. Maybe someday, yeah maybe someday.

One day I was driving up 2nd Avenue and I saw Janice and Patsy walking down the side walk. I pulled my car up next to them and asked them if they wanted a threesome. Janice said, McEwen, go to work. I drove off thinking about Patsy.

My wife and I weren't getting along now; everything was about her and her boys. I knew I had to make a change. About four months later she filed for a Divorce, I had moved from our house and onto some land that I had purchased for myself and my boys. I had a two bedroom Trailer put on the land. There was more work than I thought it would be. My boys always had something else to do, so I did most of the work on the land by myself. I didn't mind it because it gave me time to think about everything that was going

Angel On My Shoulder

on in my life. Damn,it was good to see Patsy again, it really gives me hope for a happier life. My Angel is still watching over me.

I was working the day shift and after going to court I went to Personnel to change my address. Surprise, surprise, Patsy was now working in Personnel. I pulled up small garbage can that was next to her desk and sat on it and gave her the information on my new address. I kept running my hand up and down her arm. After I signed the papers I left and went back downstairs to CID. I called Payroll which was right next to Personnel and asked her if she thought Patsy would go out with me. She did not know that I had known Patsy from the time that I was shot in 1970 and that she was a nurse that took very good care of me. Janice went over and asked Patsy if she would like to go out and eat with me. Patsy told her, she didn't know. "Well you see he's a nice guy, he's just had a bit of bad luck lately."

About 15 minutes later I called her and asked me to go out to supper with him. She said, "how would you like a home cooked meal." Fine with me, what time do you want me to come over? She said, "how about 7 PM." I told her "I'll be there with bells on." I couldn't wait to get off from work to go see her. I had to pinch myself to see if I was dreaming or what.

When I got to Patsy's house it was about 6:30 PM, she was still cooking and damn it smelt good. I had to hug her and give her a big kiss. It was just like old times, the feeling was still there. I had to tell her that I had remarried, but I also said that I was getting a divorce. It seemed that there was just too much confusion in the house and I couldn't take it anymore. She planted another big kiss on me and I knew this is what I wanted. After eating she washed the

dishes and then I told her, "well don't you think it is time to go to bed? We have to get up early to go to work tomorrow."

Angel On My Shoulder

I awoke to the smell of bacon cooking. She made biscuits and eggs and the best coffeeI had ever tasted. I told her, "you know we can't let anyone know about this, because like I said I'm in the process of getting a divorce." She said, "no problem."

I couldn't wait to get off from work to head back over to her house. Again, she had started supper and it was all that a man could ask for. We sat on the couch and watched TV until the 10 o'clock News was over. We were on the opposite ends of the couch with our legs entwined and we drifted off to sleep.

Day by day I moved more and more of my things over to her house. We both seemed to enjoy each other's company and I realized that she was a full blown tomboy. She could swing a hammer and work with a shovel. She didn't mind getting dirty and I think she enjoyed being with me as much as I with her.

I told her that I did not want to get married and she said that was OK with her. I told her that my track record with marriages was not to good and that I had walked out on every marriage that I had. I told her that even a dog likes to get patted on the head every once in a while. She came towards me and patted my head and then laid a juicy kiss on my lips. It was just like when I was in the Hospital and you came to see me. You know Joe, I knew from the first day I saw you in the ER that something just clicked inside me and I had lways hoped that I would see you again. "Well here I am," I replied.

The first thing I did was get rid of her double bed. We purchased a king size mattress. I built a stationary base with a headboard. I told Patsy this bed will stand the test of time and

it will not move all over the bedroom. I looked at her and said; "Rock and Roll is in my soul."

"Ok," she replied, "so let's give it a whirl."

Angel On My Shoulder

We built a large Dutch Barn type in the back yard. It was 24' long and 12' wide. I had to have space to put all of my tools.

We started working on the land that I had on Cane Ridge Road, cutting trees and adding onto the trailer that I had put on the land. We worked well together. This was the first woman that had worked beside me and knew what she was doing.

In August of 1986, I finally got a divorce from my wife. I rushed home to Patsy to tell her the good news. At last I think I can finally be happy and not to worry about me being married any more. Six years of Alimony wasn't what I wanted, but at least I could see the end.

Six years later when the Alimony was over, she shot herself and died. I hated this because her youngest son was home at the time this happened. This was a sad ending to her life, I really hated it because her two boys did love her.

Things seemed to be on the right track now. I feel better than I have in a long time about being with a woman. We worked together instead of trying to outdo each other. I think I have finally found my soul mate.

Angel On My Shoulder

JUVENILES AND LSD

My girlfriend's automobile was in the repair shop and she asked me for a ride home one day, I told her as soon as I got through with roll call, I would take her home.

I was assigned to the Vice Section at this time and I knew it would only take a few minutes as Patsy just lived 4 miles from Headquarters.

As I drove through Shelby Park I thought I may as well drive through the Lake area because this is where underage drinking and drugs were prevalent from time to time. As I pulled into the graveled parking area beside the Lake. I noticed a car with 3 people standing next to the vehicle. Two young girls and a young male. As I approached the subject's, I was in my unmarked Vice car and they did not suspect anything. My girlfriend got out of the car to look at the ducks and at that time I got out and walked behind my car, only to see the male put something on the top of the back tire. I acted like I didn't see him and I managed to get closer to him before he sensed something was awry.

When I approached him, I identified myself by pulling my badge out from under my shirt. I told him to "Give me some ID and you girls also." He opened his billfold and took out his license showing them to me and covering the lower right part with his thumb, as if he was hiding something. I reached and yanked the license out of his hand and noticed two small (blotter type) miniature dolphins on his license. I knew this was not right and went back to my car and radioed another Vice Officer and told him what I had found. The Vice Officer said, "Joe, whatever you do don't touch those blotter stamps because it is LSD and it can be absorbed into your body if it touches your skin." This would make a person hallucinate and become lethargic and they would do things that were not normal, sometimes they would just start screaming and running wild.

I then called for a marked unit for back-up and to transport the male subject. I approached the vehicle again arrested the subject and told the two underage girls that I was going to issue them a citation for underage drinking and that Junior was going to jail. They tried to say that the beer wasn't there's, but I said, "can you tell me why it was beside your feet." But how are we going to get home? I told them that I would call their parents and wait for them to arrive. They begged me not to call their parents, but I had no choice. I could not leave them alone because they were under age and it was starting to get dark.

My back up arrived to transport the male subject and a wrecker arrived shortly to take his auto to the tow in lot. The girl's parents arrived in about 15 minutes later and were not happy at all when I showed them the beer cans and the 2 LSD Blotters. One parent said, just wait until we get home and you will wish that you had never seen that boy. Also you are grounded. The other girl's parents said about the same thing. The girls were there and watched the car being towed.

I thought that this would give them a taste of reality.
I told Patsy, "this is a good way to start my shift, one arrest, three citations, one car impounded and I put a financial hardship on the male with the LSD. I probably saved those two girls from who knows what?

Angel On My Shoulder

UNMARKED CARS

Our unmarked cars had emergency lights installed behind the grill, to disguise the Blue glass lens, we took a pair of pantyhose and cut the lower part off and pulled them over the blue lights. This made the lights very hard to see from the front of the auto. We had the Police radio installed in the glove box. We locked it so that the prostitutes could not open it up to see if we were Vice. However, it was also a disadvantage for the undercover cop to radio for help because when a fight ensues inside the car, it puts us at a very big disadvantage trying to unlock the glove box while someone is trying to scratch your eyes out or biting your arm, especially if she weighs 180 lbs.

The most dangerous time for a vice cop is when the suspect is placed under arrest inside the car. This is when the confrontation really begins. Most of the hookers have a drug habit. They know if they are arrested – no drugs for one or two days. They become wild, start kicking, fighting, or even try jump out of the car doing 30 miles per hour, screaming rape or trying to kick the ignition key out or breaking it off. Grabbing the steering wheel trying to cause a wreck, scratch, claw, bite or reaching for a knife or box cutter in their bra. Also threaten the vice officer with a used hypodermic needle or anything else to avoid going to jail. The women are more prone to fight than a man, because these prostitutes know that a Policeman will not hit

them unless it is necessary. A bruised female going before a Magistrate would not look too good, unless there was more than one Officer making the arrest. Although some of them can fight harder than a man. Most of the time we just try to overpower them long enough to handcuff them.

Even then they will try to spit on you and sometimes try to kick you in the groin or shins. I learned real soon how fast a handcuffed prostitute could run when panic sets in. Whenever possible I would ease my auto inches beside a parked vehicle to keep the female from opening the door to escape. If the window was down it would not keep her from trying to climb out or start screaming rape. A wild female is harder to control on any arrest.

Many times they nut out. On one incident I arrested a female who weighed about 180 lbs. She was not just big, but she was strong and a fight ensued. As usual Foster was close by and he rushed to the passenger's side of the car to assist me in cuffing the suspect. I was in a Monte Carlo and during the struggle the female put her feet on the dashboard pushing back on the seat trying to keep from getting handcuffed. It takes a tremendous amount of force to break the front seat. Two door automobiles front seat are easier to break because they fold forward for access to the rear seat.

Damn these women really get violent when they know that they are going to jail, especially when they are from Memphis. The females from Memphis are the worst; some of them are small but tough as nails, but they can fight, the larger ones are really harder to control and they love to fight and fight dirty. Even our local girls stay out of their way.

We see the Memphis girls mostly on the weekends. The girls and their Pimps stay downtown. There is always a lot of activity downtown on the weekends. Also there are a lot of famous bars where the single guys hang out looking for a one quickie. We are in full force when these girls are in town and we usually have our hands full. When we arrest them within an hour they are back out on the streets of downtown Nashville. Their Pimps have the cash to post their bond's real quick. The only bad thing is, they rarely ever show up for Court. So when we catch them again, it is double the charges and they don't get a Pass To Get Out Of Jail

Angel On My Shoulder

Quick because of a previous no show and they are unable to make bond.

Angel On My Shoulder

BUS STOP INCIDENT

My partner Foster and I made an arrest for prostitution and placed the female suspect in the back of our unmarked car. We were headed for the Prisoner processing driving North on 5th Avenue.

As we approached Church Street we stopped for a Red Light adjacent to a Bus Station covered shelter. Our windows were down and standing in the shelter stood a male white, wearing a tee shirt, jeans and tennis shoes. I casually looked to my right in the general direction of the Bus shelter and the suspect said, "What are you looking at you queer pussy asshole."

Foster and I jumped from the car simultaneously and ran to the Bus shelter. I arrived first and grabbed the drunk man by his shirt, he drew back his fist as to hit me. I yanked him forward ripping the neck part of his shirt and also tearing the tee shirt about ten inches. I said, "Who the hell are you calling a queer, you shit for brains?" He lunged towards me again and struck me in the chest. About this time Foster tried to get the subject under control by hitting the drunk subject in the head with his pistol.

The suspect screamed a loud high sound, grabbed his head and broke and ran North and then right on Church Street with no shirt on. I had his shirt in my hand as he broke free from my grip. We looked at each other and I said, "Let's get out of here, now!"

This is what happens when the drunks get enough joy juice in them and they think that they are superior to anyone. We thought the drunk recognized us because we had arrested him for Public Drunk and causing a scene in one of the Bars on Broadway a few weeks prior to this incident tonight. When they sober up they are pretty decent to talk to and sometimes they tell funny stories. But this doesn't happen that often.

Driving to headquarters the arrested female in the back seat stated she did not see nothing. I told her to keep it that way and I would help her out when her case came up. When her case did come up, I had already spoken with the DA telling her that this girl had given me some

Angel On My Shoulder

information on a robbery case that I was working and when we went before the Judge , he said case dismissed.

A couple of days later a plain clothes Detective came up to me and said, "Hey Lieutenant,

I was turning left onto 5th Avenue North last Thursday night and saw 2 men roughing up some loud mouth white male at the Bus shelter on 5th Avenue." He said, "I looked the other way and immediately turned on 5th Ave. North and Church Street to distance myself from the disturbance ." You know Lieutenant the two men had an uncanny resemblance to you and your partner. In fact the truth of the matter is they looked like your twins.

I replied, "Well you know we get that a lot, especially at night." "Yeah, I guess you guys do," he added.

Lieutenant, I wish you would do me one small favor. I said, "yeah what's that?" Would you please tell me what section of town that you and your partner will be working this week so I can stay the hell away from that area. I replied, "I'll send you a memo as soon as I get back to
the Office." If, that is OK with you. You know I don't know how the two of you make all the arrests that you do. Well, you see it's just good luck. The both of you seem to make more arrests than any other twosome in the Department. "Well, what I can I say," was my reply.

My partner Foster and I just walked off and started up the steps to the Vice Office to regroup and map out the area that we wanted to hit tonight. I know why we make so many arrests. It's because we hit the streets running and we let no one get away. At times it's easy as shooting fish in a barrel. Other times it's like trying to ride a wild bull. Usually when we arrest someone they have several outstanding warrants, that we serve on them also.

When we leave the Vice Office we knew that someone was going to jail. On the other hand when Foster was late for roll call, I knew that he was either writing a ticket or locking someone up.

We had no sooner left the Vice Office that we spotted a Red car that we had stopped numerous time before for picking up a Prostitute. We stopped him and he immediately said, "Oh no, not you again Joe. I was just giving her a ride, she is my cousin."

Angel On My Shoulder

"Yeah right and I'm a tooth fairy." Joe, I know I ran the Stop sign. I said, "I'm going to give you a Ticket and you had better show up for Court. I know this car and I will be seeing you again. What is your wife going to say about this." I'll just tell her like I always do, I was stupid and I didn't stop at a Stop Sign.

As for Foster Hite, I always said that he was an one-man army. When he worked Traffic he wrote a lot of Violations and one year he wrote over four thousand tickets. While I was at the Training Academy, Foster would come to me and give me information of the Biker gangs in Nashville. This was because in one of my classes that I taught was about Biker Gang locations and their activities. I knew that Foster had as much interest into the Biker Gangs as I did. We made a great team, and it seemed as though we knew what the other was going to do.

We always had each other's back.

We received a call about a Massage Parlor that was open on Dickerson Road. When we arrived, I knew the lady that was the owner, she used to be on Murfreesboro Road. She stated that the Pimps were wanting her to pay them off, so she decided to move to the Dickerson Road area. She did not have her operating license, so I gave her a Citation. She has always supplied Foster and I with information from time to time. She's just trying to get the girl's off the streets.

She said that she was a prostitute at one time and she knew all the pit falls of being on the streets.

As soon as we hit the streets again, we saw another subject that we had arrested before regarding Prostitution. They just don't learn. Another one bites the dust!!!! Cha Ching!

Angel On My Shoulder

LADIES ON THE STREETS

In my unmarked Monte Carlo Vice car (most of the girls knew us by now) I pulled into the Car Wash on Dickerson Road. A frequent hangout for prostitutes and also a place for selling drugs.

The time was 11:15 P.M. and the wash bays were empty except for one lone female. I stopped when she waved me over and said, "Wait!" I knew the female from previous arrests. Her name was Bobbie, that's all I knew regarding her name. She was a very small woman only 5'4" tall and weighed about 100 lbs. but she looked much older than her years.

Brunette, brown eyes, tee shirt, no bra, slacks with tennis shoes (well worn) and Tattoo's all over her body. Her slacks were so tight that you could tell that she was not wearing any underwear. Her arms revealed a full sleeve of Tats and on each finger had letters tattooed on them.

She, like many of the underage girls on the streets were pitiful. After talking with these girls and getting to know them and their personality was a pattern of their childhood. Broken home with a single parent, School dropout and almost all were sexually abused early in their wretched lives, usually by their mother's boyfriend. They all have been beaten and assaulted many times on the streets while trying to make a lousy twenty dollars just to buy drugs for some low life Pimp which were mostly black and too lazy to get a real job. I had developed a real hatred towards these Pimps and at times I had threatened some of them bodily harm if they ever hurt some of these girls again. Most of the time this threat went in one ear and out the other. If the girls could not buy drugs their Pimp would furnish them and then he would take all the money they made doing tricks. This is the hold that these Pimps have on the women that work the streets. These girls were in a vicious cycle and were unable to escape or obtain help and most of all they could not give up the drugs. After they have been on the drugs for some time, their body would crave it. What a way to live, I thought. To protect and serve was an oath that kept going through my head when I would offer to help these girls get off the streets.

"Joe," she said, "do you have a couple of dollars to spare so I can buy a Cola, I have a cotton mouth and it's hard to swallow." I usually carried two dollars in my shirt pocket just for this type of situation. I handed Bobbie the two dollars and she said, "Oh thank you Joe, if I hear anything I'll let you know." I thought by helping these poor girls every now and then, they just might help me locate someone that I was looking for that had committed a crime in this area. These prostitutes were known to keep in contact with a lot of different people. By walking up and down the streets they would met some that were real flakey and some that thought they knew everything about everything.

I watched her as she walked up Dickerson Road and I thought that poor pitiful child. If I could ever hit the Lottery, I would build them a safe house where they could go and get away from this life that they were entwined with. The life they have now has no escape for them, just walking up and down the dirty streets trying to find someone so they could turn a trick for some easy money to buy drugs, beer, cigarettes and etc. Sometimes going to jail for a few nights would give them a bed to sleep in, a place to take a shower and the food wasn't that good, but it was food.

I watched her as she put the money in her crotch, she then turned and walked in the direction of a Stop and Go Market. She had no panties, no bra, no socks and only four pieces of clothes on her body and they were in need of washing real bad.

Angel On My Shoulder

I saw her leave the Stop and Go Market and she walked up Dickerson Road where she seemed to disappear into the darkness at the top of the hill. I thought to myself, her Pimp is going to pay a high price if I find out he hurts her again.

I put my unmarked car in drive and headed north looking for a violation. The night wasn't over and I knew there was something going on somewhere. I spotted a car that was driving pretty slow, I didn't know if he was looking for a date or what. I lit him up and when I approached his car I noticed that his pants were down around his knees. I asked, "what's going on?" Nothing was his reply. What's with your pants being down to your knees? Still no reply!!

I wrote him a minor Traffic Violation and I advised him to pull up his pants and head home. He stated that his wife had kicked him out. I told him that he needed to find a place to stayfor the night and get off the streets. Another lost soul.

Up and down the streets, but nothing was happening. The streets were deserted and this particular night and the pickings were slim. It was beginning to rain and as I turned the corner toget back onto Dickerson Road, I spotted another John and the girl jumped out of his car as soon as she saw me hit my blue lights. I had given this man several tickets before. They just don't learn. Another Citation for soliciting a Prostitute, even thou she got away. He got caught.

As I started driving, I started thinking back to the night I was shot and the ordeal that I went through to get my health back and how surviving this ordeal made me more alert of my surroundings, but not fearful.

I felt like calling it a night since it was almost midnight and raining a little harder now. I drove to my girlfriend's house and she

Angel On My Shoulder

made us a snack and we laid down on the couch and fell asleep watching TV.

The next morning when the alarm went off for her to get up the TV was still on. She got ready for work and before she left she came and kissed me good bye. Damn I wish she didn't have to work, but she enjoys her job. At least we have the nights together.

DIRTY NEEDLE STICK'S

I stopped a vehicle for running a stop sign. He had no driver's license, so I placed him under arrest and put him into the back seat of my vehicle. I knew he was a boyfriend of a known prostitute Michelle. While waiting for the tow truck I began inventorying his pick-up truck. I reached under the driver's seat to retrieve a small white paper sack. While pulling the bag from under the front seat of the truck, I got stuck with a used needle. I immediately began squeezing my finger to make it bleed. I did this numerous times forcing a small amount of blood to come out each time where the needle had stuck into my finger. I was so furious.

I went over to my car and asked the dirt bag in the back seat whose needle was this? He replied "That's for me to know and for you to find out." I bitch slapped him with my right hand and elbowed his chest with my left arm. Does that help jar your memory shit head?

"You, have no right to treat me like this he yelled."

"Do you want me to beg forgiveness now or tell you what's in store for you later?" was my reply.

"Yeah what," he answered.

I replied, "I know you and your truck and the area where you hang out. I'm going to lock you up every time I see you and tow your truck. After I arrest you about 4 times I'll start by charging you with a felony and then a habitual traffic offender. I'm going to make you my white whale in the coming months. That should give you something to chew on for a while, Mr. Pimp. That is your name isn't it?" I added "shortly you can watch and you can see your truck going to the tow in lot. Save your money because these tow truck drivers can use it". I added , "Welcome to my world loser!"

Again on another occasion I was working downtown Nashville one night when Foster and I had stopped a couple of well-known prostitutes outside a bar on Broadway near 4th Ave. North. It was summer and the temperature was 80 degrees. I asked Michelle "what's going on, is Dickerson Road dead now?"

"Naw, it's just I have to steer clear of two guys that are looking for me", she replied.

Angel On My Shoulder

One was wearing a lot of make-up, I guess to cover up the bruises on her face, I guess her Pimp hit her, she was wearing a short skirt that was way too short and a low cut top that showed the top part of her breasts, plus she was wearing some kind of funky high heel shoes in which she was having a hard time walking from either drugs or alcohol. The other girl was dressed about the same. Why they wear so much make-up is beyond me. She had on shorts that were too tight and too short, you could see the cheeks of her rear end. Her top looked like a bathing suit bra, too little and too tight and she was also wearing those awful high heel shoes also, but at least she could handle them pretty good. That is she wasn't wobbling when she walked.

Ok, Michelle, "Tell me why you are hiding from these two guys?" "What did you do, Michelle?"

"It's not what I did, it's what you did."

"So, how is this my fault?'

"OK Joe, do you remember stopping a guy in a pick-up truck and you towed his truck and arrested him."

"Yeah, so what?"

"Well, you see that is my pimp and he is blaming me for that."

"You know Michelle, I still don't see why this is my fault."

"Oh, Joe you just don't get it, these Pimp's think that they do no wrong and when they get caught, they blame it on us."

"Well then why don't you just leave town and work somewhere where he can't find you," I replied.

"Just forget it and just go ahead and lock me up, at least I'll be safe for a few days. "

"Yeah, I can do that, but first put your purse on the hood of my car". I told Michelle to turn around and when she did I ran my fingers across her back to see if she had any syringes hidden under the back part of her bra. This is a frequent hiding place for hypes to keep their syringes. I don't have any Lieutenant, I promise. I then opened her purse and I reached inside to retrieve a bag of white powder. Suddenly I felt a stick on my ring finger. "Son of a Bitch" I said, as I milked my finger trying to make the blood ooze out from the needle stick. Over and over I continued to say, "you fucking bitch"! Why can't you put the cap back on the syringe? No reply!!

I dumped the rest of the contents of her purse on the hood of my car. "You skank! Get in the car...NOW!! Have you ever been tested for Aids?" Her reply was, no I have never been tested. You better hope

Angel On My Shoulder

you're not HIV Positive or I'll start charging you with felonies from now on. All this time I was just bluffing Michelle, mainly because I was so pissed that I got stuck with another dirty needle, within one month. I have heard stories about Aids, that it takes years for it to surface. This is pretty tough to live with knowing that you have been stuck with these dirty needles.

All this time my partner was checking out the other prostitute. Damn Joe, you seem to be having a rough time with needle sticks these days. Just check your girl out and be careful, I replied. Damn this is a not a good night; I have to be more careful. Oh, well it's late now. Damn, I guess this just goes with the territory. You win some and you lose some but it seems like here lately I'm losing more than I'm winning. My luck has got to change pretty soon.

Michelle advised me that their Pimp would find out about this and that I would be on his shit list. I said, let him bring it on. I've handled scum like him before and I am not afraid of him.

Michelle said, you had better be afraid of him. You know Joe, he carries a gun strapped

to his leg and I've heard that he is a pretty good with it. Well, you know I shoot a perfect 300 score at the gun range every year, so let him as you say take your best shot. He knows where he can find me. I'm on these streets all the time, forty to fifty hours every week and in plain view. You should know by now that I am not hard to find.   After the two girls were processed at Headquarters, I went to General Hospital ER and explained to the head nurse what had just happened and she said that I needed a shot. What kind it was I don't know. But I do know one thing, it hurt like HELL!!

Angel On My Shoulder

MAN OR WOMAN

My partner, Foster and I were riding through the Motels, when we spotted Timothy coming from one of the rooms. Timothy was followed by a young white male who shut the behind him as he left the Motel Room.

Timothy was a black male dressed as a woman. To the experienced Policeman it was not a good disguise. However to an average man, he might not catch the difference.

I stopped the car, got out and motioned for Tim to come to where I was. The other male stood frozen in the parking lot. I asked Tim how much he charged and what type of service he had to perform on this subject. I knew Tim and he knew me on sight from our past dealings. He never has lied to me and he knew I would give him a break, most of the time. He answered in a soft voice, "He paid me $30.00 dollars for oral sex. I told him I was having myperiod." "What's that guy's name you were with Tim," I asked? "Charles," he replied.

"Charlie I yelled come here!" He walked over and I introduced myself as a Vice Lieutenant. If you answer me truthfully you may just get a ticket and you can go on your merry way, I said, However if you lie you are going straight to jail. You don't pass go and you don't get $200.00 dollars. He replied, "What is that supposed to mean?" No reply was given by me.

Well Charlie replied, "I gave Shirley $30.00 and we had sex." I laughed and "asked what kind of sex?" "Uh, Uh, oral sex," Charlie answered. I chided back, "it's a good thing you didn't try for old fashioned sex or you would of seen Shirley' dick." "Huh," he said. I didn't mumble, Shirley is a man and his name is

Timothy, I added Tim has a bigger pecker than you and me together.

Charlie said, "I feel faint and kind of light headed." I don't believe you. He added, I felt his crotch and there was no penis. "Hey stupid," I replied his dick is taped to His gut. If you would like to see, Tim would show you his secret.

Charlie said, "I think I'm going to be sick."

"Just throw up away from me," I replied.

"May I leave Lieutenant," Timothy asked in a soft voice?
"Yeah, get out of here unless Charlie wants to see your black snake."

"Okay Charlie" I stated, "let me see your I.D." I added, "about 25% of these street men and women have Aids, crabs or some STD. You shouldn't have sex with your wife for several weeks to see if your dick starts to drip."

You know you can get Aids from oral sex also. Damn, I didn't even think about that. My wife is going to kill me if she finds out about this. Let me ask you a good question?

Ok, what is it. Why is it you are out here and you have a wife at home. Well, well, uh you see we have 4 small kids and it's almost impossible to have sex. That is why I stop out here on my way home.

Man you are playing Russian Roulette packed with a ton of dynamite. You better hope your dick doesn't fall off. I asked, "How are you going to explain having to go to court for this?"

"I'll just tell her that I got a Traffic Ticket. Are you telling me that you think she'll believe that?

Angel On My Shoulder

"Yeah, she isn't too swift."

"Ok, your court date is in 5 weeks in General Sessions. Instructions are on the Ticket. The next time you go to jail, no questions asked. Just jail time and I'll impound your car," I added.

 Foster and I got into our unmarked car and left. I looked at Foster and said, humans never cease to amaze me. I added "You can never under estimate the stupidity of a human being."

"Hey Joe, that's why we catch so many," Foster said. "You know they're so stupid when it comes to sex. Especially when the little head tells the big head what to do". I replied, "I know that for a fact because my dick has made a slave out of me."

Remembering back to the first time that Foster and I encountered a man/woman prostitute, I thought it's like shooting fish in a barrel. Now the Barrel is getting pretty full, if not running over.

Angel On My Shoulder

ONE SUMMER NIGHT

One summer night my three man unit was working an area in North Nashville regarding to Prostitution. Our three man unit made 3210 arrests in a 24 month period. I doubt to this day if anyone has ever topped these statistics. I was very proud of my small unit. We worked as team and not as an individual. It takes a lot of dedication and hard work to achieve this type of productivity.

One night shortly after arriving in an area frequented by prostitutes I picked up a black female who was walking back and forth on a side street.

She got into my car and asked "was I a Cop?" "No," I replied. She then asked "if I wanted a date?" Yes, but how much? She replied, "$20.00 for a blow and $30.00 for straight sex." I said "OK" and then I turned onto another street, slowing down to a crawl and eased eased my car next to a parked vehicle on the passenger's side, only inches apart.

I told her that I'm Vice and that she was under arrest. She tried to open her car door, but it would only open a couple of inches. The fight was on. I grabbed her left arm and tried to cuff her. We were separated by the console which separated the two front seats. She pulled a steak knife out of her purse and cut my right wrist. I hit her in the left side of her head with my fist, approximately 2 times. She dropped the knife and started screaming "HELP! HELP!"

I radioed for backup and Foster arrived within 30 seconds. Foster and I pulled her from my car (a Buick) and he cuffed her while I called for an ambulance.

Angel On My Shoulder

Her left eye was swollen but it was not bleeding. She told me, you don't know who my Pimp is do you? I replied, "I don't give a fuck, he probably smells as bad as you do."

"Oh yeah, just wait until he finds out that you hit me."

I said, "You tell him to come see me and I'll hit him harder than I hit you." When we went to court she claimed that she did not know I was a Vice Officer. I admitted hitting her in order to stop her from carving on my wrist. This is a common excuse that a lot of the girls used. The Judge knew better, because I had been in his Court numerous times before with Prostitutes and he knew how they would lie, just to try and get out of the charge.

Final disposition, she received 90 days, plus probation and a $250.00 fine. Which was never paid. Approximately 6 months later she arrested again on Dickerson Road for the same thing. She also had a warrant for not paying a fine, which made this arrest even better. She could have easily stabbed me in the eye or the neck. This is what makes this job so dangerous at times.

She fought the law and I won. What a great job this is….sometimes! Cha Ching!

Several night's later one of the Vice Lieutenants called me over after Roll Call and he stated that he wanted to make some of that gravy overtime that we had been making. You know Joe, "he added with your overtime and court time you are making more than a Captain makes."

I replied, "I'm not just sitting in a chair with my ass hanging over the sides and just pushing a pencil. I and my squad earn every fucking dime we make and we don't back up to pick up our paycheck twice a month like some of these do nothings do. My team and I put our lives on the line every night and in a good week we will have about 10 to 20 fights and no one has ever escaped.

Angel On My Shoulder

I said, "you know we can always use an extra person." He asked, "what is the procedure you follow?" I told him that we ride the streets until you can find a prostitute and ask her to get into your car. I also added you have to lock the glove compartment where the Police Radio is located, hide your badge, hide your revolver and your billfold. You should keep $20.00 in your shirt pocket. When the Prostitute states a price and what you can get for the money, that is when the fun begins. You reach under your seat, grab your handcuffs and cuff her left wrist, you will probably have to fight her especially if she is from Memphis and weighs about 175 lbs. The Memphis girls seem to be the most violent and their Pimps are usually close by either in a car or on the street watching out for their girls.

"That's about it Lieutenant," keep in touch I added.

About an hour later the Lieutenant called on the radio and asked for me to meet him at a Truck Stop. He said, that when he placed the girl under arrest, she jumped out of the car and ran. I asked him, you didn't lose your handcuffs, did you? He said, no I hadn't gotten that far along. "I told him," well you can't make any gravy money by sitting in your car. You should grab her left arm next time before you place her under arrest. We both went our ways and I headed towards Trinity Lane. About 20 minutes later, the Lieutenant called me again and wanted me to Signal 8 with him at a Grocery Store in the parking lot, you know Joe, he added, "where we were at the start of this shift."

When I arrived he was standing outside his car. He stated, I grabbed her arm and told her who I was and that she was under arrest and she started to get out of the car. I grabbed the steering wheel with my left hand and she broke loose and ran up the street and disappeared around the corner. I asked him if he wanted to try again, he said sure I think I get it now.

Angel On My Shoulder

We split up and about 20 minutes later he called again on the radio and wanted to meetme at a Restaurant by the Car Lot. When I arrived, he was standing beside his car and his pants had gravel dust all over them. He said, "I grabbed her left arm with both hands and she dragged me out of the car onto the parking lot, she then broke loose and ran. I added, "these girls are scared and they are very strong when they think they are going to jail." He said, "I think I'm going back inside, I didn't realize that it was this bad out here." I told him you know we ride one to a car and we get into a lot of fights, but we have each other for back-up when possible.

He said, "Thanks Joe for the trial lesson, I'll see you tomorrow night at Roll Call." The next day after Roll Call the Lieutenant pulled me aside and he stated that he wanted to apologize to me. I said apologize for what? I didn't think it would be that bad in arresting a woman. You and your team are very productive and make more arrests than anybody in the Department. He smiled and said, I salute you!"

I said, to him that I document every arrest, complaint number, name, Charge and date. Once a month I send our monthly productivity report to the Assistant Chief, the Major over Viceand I keep a copy for my files, so if anyone ever wants to challenge our statistics. My girlfriend Patsy works in Personnel, types this up for me every month. By the way, she does this on her own time after work so that some prick Supervisor can't claim that she was taking time away from her job to help me on mine. After she finished typing the report's she would call me and I would go back to Headquarters and take her home. So, Joe I see you have your own private Secretary. Yeah you can say that, I replied. "Plus benefits, and I might say a lot of them."

Angel On My Shoulder

FALSE ACCUSATIONS / MICHELLE

I have arrested Michelle numerous times. She was a pretty blonde in her early twenties and from Toronto, Canada. However being on drugs made her dangerous and unpredictable.

The day I arrested her for prostitution was like any other day that I had taken her to jail, with one exception. She had cigarette or cigar burn marks all over her face. While she was sitting in my unmarked car I noticed she was acting strange. I looked at her out of the corner of my eye and noticed how she was dressed. Short shorts, tennis shoes and a halter that was way too small. Her hair looked like it could stand a good washing.

These girls don't care how they look, all they are interested in is turning a trick to get some drug money. They try to buy their drugs real quick so that their Pimp doesn't get all of the money they make. I've known for them to hide money in their private area, they put it in a baggie for safe keeping. So think about that the next time you touch some money and then put your hand around your face. If there is a fishy smell, BEWARE!

For some unknown reason I pushed the record button on my tape recorder which was beside my left leg and it was out of sight. I always had this with me, just in case it was needed, for a Court Case or for a complaint in Internal Affairs for false accusations made against me.

I asked, "Michelle what happened to your face?" She replied, "I be squeezing blackheads." I knew this was a lie because of the size of the burns that were on her face and they were not from blackheads.

Angel On My Shoulder

She became very angry when I told her no citations today, she was going to jail. You cannot hustle this close to a school Michelle. I've had too many complaints from the parents that were picking up their children from school and beside that your clothes are very revealing to have on when you are near a School. Besides I've warned you too many times. My tape recorder continued to run while I was transporting her to headquarters. She told me several times I would be sorry because I was going to arrest her and did not give her a citation, as I had done many times in the past. I knew prostitutes did not like to go to jail because they usually could not make bond and they would be without their drugs for many hours. However this particular girl has never given me any trouble.

The next day when I went to court the News Media was set up with all of their equipment needed for a News story. My girlfriend, Patsy was there with me. I was going to take her home after Court. She had just gotten off work. The Court was running late, so she sat down beside me. Patsy asked me what's all Hub Dub about and I stated "Beats Me." So, I asked one of the Newsman who were they waiting for? He said, "we want to see the Policeman that burned a Prostitute with a cigar all over her face, after he arrested her."

I told Patsy, "this is not good." On top of that I added, "she already had these burns on her face when I arrested her last night, which was probably caused by her pimp for not making enough money for him or some other reason, who knows." I was glad that I taped the arrest and should have not feel this uneasy because the whole incident was on tape.

I went over to the District Attorney and explained what was going on and that I had a taped recording of the arrest including her statement about the condition of her face.

Angel On My Shoulder

There were several Police Officer's in Court that day who had given Michelle a Citation for Prostitution in the past few days. They also told the D.A. that she had those burn marks on her face and that she said that her pimp did it, because she did not make enough money for him.

I was showing a great deal of agitation and nervousness and the female D.A. said Joe, "I have never seen you like this." I replied, "Hell this is a felony. It's an assault with intent to disfigure."

I also told the D.A. that Michelle told me several times during the arrest that I would be sorry for arresting her. The D.A. told me she would talk to Michelle and tell her that if she continued to lie after being under oath that the state would definitely put her in jail for Contempt and Obstruction of Justice, plus a Civil Suit from the falsely accused Police Officer. I played the tape for the D.A. to back-up my story.

After Michelle heard the tape recording she then told the D.A. she had been lying because she was mad at me for arresting her and not just giving her a citation.

The D.A. came back into the Court Room and told the News Personnel that they may as well leave because the Officer had a taped recording of the arrest and the Officer had been falsely accused. The Judge concurred with the District Attorney and the News

Media left without getting anything of this accusation. I thought, no sensational news for them today.

I sat down beside Patsy and told her I am going to start the ball rolling to take my Pension. Sweat was running down my back and from under my arm pits. I added "I cannot stand this type of stress, she could just as easily said that I raped her." Nah I added, "you know Patsy this has got to end. If she did accuse me it would be my word against hers.

I further stated that Michelle will become another White Whale for me and I will do everything to run her back to Canada where she came from and then she will be out of Nashville.

But, whenever I do arrest her again, I will have my tape recorder with me and I will have it all on tape just like I did this time.

Several months later, Michelle began to miss her Court Dates, and she had disappeared from the streets. Some of the girls working on the streets told me that she had probably hooked up with a Truck Driver because she was fascinated with the big Semi-Trucks and hit the road or that her Pimp had probably killed her and threw her in the river.

When I first saw Michelle on Dickerson Road, she was a beautiful girl. She looked like Kim Novak, beautiful smile, she wore make-up, but not that much. She had a distinct voice that was captivating when she talked. After several years on the streets she began to show a lot of wear and tear, like an old horse that had run hard and put up wet.

Michelle was never seen or heard from again. I just wondered if her Pimp did have something to do with her disappearance or if she just went back to Canada to be with herfamily or hopped into a truck and rode off into the sunset.

I guess I'll never know what happened to her.

Angel On My Shoulder

MIRANDA WARNING

I was sworn in for a Courtroom testimony regarding a recent case of Police pursuit and a stolen vehicle. The Judge was a no nonsense person but she was always fair when a Police Officer was on the stand. She knew our word was as good as it gets because the our reputation in Court is depended upon it.

The prosecuting Attorney asked me questions about the case and after he was finished he turned to the defense Attorney and said, "Your witness."

The defense Attorney walked up to me and stated, "Lieutenant I did not hear the part where my client was given the Miranda Warning?"

"I did not answer that part because I was not asked about that by the District Attorney,"

I replied. "So now you are telling me that my client was Mirandized?" he asked. "Yes" was my answer. By whom, Lieutenant? "Me" I said.

He asked, "How? From memory or a printed card with it on it?"

"From memory," was my answer.

"Memory huh?" He added, "Would you recite the Miranda Warning to this Honorable Court, as you did from memory at the time of my clients arrest?"

I said, "Are you really serious?"

His answer was "Lieutenant I'm as serious as a heart attack." He also added what's the matter, memory lapse?

Angel On My Shoulder

"No I replied," but this must be the first time you have ever cross examined me, because if it wasn't you would know that I never fail to Mirandize someone that I have just arrested. OK," I said, "You have the right to remain silent....Anything you say can and will be used against you in a Court of Law....You have the right to an Attorney during questioning....If you cannot afford one an Attorney will be appointed to you free of charge. You have the right to stop answering questions at any time."…. And finally Counselor I added, "Do you thoroughly

understand your Constitutional Rights."

I then looked to my left at the female Judge and gave her a big smile. She smiled an looked at the Defense Attorney and quipped, "He got you on that Counselor. Now let's move on....I find enough probable cause to bind the defendant over to the Grand Jury." Next case!

"But, but your Honor," the Defense Attorney tried to speak but was interrupted by the Judge.

"Did you not just hear what my ruling was?"

"Yes, but!!"

"But nothing." The Judge said once more, "Next Case!"

When I went back to Headquarters to sign out from Court, I overheard several young Officers complaining about these criminals just receiving probation instead of incarnation. I told them that the reasoning to this was that if everyone received Jail time the Government would not be able to build Prison's or Jail's fast enough. Every Prison or Jail that has been built filled up in a short time. I also said, "that the costs for building and staffing these Jails and Prisons are very astronomical." Simply put, the Jails and Prisons are packed to the brim, there are many who sleep on the floor and this causes more conflicts with the inmates. There

Angel On My Shoulder

just isn't enough room for all the Violators. Nor is there enough Tax dollars to fund the building of new ones.

So what is your point Lieutenant?

My point is that you just don't get it. I tried explaining it to you. I guess it just hasn't sunk in yet. When I left they still looked like they were

trying to understand what I had just told them.

The Captain over the Court Appearance Section spoke up and replied, I think all of you are trying to get free money by going to court. I turned around and asked him, why don't you work the streets and see just how much fun we have while fighting with just about every one that

we arrest. You know Captain; I never have to back up to get my paycheck. No reply from the Captain.

Angel On My Shoulder

THE BIKER MAILBOX STORY

My partner Foster and Officer Crumby and I went to a 3 day seminar in Knoxville, TN. concerning Biker Gangs in Tennessee. It was hosted by the ATF. It was cold and there was snow on the ground and the icy patches on the roads. We checked into the hotel and started drinking alcohol. We decided to ride around town and find one of the motorcycle gangs chapter house.

The weather was cold and snow was everywhere. We found the Chapter House with the Biker gangs name on the mailbox. Someone thought it would be a good idea to steal their mailbox which was in front of the Chapter House and that is exactly what happened. Who could that be?

The next morning when we got up, Foster looked at me and said, "Joe, even your hair is drunk and he added go look at your eyes". I went into the bathroom and the whites of my eyes were the color of an egg yolk. This being my liver was over worked due to the fact half had been removed in 1970 when I had two entrances and two exit wounds through my liver and one bullet exploded the main artery (I think it is called the Vena Cava). Actually 850 grams of my liver had been removed. I started pouring fluids down my body to flush out my kidneys and as the day went by my eyes started to clear up to where they were white again. I had been drinking Wine and Vodka the night before.

That day after the opening introduction the head Agent addressed about 60 Police Officer's from Tennessee and a few adjoining counties. Gentlemen the President of the Biker gang here in Knoxville stated that their mailbox was removed from the front of their Chapter house last night. The Biker president further stated if they did not get their mailbox back immediately he would have their Lawyer file an injunction to halt this seminar. All they want is their mailbox returned and this would go away. The Agent then looked at us and said, "Okay Nashville, get me the mailbox." Everyone started laughing. I didn't think it was so funny. I wanted a Trophy for my office. Would that be so bad and how many Officers has a Biker Mailbox to show off? Well, it is one less now, because I had to give it up.

We went to our car and retrieved the mailbox from the trunk and handed it to the Agent in charge. He took the mailbox and left the room for about 10 minutes, returned empty-handed and said, "Okay let's get this show on the road." You could hear a pin drop, because it was so quiet in the room. The Seminar went on and there were a lot of good ideas that we can take back for the Trainee's in their classes. No one said a word to us about the Biker Mailbox.

After the Seminar was over, several other Police Officers came to Foster, Johnny and I saying that getting the mailbox was a good idea. They stated that they had the same idea, but they did not know where any Chapter Houses were in Knoxville. We were asked how did we know where they were. I said, well it is like this, we stay in touch with the Biker's in Nashville and they will tell us where the other Chapter Houses are in Tennessee. You have to treat them with kid gloves, if you want any information from them.

A lot of the different Officers asked us if Nashville was hiring, we said not right now. I asked them why? The answer was, we hear a lot of things happen in Nashville and the Vice and SWAT seem to be active most of the time. One asked, Nashville is in the center of Tennessee and there is a lot of Bikers coming through, with so many Interstates and a lot of excitement.

That night Foster and I were playing pool at the hotel. It was Foster's time to break the pool balls and on his opening shot he

Angel On My Shoulder

said, "Watch this Joe!" He drew back to hit the break ball and he put all his strength hitting the cue ball. He shanked the shot by knocking the cue ball over the table and into the whirlpool 20' away. We looked as the ball circling the tub in the current that the jets were making. Round and round it went while we were laughing uncontrollably. I said, "Well Minnesota Fats I think I'll retire for the night unless you want to get soaked retrieving the cue ball!" I put a note on the pool table saying the white ball is in the hot tub. We both left for our room and called it a night. Damn, what a day this has been. I was tired, but I couldn't go to sleep so I drank the rest of the Vodka and wine. I slept like a baby.

When the Seminar was over we headed back to Nashville.

This was the end of the mailbox saga. Although it would have been nice to have a trophy for our Office or a good training aide at the Academy. Oh, well it was a good thought, it just didn't work out.

Several days later I received a call from an ATF Agent. He stated that they were going to raid a Chapter House. Before he could say anything else, I told him Hell yes I want to be there. The ATF Agent also stated that he had heard about the Mail Box being taken at a Knoxville Seminar. I replied, "damn News sure does travel fast." He gave me the location and Foster and I went there with a lot of Officer's on this Raid. I always tried to be on good standings with these ATF Agent's. They are great bunch of men.

This Chapter House had just about everything in it. Guns and ammo, drugs and a lot of stolen items. Everything was wrapped in brown paper and labeled as evidence. This was really an experience for Foster and I. You can never know enough and it really helps to see how other Agencies operate. I thanked them for calling and letting us in on this Raid, one Agent did say that

Angel On My Shoulder

the Mailbox was off limits to us. We just laughed it off. As we were leaving again I thanked the Agent that called us.

I started thinking about the color of my eyes being yellow while we were in Knoxville, so I called a Doctor and made an appointment for the following week about the color of my eyes. The Doctor told me that what was left of my liver could not handle alcohol abuse and if I continued to drink heavily them my time on this earth would be very limited. This was the day I stopped abusing my liver and still to this day I continue to be a non-drinker.

Angel On My Shoulder

MOTHER & DAUGHTER

I worked days from time to time and frequented the usual locations for prostitutes. There were several locations, but the same prostitutes had their own locations that they liked to work best, because of their regular customers. By working days every now and then we could probably get a new girl working the streets.

This particular day I pulled into the car wash and was approached by a female which looked to be about 40 to 45 years old. "Looking for a date", she asked. I replied, "sure am, if it's not too expensive". By the way I like your T-shirt, I said. The shirt had writing on the front that read "Fuck Em All". She said you'll like what is behind my shirt. What's that? Well I have a pair of DD's. Are you a cop?

No do I look like a cop? You never can tell. We'll I'm not the heat so where can we go?

I can give you a blow job for twenty dollars.

That's okay with me, get in. She got into the unmarked car and as I started going towards downtown. She said, "I have a room at the Motel and it's just a few blocks from here". I pulled my vehicle into a grocery store parking lot and pulled real close to a dumpster to eliminate her escape route. "What's going on she yelled!" Well you see I'm Vice and you are under arrest for Solicitation of Prostitution.

I reached under my left thigh and brought out handcuffs, grabbing her left arm, I cuffed her wrist and reached for her right arm to restrain her. I said, don't get all froggy on me and I won't hurt you. She just sat there frozen with disbelief as I opened the glove box and radioed dispatch my location, car mileage and time. When I arrived at headquarters I radioed Dispatch again to give them the mileage, location and time. This was a standard safety precaution when you were transporting a female to Booking.

"You lied to me, she said.

" Yeah, I'll remember that in confession the next time I'm in Church.

After booking her I headed back out looking for another lost soul. About an hour later I went back out to the car wash and saw a young female hitchhiking and she looked to be about 20-25 years old and she was not bad looking.

"What's going on," I asked? Nothing much but the rent and taxes was her reply.

You looking for a date? I replied.

"I'm no pushover but I can be had". We both laughed.

She added, I have to make $75.00 real quick to get my mother out of jail, Vice just arrested her about an hour ago and a Bondsman needs $75.00 to make her bond. I will do anything for $75.00. She got into my unmarked vehicle and this young woman told me that she and her mother had been evicted and all their belongings had been placed in storage.

"Do you want a room or do it in the car," she asked? "We can go about 4 blocks from here and there is a deserted place," she replied.

I quickly handcuffed her and then I told her that I'm Vice and that her mother anxiously awaits you. Maybe you two can be cell mates. However I was the only one who got a good laugh from that remark.

Angel On My Shoulder

Same thing again, I radioed Dispatch my location, car mileage and time. Upon arriving at headquarters I again radioed Dispatch to give them mileage, location and time. You'll soon be with your mother as soon as I get you booked in. I hope you have a good reunion.

"Fuck you," was her reply.

Just another day, I'm headed back to the same car wash, maybe I'll get her grandmother this time.

This was on July 28, 1987 and the story was run in the Nashville Banner. I was told that someone in Booking contacted the newspaper about the mother and daughter being arrested within several hours of each other. This was my first arrest of a mother and daughter on the same day. I have never heard of this happening before.

Angel On My Shoulder

THE PIMP & HIS LADY

Our Prostitution Squad of 3 men had a nickname. "The Pussy Posse" as I stated earlier.

I was cursing down Murfreesboro Road one week day when I turned to go behind a restaurant near Fesslers Lane. There I saw a male black and a white female walking out from behind a business. I was in an unmarked Vice car, a Monte Carlo. I recognized the female from a previous arrest.

I stopped my car, got out and told the couple to "Hold up!" I approached them and noticed the female had a fairly large knot over her left eye. I asked "What happened to your head?" She replied, "I tripped and fell a couple hours ago."

I looked at the female, small in stature and with a little work she could be a real looker. I then looked at the black male and said, "You're not saying much Mr. Pimp."

He snarled, "Where do you get off calling me a Pimp."

"I'll call you anything I want too. Maybe I should call you what you really are, a lazy leech that does not work and contributes absolutely nothing to society, and lives off women. I added, if I ever see this woman with a knot on her head again I am going to give you one, same size and same place. I looked at the woman and said, "If you ever want to get away from this woman beater I can get you some help."

The pimp looked at me and said "you talk real big with that badge and gun on your hip." I took my badge from my belt and pulled my pistol from my pancake holster and tossed them in the front seat of my Monte Carlo. I then turned towards the suspect and

Angel On My Shoulder

said, "Make a move you dead beat and I'll show how it feels for someone to fight you back."

He looked at me with hatred in his eyes and his nostrils flared. I looked for any movement of his fists but none came. The woman said, "Come on Charles let's go."

One final thing before you leave Mr. Pimp. Remember what I told you about abusing this woman. I took my index and middle finger crossing them and punched him in his chest several times, with my 2 fingers, pushing him backwards each time.

I watched them start walking and they disappeared around the corner. I knew I would make a believer out of this pimp if I ever run into him again.

I saw her several months later and he was not with her. I asked, "Where is that woman beater?" She replied, "He got mixed up with a bad gang and he was shot and killed."

We'll all I can say is good riddance. You know Joe, all of us girls are sure glad he is gone, we don't have to live in fear of him or give him all the money. You know, I just might take you up on getting some help to get out of being a prostitute, you know I have a 4 year old daughter and she deserves better than she is getting.

I asked, "Who does she stay with while you are on the streets." My mother keeps her. I gave her my card and told her to give me a call when she was serious about changing her life style. She thanked me. I got a call from one of my guys in my squad so I had to go. Again, just call me and I can get you some very needed help. She walked off with a different look upon her face, maybe she will take my advice and change her life style.

Angel On My Shoulder

RACHEL

Just like any other time on the streets, I liked to drive down Dickerson Road, where there is always a few girls out waiting to get with a John for some money to go buy a hit. I just can't understand their reasoning about this kind of lifestyle. We always have these prostitution stings, but we use our Police women to get the John's and usually get the same guy's quite often. I can't imagine what they carry home to their wives or girlfriends.

Oh, well it's just another arrest for me. God I love this job. Ka Ching! There is some danger, but you get such a rush when you arrest someone. Many times they have outstanding warrants. I can almost tell, because they start getting antsy when you stop them. I've heard so many stories, this is the first time I've done this, Yeah right. Seems they never learn.

Hey - there's Rachel, wonder what she's up to tonight?

I then made a u-turn on Dickerson Pike after spotting Vickie, a well-known drug user and prostitute walking South towards town. Pulling beside the female I said "Rachel what's going on?" "Nothing much Joe, just trying to find me a pigeon so I can cop. I'm not feeling too good now, it's been almost four hours since my last hit, she replied."

"I won't be but a minute Rachel I said," have you got anything for me? Yeah at the Motel on the corner, in the back, room 20 there is this guy named Tommy. The car parked in front of the room is stolen out of Alabama. It's a two tone Monte Carlo, white top, brown bottom and it's got those fancy wheels. The wheels are stolen also, he just bought them 2 days ago. She continued, to tell me that the license tags do not match up with the car. He's about 6' tall, beard, stringy brown hair, brown eyes, 190 lbs. He likes to talk and he has a slight lisp.

His body odor is something else, Joe he carries a knife on his right leg on the inside of his boot and a revolver in the small of his back. He was bragging about how easy it is to overlook these weapons, especially on sloppy Police searches. I think he's all mouth, but you never know. The son-of-a-bitch slapped me yesterday for no reason. So here he is on a silver platter Joe. Rough him up for me okay? "Vickie," I replied. "That wouldn't be nice and she just laughed.

I asked, "how long have you had those tattoos on your tits?" Not too long that's why the color is so vivid, " she answered. "Would you like to see my birds?" She then took both hands and pulled her blouse down just far enough to expose 2 full size blue birds, wings extended as if they were in flight, one on each breast facing each other.

"How much did they cost Rachel, I asked?" Not much she answered, "just a couple of blow jobs, one for each bird." He's a good artist and very detailed, I answered back. Yeah Vickie laughed, "You know Joe I made his legs buckle. I waited until he had finished the birds before I serviced him." Do you want me to get him to give you a blue bird? No Rachel, I already have one on my leg and I don't give blow jobs.

Rachel said, "No Joe if you want a bird, I'll give him a blow job for you." She added, they hurt like hell during the process and it takes about 10 days for the scabs to fall off.

Joe, I see he's standing beside his door to his room. Okay Rachel I'll see you later and thanks for the information. I'll have him in jail as soon as I see him driving the Monte Carlo."

I pulled down just a little and I saw another girl working. I stopped and talked to her for several minutes before I eased my unmarked Police car onto the street and slowly down the alley behind the motel to see if the stolen Monte Carlo was stilled parked or gone. By this time "Tommy had already left in the car and driven off. I said, "Tommy you are going to get a whammy and go to the slammy when I catch you."

I drove back to the front of the motel and Rachel was still there. He's not there, but I'll catch him driving that Monte Carlo and he won't like going to jail. I think I'll have quite a few charges to hit him with. He just might be wanted. Got to go Rachel, be careful now, it looks like we may get some rain. See you later.

Vickie overdosed one day and a Metro Ambulance responded to the Motel parking lot. My youngest son, Eric was an EMT and he and his partner made the call. While my son was checking Rachel out, she looked at his name tag, and asked "are you McEwen?" Yes I am why. Is your daddy Joe McEwen? He sure is Rachel. You know he is a good man. He treats all the girls right, not like some of the other Officers who work the streets. Most of them treat us like we were dogs. Eric finished checking her out, Rachel you have got to be careful, some of these drugs are not what you think they are. I know, but when you have to have a fix you'll take anything. You're playing Russian Roulette with your life so be careful. Thank you for helping me, I'm feeling better, but I have to get back to work so I can make enough to sleep inside a good warm room tonight.

You know Rachel, Eric said "my dad locks you up, I save your life and my grandfather taxi's you all over town." "Hey girl you know you are on the third generation of the McEwen's," he added. This must be some kind of a record, or at least an Honorable mention. "Could be," she replied.

Several weeks went by and I didn't see Rachel on the streets. I asked around about her and none of the regular women had seen her either. I think she had some type of Cancer. Maybe she'll show up soon. I've got to ask my son if he has seen her. She's another lost soul, and when they get hooked on drugs, they go kind of wild if they don't get something. What a life.

A couple of months later I was driving down Shelby Avenue and a Van pulled up beside me and the man honked his horn. When I looked over, I saw Rachel and she was in the passenger's seat. My girlfriend Patsy was with me and I was taking her home from work.

Rachel raised up so I could see her and she then exposed her tits to show me her birds. I just laughed. She had large areolas on her breasts, just like my girlfriend. I wonder what the man that was driving the Van wondered? He was probably thinking that I was her Pimp. She looked pretty good, that is her complexion wasn't chalky looking like the last time I saw her. I stayed back some to give the Van plenty of room to get some distance between us.

PIZZA PIZZA

On evening around 6 PM myself, Foster Hite and Steve Garton were hungry. We had stopped at this Pizza restaurant for a meal. While we were sitting there waiting for our Pizza, a boisterous loud mouth white male with stringy hair and a full sleeve of tattoos on both of his arms came through the side entrance of the restaurant. When I saw him I knew that this was going to be trouble, just from the loudness of his voice and his body language.

We were in plain clothes, which was our usual attire since we worked in Vice. There was no one at the cash register at this time to take his order. He started yelling and cursing about the slow service. The other customers had children with them, ranging from 6 to 15 years of age. They seemed uneasy the way he was talking and cursing. One couple even got up and left.

The manager knew us because we had eaten there numerous times. When the manager walked towards the cash register he looked at us and he raised his eyebrows. I knew what had to be done, so I got up and walked over to the loud mouth guy and tapped on the shoulder and said, "come here I want to show you something." I casually walked him over to our table and "told him to have a seat." When he sat down I grabbed one arm and my partner grabbed the other arm and forced them behind his back and then handcuffed him to the back of the chair that he was sitting in. I leaned over towards him and told him that we wished to eat our meal in peace and if you decide to become loud. I will personally stick a handful of napkins in your mouth. I told him that he was under arrest for impersonating a human being. I added in a low voice, don't get loud or you just might get physically hurt. I didn't really mean it, I just wanted to scare him and I did. Foster and Steve just starred at the jerk in handcuffs and just smiled whilethey were eating pizza. I told him to just sit there while we eat our Pizza. After we finished our Pizza we put him into the back of my car and then my partner, Foster, got into the back seat alsowith the suspect. This was done because we did not have bars between the front and back seat of a unmarked car. I told Steve to follow us down to headquarters. We had to leave one of our cars in the Pizza parking lot.

He was charged with Disorderly Conduct by Creating a Disturbance. Upon completing the booking process, I drove my partner Foster, back to the Pizza restaurant to pick up his car.The manager came out and thanked us for taking care of a bad situation. I told him that it was no problem and if he ever comes back into your restaurant after he gets out of jail, just give us a

call. The manager said, "fellows; the next Pizza is on me." I told him that he didn't have to do that. But, he insisted on doing it anyway.

Well not only do we eat for half price we sometimes get it for FREE! Cha Ching! We never went back to that Pizza Restaurant because several months later it closed down. It was really in a bad location, mostly thugs for customers. The Pizza sure was good though. One time I ate 18 pieces of Pizza. I was starting to gain weight, I wonder why?

A lot of people have a misconception about Police Officers. Police Officers love to fight and take people to Court because now they get paid a minimum of 2 hours. When I first came on in 1970, there was no such thing as being paid for court time and you had to drive our own car to and from Court and we paid for the gas. So, if an arrest was made it actually cost money out of our own pockets, plus time when off duty. At that time taking the cars home was not even implemented. Times have sure changed. However this did change a short time later for the Officer's being allowed to take the marked cars home. This made the number of arrest's increase drastically. Happy days are here again! Cha Ching!

NAIL POLISH REMOVER

While I was working the streets in the downtown area a prostitute, told me one day that the men are just not coming around because there are too many marked Patrol Cars going up and down the streets. Since you left Joe, things just aren't the same, you were always fair and looked out for us. "These new Officers are just plain rude," she added.

Sandy said that she started coming downtown because there are a lot of men that stayed around the bars and I like to stay close to 4th and Broadway. She told me that one time a guy wanted to buy her a drink. She said "OK." We sat and talked and drank a couple of drinks and then he started telling me that no street whore ever stole any money from him.

He told Sandy that he claimed to be too sharp to be conned. So he had to use the restroom.

I told him, "that I would be here when he got back." He was in their quite a while, but it was just long enough for me to pour a small amount of fingernail polish remover into his drink.

He came back and said, "Sandy lets finish our drinks and go somewhere." He added "how about doing it in my car in the parking lot?"

She also told me that when someone finishes their spiked drink there was a 5 to 10 minute window before the mark gets dizzy and passes out. She added, they walked to his auto which was about 2 blocks away and by the time they got into the front seat and she started unzipping his pants. His head rolled back on the head rest on the front seat and he was had passed out.

I have no way of knowing if this is what really happened or even if was true, but this type of story was also told to me by another girl that worked the streets.

Sandy said, she emptied his wallet and pockets of $270.00 dollars plus some change. She said that she would have taken his diamond ring, but couldn't get it off his finger because his finger because it was too tight, she stated that if she had a pocket knife with her that she would have cut his finger off and taken the ring anyway. She knew that there was a short time span to get out of there before he came to. She knew most men are too embarrassed to file a Police Report and it is very seldom reported, especially if they are married.

This Prostitute was a pretty good size woman. I doubt if the guy could have handled her in a fight. However, sometimes these girls get the shit beat out of them by the man when he catches them later on. These men do not like it when a female outsmarts them.

There is no telling how many of these prostitutes get into an altercation with men while they are on the streets trying to hustle enough money for another fix.

NEAT AS A PIN

I was cruising the Motel parking lots along Dickerson Road area and a prostitute that I had known for some time, flagged me down. She came over to my car window and said, Joe, "I had my baby and he is growing like a weed." She added, "Would you like to see him?" I said, "of course." I walked to the room; it was a typical Motel room with a bathroom which was in dire need of paint, in fact the whole room needed overall maintenance. The floor was concrete with checkered tile throughout the place. I walked over to the bassinet and when I looked at that little baby boy, he grinned exposing his gums.

I told Shirley that I did not want to touch him because, I did not want to cross contaminate any germs to the baby. Shirley said that she appreciated that and said, "Thank you."

She added, "you know Joe he's an eatin' machine. All he does is eat and shit." She had a double bed with a bookcase head board and across the top of the head board were diapers stacked very neat, and in the shelf part of the headboard there were numerous cans of formula which were stacked neatly with all the labels facing out. I looked around the room and although it was a seedy Motel, her room was clean and extra neat. She seemed to be very proud of this little baby and the way that she was keeping her Motel room. I looked at her and said, "You are starting on the right track." The next thing, get you a sugar daddy so that you can get yourself and that sweetbaby out of this environment, and away from that cock sucker that has a hold on you.

I told Shirley that I had to go, but if anybody hurts you. Please contact me. She said, "Joe you have always been good to us girls on the streets, even though we were prostitutes and a nobody to most of the people we ran into. Joe, you never took away our dignity." As I, opened the door to leave I turned around and winked at her and said luck to you and that sweet baby boy.

As I was driving off, I saw her Pimp coming across the gravel parking lot and I pulled mycar up to where he was and stopped. I told him that I had just seen your baby and he is real cute. I added, don't you think it's time that you got a real job, instead of being a half ass Pimp.

He turned away and walked towards the Motel room kicking the gravel with his foot. I just hope that he doesn't do anything to Shirley or that baby or he will answer to me.

These girls must have a strong will to put up with these no good pimps and leaches of society.

I thought that these so called Pimp's add nothing to this world. They only take and

never give. They don't work so they don't pay Income Tax or Social Security, but they are willing to take anything free that the Government has to offer. They are just like a mongrel dog, they eat and shit in public places. The girls are held like slaves and they are really pitiful creatures. The Pimp supplies these girls with the drugs to feed their habit while he on the other hand takes all the money and they just get the drugs. Little does he know that these girls hide some of the money that they make. If their pimp catches the girls, they are in for one hell of an ass whipping. I seen these girls out on the street and you can tell they have been mistreated by their pimp from the bruises on their body.

WHO LET THE DOGS OUT

Sometimes doing Intel work I would drive behind a Bikers' Club House. At one time there were 14 Biker Club Houses in Nashville. I did this to try and obtain any information regarding their organization by going through their garbage. One could find out a lot about their membership, meeting, activities and etc. That is if their garbage has not been burned.

I would also ride in the helicopter and take area photos of the Chapter Houses and automobiles that were in their parking lot.

One location of a known house was in an area belonging to TVA which was directly behind the Clubhouse. The weeds were about 2 feet tall which surrounded the huge TVA towers.

I parked my car near one of the steel towers and got out to go see what I could find and after I had gone about a short way, I realized that I left my revolver which was on my utility belt in the car. This is something I never do, however this time I did just that.

About 20 feet from the front of my car I hear some noise ahead, I proceeded very slowly and when I went a little further I saw 4 large dogs which popped out of nowhere from the heavy foliage which were coming from the direction of the Chapter house. When they saw me they stopped abruptly and just looked at me. Their ears were straight up and their tails were not wagging. I thought, this is not good. They were startled as much as I was, but probably not as scared as I was. Dogs make a great alarm system for safe houses by barking.

I figured that I was in a very bad place being 20 feet away from my car and carrying no weapon. I held both of my arms straight up making me seem larger and started backing up slowly towards my Patrol car and I yelled stop or sit repeatedly to the dogs.

The four dogs fanned out and started easing towards me. When I reached for the door handle and opened the door they charged towards me. I jumped into the car slamming the door shut and the dogs began to run around the car barking loudly.

I backed up my car into an opening and drove out to the main road where the dogs had finally stopped chasing me and they just stopped dead in their tracks as they watching me drive off. This could have been real bad if I had been further away from my Patrol car.

I'll never get out of my car again without my weapon and utility belt around my waist. As I was driving I could feel my heart pounding fast and I had sweat running down my face. Damn what was I thinking, there could have been some bikers at the back of the Clubhouse. Bikers are known to carry weapons on them some of the time and if they don't, their girlfriend's would have weapons hidden on them . Most Bikers are good size men and if a fight breaks out the rest of the Biker brothers join in.

Thinking back on this incident, I'll never do this again without someone with me. It is just too dangerous.

I had always been interested in Biker's since I lived in Louisville, Kentucky. While I was working at the A&P Warehouse, several of the men had motorcycles and even one was associated with a Biker Gang. After I purchased a motorcycle, it was an old tank shift foot clutch, with no frills. The handle bars were high in the front and the Biker's called them Ape hangers. This bike was known as a hoodlum bike.

On another occasion while I was assigned at the Police Academy I would drive by one of the Chapter houses on my way to work and write down any license tags of parked cars that were parked out front. This particular date there was a Penske Truck boxed Van which was parked out front. I had never seen this van parked there before. When I arrived at work, I called Auto Theft and told them the situation and that inside the Van was probably stolen motorcycles.

Later on that day a Detective called me and said that they had an open container ready for shipment and it was full of stolen motorcycles. I went there and took pictures and wrote down VIN numbers of the cycles.

The Detective thanked me for calling him and I then returned to the Training Academy. Several months later I can't remember what Organization, but this Detective was named Investigator of the Year. He received $5,000.00 dollars and a Plaque and a lot of pats on the back. My name was not even mentioned in the breaking of this theft of cycles that were being shipped out of the Country. No one ever mentioned that I was the one that had discovered the Penske Van that was parked in front of the Chapter House, and called headquarters.

The only person that I told about this was my partner Foster Hite. But at the same time, if not for me being so inquisitive about the Bikers and their activities this would have never been discovered and all those cycles would have been shipped out of the country to who knows where. This is a prime example of what Policemen on the streets are supposed to do and that is to be on the lookout for any suspicious activity. However, I was on my way to work and in my personal car when I came across this situation. I did a lot of investigative work before and after going to work, on my own time and in my own personal truck.

Sometimes you'd like to get a pat on the back for a job well done, but then no one would really know what you did, because you never got the Credit for it. That's what it is all about, catching the bad guy and hurting him where it hurts the most. "His pocketbook".

A lot of time Foster and I would stop Biker's on the Interstate, just to get any information that we could from them. We also would make a note of the Tattoos and where they were on theirbody. I figured that this information would come to be an advantage at some point. No two Biker's would have the same Tattoo in the same place as another Biker.

Foster called me one day about a Biker that he had stopped off I-65 North. He stated that he was acting sort of jittery. After arriving I identified the logo on his vest and I knew of this Biker Club. I talked with him and his Driver's License was valid as well as his tags on the Motorcycle. We let him go with just a warning to always have his helmet on. I thanked Foster for calling me and I went back to searching the streets for another arrest. The temperature was getting hot by now, so I headed back to the Office to do some paperwork.

JUST ANOTHER DAY

I was driving around town looking for somebody who looked like they were working. I saw a black female that was headed towards the business section. She noticed me but she had to cross the four lanes of traffic to get to my unmarked Vice car.

She came up to my window and asked are you looking for a date? I said "sure are you available?"

She replied, "I sure am." She got into the car and she asked, "Do you have a particular place to go? "

I said no, but we can find a place.

She said "that she needed $20.00 for a blow or $30.00 for regular sex."

My reply was "Sure, that sounds OK to me."

I started towards the Police Department, however before I placed her under arrest, I turned onto the 3rd Avenue, which ran beside the Jail entrance, s he became suspicious and put her right hand on the passenger's door handle. She was getting real antsy and when I told her that I was Vice and that she was under arrest for Solicitation of Prostitution. She jumped from my vehicle and started running south with me close behind. I was wearing slacks and a sport coat. I had just left the Courtroom on an arrest that I had made several months earlier.

I usually wear jeans or camouflage pants with just a t-shirt. I caught her half a block from my vehicle and the fight was on. It is very hard to handcuff someone if that person is fighting like someone on drugs. She was yelling "Rape and Please Somebody help me!"

I told her that she was wasting her time, so just shut up. But she replied, "I ain't did nothing."

"Well then what do you call Soliciting Prostitution."

"But I didn't do anything and you didn't give me any money, so you don't have a case against me."

I rolled her over on her stomach and handcuffed her left wrist. Suddenly another female began pulling on my coat yelling why are you hurting this lady? Now, I had retrieve my Badge from my coat pocket while trying to hold onto the resisting andscreaming female that was under arrest.

I tossed my Badge on the sidewalk and told the stranger that I was Vice and this woman was under arrest.

I then added, now get away and quit interfering with an arrest. The lady replied, "you don't have to be so nasty about it." "Lady just go away and but out," was my reply.

I pulled the black female up and muscled her into my unmarked car. I placed her in the passenger's seat and climbed over her to the driver's side. This was so she couldn't jump out of the car again. I then took her left hand which was handcuffed and cuffed it to my right wrist to the dangling handcuff.

While waiting for the door to open to the Booking Room, she tried to kick me in the groin. I grabbed her by the hair of the head and pulled down so that she could not do anything. While pulling her down I shook her head and when I turned loose, I had a hand full of hair.

This is known as a hair mare. I told her that I could charge you with resisting arrest, but I won't unless you act up again.

Suspects that are arrested on Friday will have to stay in Jail until the Jail Docket on Monday, especially if they are from out of town. Final disposition in General Session's Court on Monday she was credited for 4 days served, suspended 26 days and a $200.00 fine. I don't know why these women from Memphis don't learn. They will spend 4 days in Jail when they come to Nashville, to pull their tricks on the weekends, plus their Pimp doesn't get any money also.

We know most of the prostitutes on the streets of Nashville by name and usually they always try to get us some information on drug sales, but we rarely ever get the real truth out of them. Some of these women looked pretty several years ago, now they looked like they were in their 50's or 60's. Their skin was getting rough and they all looked worn out and haggard looking, especially their teeth, going, going, gone.

Drug's and whatever else they use or take really cut's their life expectancy. A lot of them have the sack around their heart which becomes inflamed. I guess they also die from being infected with HIV or a multitude of diseases. I don't really know this except from what I have been told from several of these women on the streets. Their time on the streets is usually short lived. The Pimps have it easy because all they do is collect the Money.

HAIR TODAY GONE TOMORROW

My partner Foster Hite and I made an arrest of a he-she in North Nashville near the Interstate one night. We had received some complaints that some guys were losing their billfolds to some black prostitutes. These he-she's would get their money in advance because afterwards they would have to high tail it to get away from the men after lifting their billfold.

When these prostitutes when performing oral sex on their customers, they would reach down to the customers ankles and retrieve his billfold from his pants. They had also been known to tie their shoes together so that they could not run after them. The customer was in such a state of ecstasy that he never missed his billfold until he started to pull his pants up. By that time the he-she had hopped out of the car and was long gone.

This particular night we spotted one of the he-she's on a side street off Jefferson Street. We got out of our car and called him or it over to our car and I said "what do you have in your pocketbook?" "Same old stuff the he-she" replied.

I said, "well let's take a look." I opened up the purse and inside I found a prescription bottle with the label scraped off and there were 10 pills inside the bottle. I placed this person under arrest, handcuffed him or her and made the suspect lean against the side on my unmarked car. When I walked to the back of my car, the suspect looked like he or her was getting ready to run, so I leaned over the trunk and as the subject started to run and I grabbed him or her by the hair of the head. Keep in mind this person was handcuffed with his arms behind his back and also wearing high heel shoes. The suspect took off leaving me holding only a nasty wig.

I jumped in my car and told Foster to go towards Jefferson Street and I would meet him up there as I was driving off. We couldn't find this person at this time and I told Foster that "we just lost a good set of handcuffs."

I asked "Foster can't you run any faster than that?" He said, "well what happened to you?"

I said, "I'm 25 years older than you, that's what happened to me." We drove down about a half a block on Jefferson Street when a Restaurant owner flagged us down. He said that some guy in a dress just ran into my Restaurant and then ran into the restroom and he had handcuffs on. We went into the restroom and grabbed our suspect who already had his hands in front of him with the handcuffs still intact. I thought that is what being young and limber can do for you.

He said, "how did you find me?"

I answered by saying we just followed your scent and the swarm of flies. I added, "You leave a trail like a slug wherever you travel."

He answered; I don't think that is very nice.

OK, was my reply then what would you like me to

to say about you. No answer from him after this. I placed it under arrest and we went downtown to the Prisoner Processing and there he was charged with having an illegal prescription, fleeing and eluding. The next day in Court, he was still in his dress, but no wig. I threw it in the garbage, so he'll just have to buy another one. The Judge found him Guilty and fined him $250.00 and time suspended. Cha Ching!

We never saw him on the streets again. Heaven only knows where he went. I'm hoping that he went to somewhere far away. I do not like arresting these He-She's because they are disease ridden and very dangerous because we forget that we are dealing with a man, because they are men in women's clothes.

SHELBY PARK GOLF COURSE

One night on the way over to my girlfriend's house after I had finished my shift and decided to drive through Shelby Park where I used to play golf in my younger years. Sections of the road serpentined through 5 separate golf holes. When I came around a curve in the road I saw an automobile on the 16th hole putting green. The car was circling around and making ruts in the putting green surface doing severe damage to the surface of the green.

I was in my unmarked Vice car and I had blue lights in the front grill. I called for a back-up and then I headed onto the fringe of the 16th green and I bumped the siren several times with my headlights on high beam.

I hurriedly copied the license plate number down on a piece of paper. I then opened my door and approached the suspect's driver's door. I asked, what the heck is wrong with you?" I told him give me some I.D., from both of you guys. But, I wasn't driving the car sir was his reply. Maybe not, but you are in the car and that makes you guilty of this crime also. It's known as Aiding and Abetting.

I asked how old they were. As I thought, they were both under 18 years old. I said give me your phone numbers of your parents and it had better be the right one. I don't imagine your parents are going to be too happy about this situation and of the cost that somebody is going to have to pay to fix this mess. Do you clowns have any idea what it costs to build one of these greens? It takes thousands of dollars and a lot of labor which isn't cheap.

I advised these two that they were under arrest for malicious destruction of property. I asked the driver "who does this car belong too?" He replied, my dad. I said, "I wonder what pops will think about this property destruction while you were in his car." I added, "he can pick up his car at the tow in lot." The young driver said, please don't tow my dad's car because he will kill me when he finds out what I have done. I said, this is a done deal and I'm calling the wrecker now. I could see that these two boys looked scared not only about being arrested but of what their parents were going to do to them.

I told them that the wrecker should be here pretty soon. You know someone is going to have to pay for these damages and since you are juveniles, I guess it will fall upon your parents to pay for these damages.

The back-up arrived and I moved the vehicle from the 16th green to the 17th fairway so that the tow truck driver would have room to hook up the car for towing.

Officer, you know that my parents aren't going to like this. I bet you don't know who my parents are, do you?

No, I don't and it won't make any difference, because I caught you both tearing up this putting green. We can rake it out, Officer. I replied, It's going to take more than a rake to fix this mess. I'll bet at least $4,000.00.

The two juveniles were taken to Juvenile for processing.

Instead of getting to my girlfriend's house at 11:15 PM, I pulled into her driveway at 2 AM. I entered the house and she was lying on the couch with the TV still on. I turned the TV off and went over and kissed her on the cheek, which woke her up. She fixed us both an egg sandwich and we both fell asleep on the couch.

A couple of weeks later when I went to Juvenile Court on these two boys who tore up the 16th green at Shelby Park. The damage was estimated around $4,000.00 dollars, in addition there were court costs plus 6 months' probation.

Their father's came up to me and thanked me for the way I handled their arrest. They said you gave them a good talking too about their safety and you were not a bully, you just seemed to care about their safety.

You know I have two boys and they get into trouble also, but not like this. You can punish them but not too hard. I talk to them with reason and their punishment is working around the house helping with the mowing of the grass, cleaning out the pool and whatever else I can think of. You can punish them, but you have to be careful not to push them too hard. One of the father's told me that his son was going to be punished and his driver's license will be taken away for 6 months. The other father told me the same thing about his son who was driving at the time when the incident happened. He stated, it's ankle express for some time Officer.

I was thinking as I was getting in my car, yeah I really would hate to be in those two boys' shoes right now.

This was my day off and as I drove back through Shelby Park to my girlfriend's house, I was thinking about all the times that I spent playing Golf at Shelby Park. I guess I'll always have memories both good and bad.

ANOTHER ARREST

During my last years at the Police Department, I was a Detective Lieutenant in the Vice Squad Division. We targeted drugs, prostitution, motorcycle gangs and traffic violators and those we knew had warrants on them. At times it was like catching flies, they seemed to pop up from nowhere. Many of them had numerous warrants, for all types of violations.

I portrayed an older guy looking for a date to both men and women. This was nerve racking and my sweat glands seemed to shift in high gear when a suspect got into the car, man or woman I didn't know if they had a box cutter in their bra or a knife in the man's pants pocket or an ice pick taped to his leg or a gun in his Cowboy boot. Everything is fine until you make a case and you tell them that you are Vice and that they are going to jail. This is when all hell breaks loose sometimes.

Picking these guys up was easy if you knew where to look. They stood on street corners or the middle of the street waiting to hop into any car that slows down. It was like shooting fish in a barrel. Our unit made a lot of arrests, sometimes faster that we could process them.

This was very dangerous and my sweat gland's seemed to over react after the initial arrest. I could feel the moisture going down my back and my armpits got extremely wet during this process. During this time I was 50 years old and I started to think that I was getting too old for this shit. The men were the most dangerous when they knew that an arrest was imminent.

One night I encountered a big guy and after he got into my unmarked vehicle he grabbed my right leg and squeezed it hard, then he flexed his arm muscle, damn it was big. I knew that it was getting time to hang it up; I thought I'm getting too old for this shit.

This guy thought I was gay and looking for company for the night. He claimed to be an ex-Marine and he said he loved to fight. I prepared for the worst and I tapped my brakes three times to signal Foster or a backup man who usually followed me for safety reasons. This was to let Foster know that a deal had been made for some type of sex act for money.

We were headed out 4th Avenue South when my Foster lit us up and bumped his siren. The ex-Marine said, "what's going on?" I said "be cool, I might have run through a caution light at the last intersection."

I pulled to the side of the roadway and stopped as Foster approached my car on the passenger's side. I lowered his window and told the suspect that he was under arrest for solicitation of prostitution. I told him at this time I was an undercover Vice Lieutenant. He stiffened up as I grabbed his left arm and Foster reached into the car and grabbed his right arm stretching it out the window and bending it backwards to try and restrain him. I said in a loud voice, "don't make it any worse than it is or I'll have to charge you with resisting arrest."

It took all my strength to bend his left arm behind his back. Foster and I handcuffed the suspect after a brief struggle.

Several days later in court he testified that I let him fondle me while we were riding around. His Lawyer asked for dismissal because of my supposedly lewd conduct. The D.A. then put me back on the stand in rebuttal to the suspect's testimony. I then produced a tape recording of our entire conversation from the time he entered my vehicle to when he was being placed under arrest for solicitation of prostitution. The suspect's Lawyer looked very angry after hearing the tape recording and pleaded No Contest for his client. I told his Lawyer after Court, you have to stop believing what your clients tell you, Counselor.

Results – he was fined, plus court costs and 6 months' probation (supervised Probation only because of how he lied under oath.)

That night I told my girlfriend, Patsy, that I cannot continue this type of undercover work due to the stress, and anxiety attacks.

Fighting with the suspects that we arrested were becoming more common and from the way this guy was acting, I though another front passenger seat was going to be broken.

Luck was on my side tonight and everything worked out to our advantage. I thought, I'm getting too old for this shit. I could feel the sweat running down my back.

I had a case pending before the Grand Jury and I saw the Medical Examiner in the hallway outside of the Courtroom. He asked me how I was doing; I told him that I was having some anxiety attacks and that when I arrested a subject I could feel the sweat going down my back. He told me that I had probably lost 15 years from my longevity, due to the fact so much of my liver was removed from the gun shots I received on March 6, 1970.

I really began to seriously consider taking my pension in the near future, especially after what the Medical Examiner had told me.
This really rattled me, I know that I have got to consider my health. At the same time I love what I am doing and I don't want to give it up. I think I am between a rock and a hard place on this one.

PROSTITUTION STINGS

Many times during the summer months , we would target a certain spot that we knew was frequently known for guys wanting a date. This sting Prostitution Sting was run mostly on Dickerson Road. This is the area that most of the girls work. We used female Police Officers for decoys in front of a sleazy Motel.

The decoys would walk on the edge of the road waiting for someone to come by and proposition them for sex. This was like shooting fish in a barrel. We literally could not process the paper work as fast as the John's were arrested. Of course, whenever they were caught they said that this was entrapment and this was the first time that they had done this.

Yeah Right!!

Many of the John's said to undercover Police women, "You're awfully clean looking to be a prostitute. They would add the girls usually have rotten teeth and tattoos everywhere on their body. One guy told the undercover Officer that he saw a tattoo of a popsicle on her lower right abdomen with the wording that read, LICK THIS.

Our undercover females would reply with, we are from Memphis, Tennessee and our Pimps won't allow us to have any tattoo's on our body.   The guys would come back with, well what about your teeth. What about our teeth, replied the undercover female. We try to keep ourselves in good shape, so do you want to party or do you just want to talk? Hell, let's party was his reply, how much for a straight lay? The girl would tell him how much and then she would say I have a room on the back row of the Motel and she would give him a room number. The guy would drive his car around, but the girl would stay on the edge of the road and wait for another John to come by. When the John would drive around back and he was greeted by several Officers which would tell him that he was under arrest for Solicitation of Prostitution or sometimes we would tell them "No Pussy Today."

Their reply was, but I didn't do anything.

"Yeah right, you can tell that to the Judge," was our reply.

Upon walking to one of the John's car, I looked into the inside of his back seat and noticed a lot of female underwear. I asked the perp what do you do with these panties? Do you sniff the crotch or chew on them? No Reply from the perp.

These sting operations for 2 or 3 days would result between 200 and 300 arrests. All types of men were caught in these stings. Preachers, Deacons, Businessmen a few Metro employees, 1 Fireman, 1 Retired Law Enforcement Officer, a few Military Personnel, and men that were in Nashville with their wives on business or vacation.

We did catch one Deacon on a Monday night and the same man on the following Wednesday night after he had been to Church. They never learn. Praise the Lord!

Sometime later I saw the panty perp at a Flea Market selling used merchandise. No panties. He did not recognize me at that time. However if he did it would not have made any difference. This type of person has no shame and does not get embarrassed very easily.

To this day there are still stings and the John's never quit. Some of the John's are caught time after time.

Prostitution is as old as time itself, it cannot be stopped and in my opinion it should be legalized along with gambling and Massage Parlors and it should be taxed. I doubt this would slow it down, but it would surely make the Municipalities a lot of money.

WHERE'S MY PANTS

One prostitute would make a date with an older Guy. She said that they can't run as fast as a young Guy. They would go to a Motel Room and she would help him get undressed and teasing him along to distract him for what was about to happen. She then would tell him to lie on the bed and close his eyes while she got undressed. She would make all kinds of funny noises. Again she would tell him to keep his eyes closed and she would tell him when to open them. He replied, "this suspense is killing me, come on to your daddy and I'll make it worth your while." You see what I have. Oh yeah, and I can't wait either. He would reply, "the suspense is killing me and I want to treat you right."

She would then grab his pants and shoes and run out slamming the door. The startled man would holler "what is going on!" She would get into her pimps car and drive out of the Motel's parking lot. Leaving the Sucker with no shoes and no pants. The prostitute also writes down his name, address, SS#, phone number and anything else that they could use against him, should he decide to make trouble or press charges against her. Most of the men were married and prosecuting a prostitute was usually not done. Mainly because that the male would be too embarrassed. Especially when they go to Church.

She would then throw the billfold into a mailbox and his clothes went into a Drop Off Box for Charity. Of course she also took his money and credit cards.

The Credit cards would be used very quickly. This was done before he had time to call and report them stolen, that is if he remembered the names of the Credit Cards. He would probably be so startled at what happened this would give her more time to buy things. She kept the purchases under $50.00 so she wouldn't have to show any identification. If they asked, she would say it was her Daddy's card and they would leave the store if a problem arises.

After making several purchases at different stores, she would sell the Card or Cards For $50.00 or less, or whatever she could get. There was always somebody willing to to purchase them. These women had so many tricks to play on these men and they played them very. As the old saying goes, "there's no fool like an old fool."

ESCORT SERVICE ROLE PLAYING

The reason Vice does not continually work the Escort Services is because it takes so much time and Personnel in order to make just a couple of arrests in one night. On this particular night, we rented a room at the Marriott Hotel with an adjoining room which had a door that the other Officers could have easy access to this room. This would make a quick entrance to the room when the deal had been made and the Officers would take down the female Escort.

We needed two plain clothes outside the Hotel, if the arrest was made for the driver of the female Escort. I was chosen to play this role of the John, because I was the oldest.

Four or five more Officers were needed in the adjoining room to monitor the hidden camera and the audio equipment. I picked an Escort Service at random out of the Yellow Pages and called them and told them that I needed some company. I was asked if I wanted any particular type of girl, I said that I preferred a slim blonde. I gave them the address and my room number and the Escort Service said that someone would be there within the hour. I had a velour bathrobe with my initials engraved on it, I laid this across one of the beds. I sat at the small table and waited for the Escort to arrive. In about 45 minutes, I heard a knock at the door. I opened the door and stepped back and let the female into my room. She sat down on the bed and I sat at the table, we introduced ourselves to each other and she then stated that there was a $200.00 fee for one hour of company. I said, what do I get for this $200.00? She looked at me and grinned and said a "lot of happiness." She asked me for my Driver's License. I replied, "it is in the car locked up because about 6 months ago, I had it stolen by an Escort." She asked for my name and I gave it to her and she picked up the phone and called the Escort Service, she told them the story that I told her and added that he looks OK to me. She then looked at me and asked me if I had the $200.00? I reached in my pocket and pulled out a sizeable amount of money and counted her out the twenty dollar bills, in which she took and placed in a zippered compartment in her purse. She said also, tips are acceptable. I said we "will see."

I stood up and started unbuttoning my shirt and she kicked off her shoes and slipped out of her dress, leaving on her bra and panties. She had a few Tattoos on her, but the one that caught my eye was a very large Peacock on the back of her right shoulder. I unbuckled my belt and let my pants drop to the floor, but I still had my underwear on.

At that time the adjoining door opened and in comes the Calvary. She was advised of her rights and also told that we were the Police and she was under Arrest for Solicitation. I retrieved the $200.00 from her purse, which I had just given her a few moments earlier. I asked her where was her driver? She was visibly upset and said that he drops me off and leaves and returns in about an hour and a half. I got dressed and she put on her clothes. I asked her just how much money she makes in a month. She replied, last month I made about $11,000.00 dollars, sometimes I make more and sometimes I make less.

The caper took about four and a half hours for this one arrest. Two of the Officers took her to Headquarters for booking while the others stayed at the Hotel room to pack up all of the equipment. There was no need for us to try for another arrest because these Escort Services have a network and when someone is arrested it spreads like wildfire.

This Escort did not give us any trouble, she was very personable and articulate and she told us that working for an Escort Service was safer than working the streets and the money was much better. One of the Officers told me that when they arrived at Headquarters the Escort called her office and told them what had happened.

SUMMARY: One arrest, eight Officer's tied up for 5 ½ hours, all for a fine and suspended sentence. In my Opinion it should be legalized, because everyone knows that it is the oldest profession and it cannot be stopped!

ANOTHER NIGHT ON THE STREET

While working in the Vice Section I received a complaint from a Motel on Dickerson Road. These motels are old and seedy, run down and bug infested. The grass looks like it has never been mowed. Paint peeling of the outside walls and the gutters are packed with so many leaves they are hanging up there by a thread. This is a typical whore house. The manager stays behind a closed in office where you slide the money into a tray and to get the key for the room.

I don't know why Codes won't just condemn these places. My calls to them are not answered. I guess it is because I leave the message ending that this is Lieutenant Joe McEwen from the Vice Section of the Police Department. I guess there are so many calls on more important matters in Nashville, due to the bustling construction throughout Nashville. This construction hasn't slowed down in 20 years and it looks like there is no end in sight.

After roll call, I thought I should get on out there and see what is going on. Hell, I know what is happening, some of the girls are getting a room and doing tricks in it and when they leave the place looks like a tornado hit it. There may be damaged walls, some blood on the sheets along with another disgusting matter. The maids that clean the room wear masks and a double pair of gloves, why, because they have young children at home and they don't want to carry anything home to them. The Motel manager shouldn't complain, he's renting those dilapidated so called rooms six and seven times a day. The beds probably don't even have time to get cold.

I met the manager of the Motel and he told me the girl in room 203 was bringing in an excessive amount of males to her room throughout the day and night. Well, I explained you are renting these rooms by the hour instead of daily rates. So, what do you expect? You don't have to answer me in a way like that Officer. Oh no! How would you like me to answer a stupid reply like that? Just forget it Officer and get the girl out of the room. I can't because she has paid you what you asked her to pay and it is her room.

I parked just adjacent to the Motel. I was in my Vice car which was a Monte Carlo with T-Tops. It was a pleasant night so I removed the T-Tops and placed them in the trunk. Within 30 minutes of parking my car a tall blonde came up to my side of the door. I acknowledged her and she asked if I was looking for a date. I said, "You sure have a big set of tits." What are they double d's? I asked. She was the type that could gang bang all night long and would never get winded or break a sweat. She would be a real money maker for some pimp. I looked around and I didn't see any guy that looked like a pimp. Her slacks looked like they were painted on and she had a wide black belt that was cinched tight around her waist. Very heavy make up on, dark piercing eyes and pouty red lips and a low cut shirt which was exposing the tops of her breasts. This is a hard look for a girl in her mid-twenties. Then I asked "her how much and what do I get for my money?"

She leaned on the car door still exposing a large portion of her breasts and said and for 20 bucks a blow job, 30 dollars a straight lay, 40 dollars for half and half in my Motel room. Let me get this straight now, I don't do anal sex.

"That's fine with me," I replied. " I don't care about dotting the eye anyway."

"If you want to go 2 times the prices double, payment in advance, no exceptions," she replied.

"OK get in," I said "don't forget to buckle up."

My Vice partner Foster was parked across the street just a short distance away. He was watching me with his binoculars, this was just for safety precautions. These girls have been known to get pretty violent when they think they are caught by the Police and they do carry knives or box cutters with a razor blade. I know because I have been cut across the wrist with a steak knife and I know what to look for now. When they start for their purse it's not a good thing. Box cutters seem to be there weapon of choice because they can put it in their bra or if they are wearing socks they slip it under the elastic. The needles are kept under their bra in the
small of their back.

I put the Monte Carlo in gear and started towards the road. "I'm going to get us a 6 pack, do you need anything?" I asked.

"Yeah you can get me a pack of cigarettes, Winston filters," she answered.

I drove a short distance down the street and immediately pulled in front of Foster's vehicle, stopped the car and turned to the girl and said, "I'm Vice and that is my partner behind us and you're under arrest for solicitation for prostitution." I spouted off the Miranda Warning real fast, handcuffed her and proceeded to go downtown to Prisoner processing with Foster driving directly behind as a witness to show that I did everything by the book. These girls will lie big time, trying to get us in trouble. Some examples were, rubbing their crotch, fondling their breasts, saying that I exposed myself to them or burned them with my cigar. I usually tape my conversations with the girls, whenever possible. Sometimes I don't have time to key it in or pull it out from under my seat. The tape recorder picks up all sounds, windshield wiper noise, car horns, gravel noise, motor, air conditioner or the heater . Unlike the TV, where you hear no sounds or effects.   But tonight, I left my recorder on my desk in the Vice Section. You can bet when I get downtown I will get my tape recorder.

On the way to booking, she told me that I was going to be sorry I arrested her. I said, "Sure I will." I answered, "I already am because your breath smell's pretty bad. You might consider buying some mouthwash or chewing gum."

While processing the prisoner, I ran her record and found that she had 4 outstanding Warrant's on her, this made it even better, now she can't make bail. We waited until she was processed and all the paper work was finished and then Foster and I went back to work on the Streets of Nashville after picking up my tape recorder from the Vice Section.

Two days later when her court case came up there was a newspaper article concerning her arrest. She told a reporter that after she got into my Monte Carlo I exposed myself to her and asked her to masturbate me and I would let her off with a written citation. Of course Foster saw the entire arrest and his testimony is what saved me. Once again, I knew that it was time to start considering thinking about taking my pension. Things were beginning to get out of hand and causing me embarrassment.   The next day when I visited my Aunt she said that she had just read the article in the Newspaper about the arrest I had made the night before. She looked at me like she had her doubts about this incident.

When the trash I become involved with tells the media lies about me when they were arrested, for some strange reason many people think that if something is in print it is the truth.

NOT SO! Sometimes it is very far from the truth. Each time I make an arrest or stop someone it becomes more difficult. The thoughts of the night I was shot comes to mind all the time while I am running the streets looking for someone to take down. I guess the Post Traumatic Stress
Disorder is kicking me hard. The shortened name is PTSD.

A seasoned whore when getting into the car will immediately try to open the glove box to see if there is a radio inside of it, pull down the sun visor, check the back seat and look for any tell-tale signs of me being a Vice Officer. This is why we change cars so often. We wear disguises, like clear glasses, not sunglasses, different hats and no rings on our fingers. They rub their hand over your chest area to see if you have a badge hanging from your neck under your t-shirt.
Time to go! No more Cha Ching!

POLICE OFFICER DEATH'S

There are numerous incidents involving Police Officers, one in particular was Officer George Wall who bought my house out in the country after me being shot and placing my house up for Sale. One night when George and his wife were arguing, he killed his wife and then turned his gun on himself, committing Suicide. This was done while his children looked on in horror!

Police Officer Curtis Jordan was killed in a domestic dispute that he answered. The suspect was sitting on a couch and he reached between the cushions and retrieved a butcher knife and stabbed Curtis just below his vest. He died several days later after numerous transfusions. My two boys Joe Joe and Eric played Basketball with Curtis in the Police Academy Gym when they came to work with me one day. They knew Curtis on a personal basis. This was a hard blow for my two sons. I told them over and over that life comes at you hard, very hard.

On occasion Officer Bill Bowlin would come to my house in South Nashville. Bill would come by about once a month on the weekend and we would just sit and talk about Police Work and just how much being a Police Officer meant to him. Officer Bowlin was Major Bowlin's son. Major Bowlin was the Director of the Training Academy. Bill was a model Recruit and I showed him no favoritism during his 26 weeks at the Training Academy as a Recruit. It wasn't long after this time that he answered a call in Inglewood with a dispute over a lawnmower. Some elderly man shot Bill in the head and he was killed over a $15.00 lawnmower.

Another close friend of mine was Officer James Long, who was killed in a car crash while off duty. He use to come down on occasion and just talk while I was working an extra job at Shoney's. I remember one July 4th at my house when James showed up and we all sat down and ate fried chicken that Patsy had made. We were very close and his death hit me hard.

I remember one time he rented a Limousine and went to pick up my son Joe Joe from work. One day in late Spring, Patsy and I stopped at Taco Bell on Gallatin Road in Nashville, to get a bite to eat. As we pulled into the parking lot I noticed a Metro Police Car parked at the side of the building. I pulled up beside the Police Car and noticed that it was Officer Paul Scurry.

I was one of Officer Scurry's Training Instructors at the Academy when he attended the Police Recruit Training. I asked him, "How are you doing and what's going on?"

He said "that he was looking forward to going to Uncle Dave Macon's Days in Murfreesboro this year."

I told him that we lived in Murfreesboro. I asked Paul where he planned to stay when he was coming to Murfreesboro for the Music Festival.

He said, I hadn't thought about it yet. I told him that he would be welcomed to stay with Patsy and I. You will have private room with a TV and Patsy is a very good cook. Just look at me. I told him that he could park at the lower parking area of the Library for free and Uncle Dave Macon's events are just 2 short blocks away from the parking garage. He said "he would to stay with us if it wouldn't be too much trouble." I told Paul that it was no trouble and that we would love to have him.

I gave him my business card with my phone number on it and told him to call us about a week before he came down and his room would be waiting. We left Taco Bell and went back to Murfreesboro. Several weeks later, I learned that Paul was murdered while attempting to arrest some thug who was held up in an apartment in Madison. I didn't know all of the details and I didn't want to know them. It is an entirely different feeling when a Police Officer is killed. When you have connections with someone, it is a totally different feeling. I was with Paul 5 days a week for 26 weeks during his training. He was in his mid-thirties with his whole life ahead of him.

This is just a very few of the many Officers that have died one way or the other while on or off duty. Police work is a brotherhood that bonds Police Officers together.

MARRIAGE AND HEALTH PROBLEMS

Well, 6 years later in 1992, I asked Patsy one day, don't you think it is about time that we get married. She replied, "but Joe don't you remember that you said you didn't ever want to get married again." I replied ICMM. Patsy said, "what does that mean?" It means I changed my mind.

In 1993 we decided to look for a bigger house and looked everywhere and finally finding a lot in Murfreesboro, this was in a good subdivision. From day one we were therehelping with whatever we could and just making sure that our home would be built to last.

In 1994, after going to a yard sale and buying a cement mixer. I felt a pain in my jaw and my left arm was numb. I told Patsy, "I'm in trouble, do you have any aspirin with you?"

I stopped at a 7-11 and she went in and got a coke and she gave me three baby aspirin and I felt a little better, but that it didn't last long. We headed over to my youngest son Eric, who was a Paramedic Fireman for Metro in Nashville. He said, "Dad we have got to get to an Emergency Room ASAP." We drove to Lavergne to a small Hospital and they took me in right away. The Doctor came out and told Eric and Patsy that he thought I had a aorta infarction.

Eric told him that his dad was shot in 1970 and that is what he saw on the X-ray was from the gunshot scars. They gave me some morphine and told me that we had to go to Vanderbilt ER right away. I said that I wasn't going to pay for an Ambulance ride. I told the Doctor that I was going to drive my truck and that Patsy could hold the IV up. But we went to Nashville in an Ambulance and the Paramedics gave me Morphine two times on the way.

When we reached the Vanderbilt ER they began to check me out and they drew blood. By this time I was feeling better and they were about to let me go home. A Dr. came in about the time I was getting off of the bed and getting dressed and he said, your blood work up showed that you had a Heart Attack, and then the Dr. said get him to Intensive Care ASAP.

This really scared Patsy. The very next day they put a stent into my left circumflex which had a 90% blockage. This operation was performed while I was wide awake. I stayed in the Intensive Care Unit for two days. Patsy could only come in to see me just for a few minutes several times a day. She stayed in the waiting room just outside the ICU. I was told that she slept in a chair right outside the ICU and that she never left the Hospital until I was released. She told me that a nurse gave her a pillow and a blanket.

When Patsy was allowed to stay in the room with me, I asked her, why is everyone sticking their finger up my ass hole, four men and one female shoved their index finger up my ass. It was a heart attack that I had not my prostate. Joe, you forget that you are at Vanderbilt and this is training hospital where the students are learning to be a Doctor. When we finally went home, the men were installing a carport cover that we had ordered.

A building Inspector came by and asked to see our Permit. I told him that I didn't know we had to have one and that I had just gotten out of the Hospital from having a heart attack.

The Inspector said, well you have to get a permit. Patsy went downtown and she got a Permit and when she got back home she showed it to the Inspector and he said go ahead and erect your Carport cover.

We have worked on our home trying to improve it so that we could live out our golden days together in our own castle. She is still by my side and whenever I would go outside to dosomething in the garage I would have a hard time trying to remember where I put my tools. I never did put them back where they were supposed to go. I would ask her and before you know it she is out the door and somehow she finds what I am looking for.

Life is really good when you have a mate that works with you and not against you. She is beside me all the time and I wouldn't want it any other way.

In February 2002, I received a phone call from the office Chief of Police in Nashville, TN. They informed me that I was to receive the Purple Heart for being shot in 1970. Deputy Chief and Acting Chief of Police Deborah Y. Faulkner told me that it was an oversight that I had never received a formal reward for that night in 1970 when I was shot and almost lost my life. I told her that the friends that I had made while working for the Police Department meant more to me than an award. But, at the same time I really felt honored by receiving this award. I told Deputy Chief Faulkner that not a day goes by that I do not think about that night. My two sons and I use to cut Deborah's grass in South Nashville. We were both Police Officers at this time.

I truly believe in Guardian Angels because I had one on my shoulder several times. One was with me the night I was shot 5 times. The Doctors that operated on me was astounded that Imade it through the operation and walked out of the Hospital 22 days later. In the coming years my Angel is still watching over me. I still suffer from severe cramps of the stomach muscles.

I guess that this is what you could call posttraumatic stress syndrome. In 2004, I began to experience shortness of breath by just walking. Patsy insisted on me going to the Doctor. Well, I went and did a stress test. They found out that I had 5 blockages and the Doctor said that he would try to stent the blockages. The Dr. told me that this was beyond his expertise and he had me go to a Cardiologist. The next day I saw the Cardiologist and he asked me what do you want to do? I said, right now I feel pretty good and what would happen if I chose not to have my chest cracked? He said well, "sometime in the future you will be walking around in your back yard and fall over dead."

I said, "Operate as soon as possible". I went in the hospital the next day and the surgery was a rough one. When I awoke, it felt just like when I was shot in 1970. I had tubes everywhere. Patsy cried when she saw me in the ICU. She was a trouper; she did not leave the Hospital until I was released 8 days later. Several times I felt like I was upside down in the bed, hell I even fell out of the bed and hit my head and it made a huge bump. The Nurses were coming in every few minutes checking on me. They asked me who the President was and I told them, "it is Bush." They drew a circle around the knot on my head, to see if it would go down on its own. I looked like I had been one hell of a fight, but it did go down. My left leg gave me a lot of trouble, because the vein was removed so they could place the vein in my heart to fix the five blockages. Two of the blockages were so close together, they were tandemed together; therefore there was a triple bypass and not a quintupled. I already had one stent put in my left circumflex vein from 1995.

In July 2007, I thought I was having a kidney Stone attack so I went to the ER and they ran a lot of tests and X-Rays. They removed the Kidney Stone, but they also told me that I had an Abdominal Aorta Aneurysm. They call this a triple AAA. This really upset me; I thought what else is going to happen to me. In May 2008, I saw Dr. Martin at St. Thomas to confirm that the Abdominal Aorta Aneurysm had not gotten any bigger. It had gotten just a wee bit bigger, but Dr. Martin said not to worry, that he would keep checking every 6 months to see how it was doing. Did he just tell me not to WORRY. I made my regular visits and it seemed to be doing OK.

In January 2011, I thought I was having another Kidney Stone attack and that it was moving around and I was in a lot of pain. I went to see my Urologist and his Office was full of patients waiting to be seen. I did not have an appointment so I had to wait until they could fit me in. We had been waiting for some time and I told Patsy, "let's go." My patience was getting thin at this point. She said, "no we have waited this long and we could be next." Well, it wasn't before long until they called me back and they gave me a Cat Scan. I went to the restroom and Patsy said that the Doctor came running down the hall and he was asking her where I was. She told him that I had went to the restroom. When I came out the Doctor told me that he had already talked with Dr. Martin at St. Thomas and that I needed to go to the ER as soon as possible. I asked him why? He stated that it wasn't a Kidney Stone, but the Abdominal Aorta Aneurysm was now 5.3cm. which they said it was as big as a tennis ball. I told the Doctor that the last time I saw Dr. Martin it was 4.5 cm. Joe, get out of here , St. Thomas knows that you are on your way.

After checking into the ER, we waited for quite some time. Neither Patsy nor I had anything to eat or drink since the night before and that was at 9 PM. The nurse got us both a sandwich and a cold drink. She said I couldn't have anything else because I was going to operated on the next morning. There were no empty rooms so they had a make shift set up in the prep room before surgery.

Patsy had to go downstairs and wait, they would not let her stay with me. I needed her beside me, because she keeps me under control. Being in a hospital made me think about the night I was shot and all the turmoil. I was not a happy patient. I had no TV, no phone and no restroom. It was just a lot of beds with curtain partitions between the beds. If I had use the restroom, a male Nurse would walk me down the hall. I was hooked up to an IV so I had to roll that alongside me.

The next morning I asked one of the male Nurses to call downstairs and get Patsy come up here. Patsy came in and I was so glad to see her.

Dr. Martin came in to tell me that he was going to operate as soon as possible. He then took Patsy outside in the hallway and told her that that if he nicked the aneurysm that Joe would bleed out in about 10 seconds. Patsy did not want to hear this.

Patsy came back into the make shift room just as I was being wheeled into the prep room for surgery. She gave me a big kiss and then they wheeled me out. I could tell in her eyes that she had been crying.

She called Joe Joe and within the hour he was at the Hospital and he saw that Patsy had been crying. He assured Patsy that his dad was as tough as nails and that he would be alright.

Joe Joe, also told Patsy, have you forgotten that dad has a Guardian Angel watching over him.

After surgery I went to a room and Patsy and Joe Joe was waiting on me to come. It was a rough night, but I made it. I wasn't in much pain because of all the drugs that they had given me. I slept through most of the night and then the next morning Dr. Martin came in and said, "Joe you can go home, but you have to take it easy for a couple of days." I told him no problem.

Joe Joe came by to check on me and he told Patsy, you see I told you that dad was tough as nails. The nurse came in and said, "Joe I have to take you catheter out."

I begged her to leave it in. I told her that I always have to leave the catheter in because I have trouble urinating after any surgery. About that time I felt a little tug and it was out.

I felt pretty good so we went and ate breakfast and then to Kroger's to get my prescriptions. We went several other places, I was feeling no pain. Patsy said OK Mighty Mouse enough is enough, we are going home.

When we got home, I felt like I needed to urinate. I tried and tried with no luck. I called several places to see if they had a catheter and only one store had one. So we went and got itand when we got back to the house, I was in so much pain. I forgot to wash the area real good so I got an infection. Later as soon as I put the catheter in it was instant relief.

Things have a way of working out OK; it was just that I don't have very much patience. I guess it is from being on the Police Force.

All in all, Patsy was right there by my side like she has always been. She is my Rock. She knows that if she is sick, I'll be right by her side. Through the years we have bonded and we are Co-Dependent with one another. This is my mate for life and I know that she feels the same way about me.

MEETING EVEL KNIEVEL

In the May of 1998, Patsy and I went to see my oldest son, Joe Joe in Clearwater, Florida. He had an apartment on the 7th Floor at the Crystal Bay Apartments.

After we had settled in he asked me, "Dad do you know who lives down the hall from me?" Just how do you expect me to know who lives down the hall from you? OK, I'll tell you, it's your man Evel Knievel.

My reply was, "no way." I asked him if he was kidding me."

Joe Joe said "No way dad, he really lives just down the hall on the back side of the Crystal Bay Apartments."

We went out on his balcony and he pointed to the right and said, you see that car down there.

"I said which one?"

"Do you see the red Mitsubishi with the Florida tag K-TWIN."

"Yeah, I see it."

"OK the car that is parked to the left of it belongs to Evel and also the Motorcycle that he rides is right next to his car."

I couldn't hardly believe that I might get to meet Evel. I have watched all of his stunts on TV. Later on that day we went to the beach and when we returned Evel was just pulling into his parking spot. When Evel got close to the entrance he said, well Joe "I see you have your Dad visiting you. I can tell it is your dad because you look alike." I shook Evel's hand and I asked him if I could take a picture of him and me, he said sure thing. This really made my trip to Florida meaningful to get to meet Evel Knievel. He seemed to be a really nice person. He showed me his walking cane and when he unscrewed the bottom of it off, well to my surprise this is where he kept his refreshments. He looked pale and weak and he was on the list for a Liver transplant, which he received later on.

THEODORE ROOSEVELT AWARD

One Thursday night in August 2011, I received a phone call from a Retired Police Officer who was my dear friend Foster Hite whom I have known about 30+ years. When the phone rang, I picked it up and said, "Hello."

The caller said "Hey Joe, what are you doing?"

I replied, "Nothing, just watching TV".

He then asked, "have you heard from the Police Chief's Office?" Debbie has been trying to reach you.

"I said no! Why what has happened?"

Well he then said, "You need to call the Chief's Office in the morning and talk to Debbie."

I couldn't sleep all night thinking and wondering what this could be. I called the Chief's Office the next morning and asked them "What is going on?"

Debbie told me that I had won the Theodore Roosevelt Award and the ceremony would be September 1, 2011.

"I asked her "are you serious."

She answered, "yes Joe it is for real."

I could hardly talk. It hadn't really set in what I was just told. My wife had to take over the phone because I couldn't talk, I started crying. Patsy talked with the Debbie who gave her all the information about the Ceremony.

Well, it seemed like it took September 1, 2011 forever to get here. Upon arriving at the Hermitage Station, I couldn't believe the amount of people that attended. Old friends I hadn't seen in a long time. We told great stories of our days on the force.

When the ceremony started, I had the privilege of meeting Sen. Jim Summerville of Dickson, TN. He was very instrumental in the presentation of this Award. I have never met a finer man with such conviction of giving Police Officers that were wounded in the Line of Duty and then returned to perform their duties and get the recognition that they deserved.

Judge J. Randall Wyatt Jr. gave a short speech about us going to Father Ryan High School. He was a sophomore and I was a senior. I have known Randall for over 60+ years. Randall told about how our paths crossed in Norfolk, Virginia. He stated that he was walking down Main Street and he noticed me walking his way. We stopped and chatted briefly and I invited him to come to my apartment for supper. We talked about old times, our Boot Camps and the days at Father Ryan. Little did I know that I would visit him in the Hospital years later when he was seriously injured in an automobile wreck and then he would visit me when I was shot and seriously injured and in Intensive Care. He told of how I would bring a pillow to sit on while I was enrolled in his class at Acquanis. Judge J. Randall Wyatt Jr. was very proficient and well respected throughout the Police Dept. In my entire career with the Police Department I have never, ever heard one word against Judge J. Randall Wyatt Jr. He is so well respected in Davidson County and is considered to be a self-made man, been there, done that type of person.

On March 6, 1970 I was shot 5 times and I survived this ordeal and I returned to the Police Department 17 ½ months later. After I returned back to work, I put my focus on being the best Police Officer I could be. It took me a few years but I was eventually Promoted to the rank of Sergeant and then to the rank of Lieutenant. All of these promotions were acquired while under the leadership of Chief Joe D. Casey.

This is truly a day that I will cherish. So many Officers were present and each one had a different story to tell. Some I remembered and some that I had forgotten. There was even some officers that I had never seen before, but they knew of my shooting and wanted to come. I am so thankful for the time that I had the privilege to serve in the Metropolitan Police Department.

My Grandfather served with the "Rough Rider's" and Teddy Roosevelt in the Spanish American War. He was shot in his hip and used a cane throughout his life. He was a Dentist In Hopkinsville, Kentucky.

STRANGER THAN FICTION

Things happen for a reason and some you can't explain why they happen. When my ex-wife died in 2007 at a Nashville Hospital, my two sons, Joe Joe and Eric never saw their mother the day she passed away. All they could find out was that their mother was taken from the Hospital and sent to somewhere in Memphis, Tennessee. Their sister Lisa, was very controlling after she had the Power of Attorney which was signed by Dean. This was shortly before Dean died. Joe Joe did see his mother the night before she died and one of my stepsons prayed for Dean and she looked up and said his name and she also acknowledged Joe Joe. She had been in a coma and all of a sudden she awoke just long enough to tell Joe Joe that he was not to worry and that it was OK. This really hit Joe Joe hard, but she did call out his name and he gave her a hug.

A couple of years later Joe Joe told me that he needed a lock for his storage shed that was in his back yard. This is where he stored some of his yard tools and ladders. He told me, that if I didn't have one and I just happened to find one that didn't cost too much to please get it for him. I bought one at a yard sale and it was a combination lock and was only 50 cents.

I gave it to him a couple days later. He called me later and asked me if I knew what the combination was to the lock?

I said, was it not in the package with the lock. Yes, it was dad and you won't believe what it was.

I asked him, "what is it?"

He stated that it was 3-18-36. He added, "this is mom's birthday."

I said, "I know that those numbers are the date of her birthday, because I am two weeks older than her and my birthday is 3-4-36." I have never heard of anything like this happening before. How could this possibly happen? Could this have been some type of a Spiritual Intervention? Dean really did love both of her boys dearly. This is still a mystery today.

In the summer of 2009, my sons were taking pictures in Eric's home and Joe Joe's dog Panama, was looking up to the ceiling and barking and her head was moving back and forth and she seemed to be watching something. There was nothing that Joe Joe or Eric could see.

It was a mystery until they had the pictures developed. On every photo that they had taken of Panama there was a white ghost like image on the top half of the picture. Strange but true.

During the summer of 2011 in our home, Patsy and I could not find $200.00 in cash that we had put up for an emergency use. We began to look high and low in all the spots where we had put back money before, but it was nowhere to be found. We knew the places that we had placed money before in the Kitchen, but it wasn't there either. We sat down and started thinking where could this money be? We searched and searched but each time we came up empty.

The kitchen eating bar is where we take care of all our household finances. The money was in ten dollar bills. A couple of days passed and one day we were sitting at our kitchen bar and working a crossword puzzle. For some strange reason I glanced to my left at the China Hutch and my eyes focused on the middle of the Hutch and in plain view was the missing $200.00. Nothing was around it and it stuck out like a sore thumb. I can't explain this and I have given up trying to dwell on how it had gotten there. It was in a plain envelope with $200.00 written on the outside of the envelope, this was the same envelope that we had placed the money in originally.

In 2012, the latter part of December a lifelong friend from Florida came to see Joe Joe and LaRae (Joe Joe's wife) for a visit. LaRae had known Sonja for a real long time, in fact she use to babysit for Sonja's children when they were young. Sonja spent a week with them. When Sonja awoke one morning she told Joe Joe that she had a dream last night. In the dream she saw an image at the foot of the bed where she was sleeping. Dean (Joe Joe's and Eric's mother) told Sonja to tell Joe Joe that she was alright and not to worry about her and to look for the angels.

Dean seems to be watching out for her boys even from the beyond.

A VOICE FROM THE PAST

Late November 2012 my phone rang and the caller asked who was speaking? I said "who do you wish to speak to?" She said "is this Lt. McEwen who used to work for the Police Department in the Vice Section?" I replied "yes it is."

The caller said "23 years ago you saved my life." I said "how so?" She said "that I would always fuss at her whenever I caught her on Dickerson Road while I was working Vice." She added that I said if she was ugly or looked like a bulldog, I could understand why she was working Dickerson Road." I told her she was to pretty to be doing this and if she continued to this lifestyle she would end up murdered or beaten up real bad and left to die in the street or on some dark alley. She said, "I would look her in the eye and tell her to get out while she still could."

I told this woman that this is very emotional for me to receive this type of call and that I appreciated it very much, it is always nice to know that you can help make a difference in someone's life.

She said that she raised her four children, married, got a job and joined the Church and I was right about her leaving the streets. She told me about a close friend of hers that was murdered in New York over a drug deal. I remembered the girl she was talking about. She also told me that she knew then it was time to do something, and she did.

I asked the caller "how she found me?" She told me that she went on Facebook and You Tube and saw where I had won the Theodore Roosevelt Award in September 2011. She also added that I still looked like I did when I was working in Vice. She said, "that she hoped that by calling me on the phone wasn't a bother and she also apologized for calling." I told her breaking up. She said that she had been looking for me for quite some time, but she was hesitant to call me at my home. She closed by adding that when she saw me in Night Court with my glasses around my neck that I looked just like her dad.

This phone call made me think about all the women that I had locked up during my 20+ years with the Police Department. I just wonder how many of them actually took my advice and found a job where they were not in harm's way every time they come in contact with a man looking for sex and whatever else it took to give them pleasure.

This was truly a welcomed phone call.

After we ended the phone call. I thought my life is on the fast track and picking up speed. In a way I miss all the excitement, but I have another life now and I'm truly happy. You know even a dog likes to get patted on the head every once in a while.

In May 2013 the phone rang one morning while I was watching the Price Is Right. This lady whom we will call Iris, her real name will be omitted for obvious reasons. She asked me, am I disturbing you or is this a bad time to talk? "I replied, no and how have you been." We began to talk about events 30 plus years ago when I was a Lieutenant in Vice.

I asked her about some of the girls that was worked the streets back in the early 80's. She told me that every single one of the girls were dead. She mentioned that they either died from drugs or were murdered by their Pimp. I asked her again, are you sure that they are all dead? She emphasized that every single one of the girls that worked the streets back then are gone. I told her that this is really sad, but a person does not grow old if the use drugs or

mainlining. She told me that she was truly blessed for knowing Steve Garton, Foster Hite and myself during the late 1980's.

Again, this was very emotional time for someone to look me up again and tell me about how she was treated and the respect that she was given from me while preaching to her preaching to her to get off the streets while she could. She said, "Joe you would be surprised about how the other girls working the streets remembered the things you told them about getting off the street and how dangerous a situation that they put themselves in an leading the lifestyle that they have chosen."

We talked for about thirty minutes and she gave me her new phone number and I told her that my phone number wouldn't change because I've had it for 25 + years.

I wished her well and we hung up.

I guess by talking to some of these girls and women that worked the streets did listen to me about changing their lifestyle. I feel sure that some of them overdosed or were killed by their Pimps or someone that picked them up for a quickie. They came from families that either didn't care about them or they chose to do this for the money and drugs. I suppose that no one will ever know why they chose this line of work.

SUMMATION

My life has been a physical and emotional roller coaster. I have had the honor of meeting and working with so many exceptional men and women. I have met many famous people throughout my life.

I have made many mistakes, some more than once but I have always tried to improve myself and learn from my bad mistakes. I have truly been blessed my entire life and even though I have hit many low's, I have always managed to bounce back. My dad always told me that it's hard to keep a good man down. Maybe bent, but not broken.

My dad being a Professional Musician lacked in use of tools and construction skills. I have learned my Mechanical and Carpentry skills through the School of Hard Knocks.

While stationed in Orange, Texas I learned how to use a cutting torch, gas weld and arc weld and I learned how to paint automobiles and do minor auto body repair. I worked free at a body shop in Orange, Texas.

My mechanical skills began in Louisville, Kentucky when I was working at a Gas Station , part-time. I built a Race Car and won 28 Trophies Drag Racing one year. I built a 3 Car Garage, in ground swimming Pool (I studied a How To Book for 6 months). I also enrolled in an Upholstery Class, added a room onto my home. I built a trailer to move my furnishings to Nashville. The axle made from a drive shaft, cut down, etc.

Onto Nashville where I built a 3 Car Carport (33 feet) on the rear of my home in the Country. Moved to Brewer Drive where I built another in ground Pool plus a Den and a Bedroom on the rear of my house.   Next house a 3 Car Garage and another in-ground Pool. Later at Patsy's house we covered her Patio, plus a huge Dutch Barn in the back yard, removed a wall between the Kitchen and Living Room. Next on Cane Ridge Road I built a 2 story addition onto a Mobile Home plus another 2 bedrooms, 2 Baths, Kitchen and a 2 Carport. This was on 5 acres with lots of maintenance.

Patsy and I sold our house in Nashville, TN. and we moved to Murfreesboro where we had a house built. This is the first time that I had ever been able to work on a house from the start. Patsy and I did a lot of extra work on the house while it was being built. I added crown molding in every room including the bathrooms. We also built a 12' X 40' shed on the back of our property. It didn't take it long before it was full. I guess you can never built something big enough. The list is endless.

Like the old saying goes "Life comes at you hard."   I'm like an old Edsel with 300 thousand miles and just plain worn out. My 80th birthday is just around the corner. I hope I get there. I have skirted death on many occasions and somehow I by passed the Reaper every time.

I hope that whoever reads this book will get some enjoyment from it.

Made in the USA
Monee, IL
14 January 2023

25298692R00267